Dot.com
Success!

Dot.com Success!

Surviving the Fallout and Consolidation

SALLY RICHARDS

SYBEX®

SAN FRANCISCO • PARIS • DÜSSELDORF • SOEST • LONDON

Associate Publisher: Cheryl Applewood
Contracts and Licensing Manager: Kristine O'Callaghan
Acquisitions and Developmental Editor: Kathy Yankton
Editor: Kari Brooks
Production Editor: Kylie Johnston
Book Designer: Kris Warrenburg, Cyan Design
Electronic Publishing Specialist: Kris Warrenburg, Cyan Design
Proofreaders: Nanette Duffy, Dennis Fitzgerald, Laurie O'Connell, Nancy Riddiough
Indexer: Lynnzee Elze
Cover Designer: Yvo Riezebos Design

Library of Congress Card Number: 2001087090

ISBN: 0-7821-2851-3

Manufactured in the United States of America

10 9 8 7 6 5 4 3 2 1

A great debt of gratitude goes out to Carol Sands, angel extraordinaire, a wonderful friend and mentor who taught me the ropes. Thank you!

Contents at a Glance

CONTENTS

FOREWORD

I think being a successful entrepreneur is just a matter of perseverance. I've started eighteen companies—five were not successful—but I've had my successes. I've been in this game for a while, and I've received funding before. Many entrepreneurs believe it's only a matter of strolling into a VC's office, pitching them, and then getting money in your account three days later. That's not the way things happen. It's going to be difficult, and you have to be relentless—and most of all, you have to listen. Funding is there if you really figure out what you're doing wrong. Look at each presentation you make and every business plan you write as a learning process, and seek experienced people to give you honest feedback. This is going to be very hard, especially for new entrepreneurs who think they have it all figured out.

As an entrepreneur, you also have to really understand the economics of your business; there are too many ideas that aren't thought through. Many entrepreneurs don't understand the business end of starting a company.

Whenever I hear an entrepreneur say, "I have a great idea," I say, "Tell me about the economics." They answer, "I'll hire an accountant to do that for me one of these days." When you're in France, you better speak French. Before you think about starting a business, you better know the economics of your revenue model.

Many business plans talk about a great product, but they don't talk about a great company. Some products are not sufficiently large enough to be a great company. There are also a lot of product ideas that are fundamentally not defendable, even with patents. Patents are difficult in such a fast-moving world. Often enough, the life cycle of a product is shorter than the patent process. And sometimes you can't get big enough with the product without the danger of a bigger company coming in and taking over the market. I see business plans all the time that are nothing more than marketing research for the big corporations. You have to think all of these things out and make strategic partnerships early if you want to succeed.

New markets are also difficult to target. For instance, when I started Atari, the board game industry was under a million dollars. Now the video gaming industry is worth about $23 billion—three to four times the theatrical ticket sales of the movie industry. But at the time, many of the investors I went to didn't see that vision down their shotgun barrels. How could you see that coming at the time? How can you foresee these types of trends? You have to know in your gut that your plan will work, and build a well-structured company that will produce profits.

And even if you've been starting up companies as long as I have, something may happen to broadside you. Even large corporations make bad decisions; every decision has the potential of being a mistake. Things happen. I remember talking with Bob Noyce about such an event in Intel's history. I was a chess player, and he was a chess player—a good chess player—and we had became friends. It was after Intel had taken a big write-off. They had manufactured the Michroma watch modules. He said, "You know, just as the other guy's business looks too easy, it just means you don't know enough about it."

There are natural limitations to fantasy; reality will finally set in. There will be a natural shakeout because companies have to be profitable. Right now there is a tremendous bubble of money going into companies for capital spending to support losses, and this will not continue indefinitely. The market will cleanse itself, and there will be a shakeout, a consolidation, and a contraction. This has happened several times. I remember when there was 23 million square feet of unused light industrial space in the mid-'80s. The market went up and then crashed, because a lot of companies that were venture-backed or IPO-funded didn't make their projections, and all of a sudden the buildings that were full of people one day were empty the next. It's a cycle—it'll happen again.

The reality is when you're playing chess, you win some and you lose some. But you have to set the pieces up and start a new game. Life is a process, and it would be really boring if it was just one win after another. You don't really want to struggle, but it's part of the process. My dad used to say, "If it was easy to make a million dollars, there'd be more millionaires."

As an entrepreneur, you have responsibilities to yourself and others. You need to know, as much as solid research allows, that you have a solid business plan that has an opportunity to make a profit. Then you can go out and pitch your dream—your company—to others. It's not an easy process by any means, so be prepared to work harder and dig deeper than you ever have before. Being an entrepreneur is difficult; if it weren't, there'd be more of them out there.

Good luck in your entrepreneurial endeavors!

Nolan Bushnell
Founder of Atari and CEO of Uwink.com

Who Loves Ya, Baby?

W hen you're obsessed, you're obsessed. I see it in the eyes of people coming from the offices of the VCs and angels I visit. I see it in the vacant looks of people (wearing dot-com T-shirts) shopping for groceries at 2 A.M. at Safeway and in the eager hand gestures of people in team-packed SUVs that pass me on Highway 101 on their way to pitch sessions.

If you're reading this book, chances are that you're obsessed with the whole idea that you, too, will one day become one of those dot-com millionaires who are a bit more difficult to find these days. It used to be that you couldn't stand on a street corner in Palo Alto without throwing a rock and hitting one of them— not that you'd do that on purpose. It's gotten to be more like *Where's Waldo?* these days.

So how will you hone your concept and all of its finer points to get it in shape for the *Big Pitch*? The reason I wrote this book was because I was getting so many phone calls and e-mails from friends and complete strangers asking me to read their business plans and give them feedback. Basically, I saw a great need. Calling endless numbers of people back and giving them advice is a great thing to do if you're independently wealthy. Then I could sit around all day on a chaise lounge next to the pool, pop bon-bons, and turn the pages of business plans I was reading purely from the goodness of my heart. *Not.* I wrote this book because now, when someone asks me to take a look at their plan, I can say, "Hey, I wrote the book on it. Here's the Amazon link (assuming Amazon is still around when this book is in its heyday). Knock yourself out!"

People need mentors, especially when they're not familiar with the terrain. And I always end up passing the good teams on to other people who might be able to mentor them through the process. Recnetly I thought, *What I need is a manual full of mentoring advice from people who really know what they're talking about.* So I went about the task of finding these people and making this book happen.

Sherry Bonelli, my acquisitions editor at Sybex, saw what it was that I was trying to do and immediately put the wheels in motion to publish the book. Sherry went on to another publisher halfway through the book, and I was extremely lucky to have Cheryl Applewood take over the editorship of this project. Both Sherry and Cheryl are women ahead of their time when it comes to choosing books that are on the cutting edge, and they are both dot-com savvy. And I love that they're women. In this industry, women seem to have an intuitive sense about what the future will look like, and we're starting to see many more of them taking the helm of dot-com companies and the industries that support them (many of whom I've interviewed for the book). This book provides many mentors—top CEOs of major dot-com companies, as well as others who are leading the industry in peripheral dot-coms.

I skulked around dot-com parties and was invited to the insider meetings to help get my head around the entire process, and at times I found many contradictory truths that lead to many layers of complexity. I had to peel back the layers, one by one, until I found that there were no truths in this business except that Lady Luck plays a very grand role.

For your reference, dot-com companies not only are ones that have ".com" after their names, but also the companies that support the industry. So there are companies included in this book that do not do e-commerce, but instead are symbiotic to the dot-com industry. Many of the dot-coms that survive the upcoming consolidation and fallout will be these strong, symbiotic companies. There are many changes ahead for the industry, and the winners will be those who saw the stuff coming down the pike and waterproofed their dot-coms for the future.

I wanted to write you a book you could pop into your backpack, take to work (hopefully you'll still have a day job at this stage), and read bits and pieces at a time to inspire you on this road you've decided to take. I hope you get what you need from *Dot.com Success!* and will continue to be inspired when you've finished it.

If there's one thing I've learned from all of the people who've generously given me interviews for this book, it's that you absolutely, *positively* must have passion for what you're doing. If you're doing it for the money, you may get there, but it will probably be as painful as using a stick in the eye, instead of an alarm clock, to wake up in the morning. If you do it because you're passionate and believe your dot-com baby will grow up to do things that will change the way your market does business on the Web, go for it. But most importantly—*you must have fun.*

This industry will chew you up and spit you out without a second thought if you're not doing this work from your heart. Just because people are out to kill you—I mean the competition, not *you* personally—you need not stress out on this business of being an entrepreneur. People have done this kind of thing for millennia in every way, shape, and form, so put this into perspective. Get a grip. You're not going to die if your company doesn't pan out. You will do what an entrepreneur does best and reshape your plan, or start a whole new business where you didn't see a market need before, and *keep on keepin' on*, as Bob Dylan, the original entrepreneurial musician of the '60s—the one with the long and money-making career—says.

This business of being the boss comes with a lot of responsibilities. You need a few mantras to get you through those long nights of sitting up with your coders (or all alone, if you are the coder). Just as those noir detectives like Sam Spade lived and died by an unwritten code, you too will have to develop a code to get you through. I kept hearing the same things from successful people, and I made a list of the most common:

- Be tough.

- Never give your company away for bad terms just to get cash. A startup is very much like a book—if you have to self-publish, chances are your book isn't good enough to interest a publisher. So get some feedback, and change it to fit the market.

- Put your foolish pride in a paper sack, and leave it in the attic.

- Work hard at building relationships and good ideas so you won't have a problem finding fair term sheets.

- Be completely honest and open during due diligence— all it takes is one little lie or withholding to blow your deal so completely out of the water that you'll need to move to Ohio (sorry to those of you who are reading this in Ohio).

- If you don't like an investor, don't take their money. This isn't brain surgery. You will be working, in most cases, very closely, with that person for a long time. Remember that *having fun* is part of the entrepreneurial journey.

- Don't be afraid to have an exit strategy. You'll need it for your business plan, so think beyond an IPO. The words "merger" and "acquisition" are your friends.

- Be in love with everything about your company. And yes, just like lovers, you will have fights and want to walk out on your company from time to time. But never lay your head on your pillow without settling a disagreement or getting something out in the open. You will feel better about it in the morning when you have to speak with your company again.

- Be generous with your stock to those who help you build your company.

- Be patient, but not complacent. If, in your gut, you feel that the market is going somewhere else, cut it off at the pass. Take risks—that's what this whole thing's all about. If you do it right, you'll be a visionary. If you completely blow it, hopefully you'll live long enough to prove what they say about you is wrong.

- Make technology and market shifts from the strength of research and feedback, not from fear. Failure can smell fear 10,000 miles away… and it *will* get you. Knowledge is power.

- Never demand someone's help—it is not their duty, or your god- (or goddess-) given right to ask for it. People will help you because you've sold them with your passion, concept, and vision. And when someone does help you, make sure you are one day in a position to offer them something in return, not because you have to, but because that's the way it's done.

- Never expect more from your partners, employees, VCs, or angels than you would expect of yourself. You'll have a real problem here if you're running yourself into the ground with expectations. Pace yourself—you have a long road ahead.

- Make sure you provide your employees with coffee (the good stuff) and bottled water. If it were me, I'd bring in a few cases of Jolt cola each week, too. And push them to get out of the office every few hours to get some fresh air. Praise them when they've done good work. And if you can afford it, take them out to lunch once a week. These people are in partnership with your dream—they care, nurture, and embrace your company just as you do your own dream. And after your company gets too big to do weekly lunches, make sure they get powerbars, popcorn, soup, and hot cocoa in the kitchen. You would want someone to do the same for you.

- Pay fair wages. People cannot live on stock options, free soup, and pipe dreams for very long before they start to wander over to the company down the road for an interview.

- Build loyalty with those around you. These people are your friends (or should be). Treat them with respect and generosity, and take their personal feelings and needs into great consideration.

- Revel in your small successes. Even if you don't win the wars, celebrate the battles won.

These are some pretty tough mantras to live by. Can you do it? You'll do it if you want to keep your sanity, or you'll find some other reasonable facsimiles of these all on your own. How important are the things I've mentioned? I have known companies to lose people only because they didn't provide sodas and coffee. These are the basics of life. If you're expecting people to give you 120 percent for your dream, you should at least give them the basics.

There's also a bit of a disclaimer that I must stick in this preface. This book is a living, breathing part of history. We're livin' in Internet time, baby. By the time this book comes out, anything could have happened, and it will. Be flexible and learn from the lessons in this book. Some of the people in these pages may be out of business, or extremely rich, by the time your eyes hit this page, so learn. And most of all, enjoy yourselves. Grasp the fundamentals of what these people are telling you; I've chosen a lot of people who've shown incredible chutzpah, so I have a feeling everyone within these pages will land on their feet. And hopefully, so will you.

Being an entrepreneur is the best job in the world—you need to be brilliant, passionate, fair, honest, and forthright. Expect to fall in love with your company, and everything else will follow.

Happy e-trekking in this wonderful space we call an industry!

ACKNOWLEDGMENTS

For all the entrepreneurs who shared their trials and tribulations with me—especially Richard Verdoni (PreludeTrilogy.com), whose garage I spent a great deal of time inside, hangin' with his dot-com friends and watching him endlessly shape and reshape his company and others'. Richard, I'm sure you'll be a dot-com success sometime soon! And thank you to all of the professionals who shared your wisdom and where-withal—and your much appreciated time—with me.

A huge thank you! to Guy Kawasaki (Garage.com), whose boot camps opened my eyes to this incredible era of dot-com—you rock! I could hardly believe my luck when serendipity (and Loni Reeder) brought Nolan Bushnell to town! Nolan, many, many thanks for your inspiration and candor. Alan Cole-Ford, you taught me the value of early-stage technology and how nicely it dovetails into broadband dot-com entertainment. I'm keeping an eye on you! Hey, Paul Hoffman! Thank you for your ongoing encouragement and "insider" insights into the Internet industry, and letting me bounce ideas off of you at all hours of the day and night. Pat "McCarron" Hagen, as always, thank you for your ongoing services as my personal ethicist and your very much appreciated go-be-do directive. Thanks Chris Williams for your insights on Internet security, you can see your influence throughout the pages.

A lot of really wonderful things happened when I did the research for this book. The greatest thing of all was the opportunity to meet the people who make up this incredible industry in which all of the players are bent on winning and go to extraordinary lengths to do so. All of you welcomed me into your garages, offices, homes, lofts, and limousines, and you leveled with me about what was really going on in this space. I interviewed hundreds of people for this book, and not all of your interviews got in. I'm sorry, maybe there'll be a sequel.

And to the wonderful women who brought this book together: my fabulous agent, Margot Maley Hutchison, of Waterside Productions (Waterside.com); my visionary acquisitions editor, Sherry Bonelli, who worked with me on the proposal to get this book off the ground; and a mega-huge thank you to my editor and Associate Publisher at Sybex, Cheryl Applewood, for her straight-up guidance and really great sense of humor (it made the process much less painful!). And Merci! to Sybex President, Rodnay Zaks, who sees the trends in technology a little before the bend in the road. And a very grateful tip of the hat to the entire crew at Sybex who pulled this project together, got it onto and off of the presses, shipped it, and put it on the shelves and into your hands. You guys have worked hard to make this book a dot-com success! Thank you!

Thanks to all the folks (especially Stephanie Hare) at the British Banker's Club in Menlo Park, who kept me fed and hydrated on those long days of tapping away at my laptop when my (albeit likeable) neighbors from hell had ongoing construction throughout the spring and summer. And mugs up to the crew at We Fix Macs, Palo Alto, who had my very broken and traumatized G-3 up and running to meet my deadlines—you all are worth your weight in gold (and charged me accordingly)!

This book was written for all of the green entrepreneurs who will go forth and persevere in this harsh environment to become dot-com successes. You will be the next generation who were inspired by the greatness (and luck) of those who got in under the wire and tempered with the humility of the failed dot-bombs you see all around you. Take wisdom from the people in this book, find a market, build a brilliant business plan, go forth, and conquer!

And let's not forget the beautiful UPS man who broke up my days and weeks of writing in solitude with his gorgeous smile and quirky sense of humor. Thank you, Jeff Bezos, for partnering with UPS and having a great service in which I could find the books I needed and have them sent overnight (I hope you can pull it together). Thank you to the people at Waiterson-Wheels.com, who made sure I was fed and wouldn't be found slumped over dead on my keyboard; all of the wonderful people running great web cams so I could watch the great outdoors and busy cities online and pretend that I spent some of my summer on vacation; and all of the online clothing catalogs that were able to provide me with a new wardrobe every time my laundry pile got too overwhelming. The Internet is such a wonderful thing, I can hardly wait until someone puts a chip in my head, or at least my refrigerator!

And a special heartfelt thank you to the people in my life who put up with me going underground for three months while I wrote this book.

Sally Richards
Sally@SallyRichards.com
www.SallyRichards.com

B2ME
The Dream

Internet companies are crashing all around us. Every day we hear about another one biting the dust—even sites like Pop.com, with such high-profile investors as Steven Speilberg, have bitten the dust while still in beta. Entrepreneurs who haven't already gotten in under the wire at this point seem to be dot-com screwed. Although there's as much investment money as there was before April 2000, most investors have become cautious lemmings in an effort to follow the pack and are choosing safer, proven-out investments. For the most part, they're staying away from companies whose names contain the words dot and com. Phrases like "early stage" and "bridge funding" are not as sexy as they used to be.

And the chances of you—a new entrepreneur—getting into a venture capitalist's office to pitch? You ever hear of a cold day in hell? That is, unless you have the inside insights this book provides.

WHERE DOT-COM IS TODAY

Today's market is hostile. It demands to know when you plan to be in the black. You've entered a *Mad Max* environment in which you will be sent to the dot-com Thunderdome with everyone from analysts, the press, investors, and especially your users, chanting, "Two dot-coms enter, one dot-com leaves!" The fallout and consolidation ahead will be treacherous for anyone who decides to target a market and kick into gear.

So knowing all of this—and many of you may have been trying to get funding for several months already—what drives you to persevere? What you may understand by now is that you live in a different world from ordinary people because you want to live an extraordinary life. There is no shame in this endeavor; it's all about rising above the noise—a noble pursuit. You are probably thrilled with the whole underdog concept, and you're determined that it will be your company that wins in the end. If only you can just get your foot in the door. You want to be rich in this *new economy*—to be rich in this *space* (what insiders call the Internet industry). It's an industry with a different vocabulary made of acronyms and phraseologies with different rules, protocols, and expected behaviors. Entrepreneurs invent concepts, services, and companies the rest of the world can't live without—at least not comfortably or efficiently, right? If this is you, then you're reading the right book.

"If you try hard enough and long enough, you can do anything. What different individuals can accomplish is a product of their ability, their beliefs, and their passion."

—STEVE KIRSCH, founder of Mouse Systems, Frame Technology, Infoseek, and Propel

The other morning, it finally hit me just how different things are in Silicon Valley. I was driving down Highway 101 with a friend, one of the few I have who isn't steeped in technology. We had both taken the day off and were on our way to San Francisco from the Peninsula. For the most part, we'd been stuck in traffic that was traveling two miles an hour at best. I noticed she was staring off at the billboards in the wetland marshes; she was making a thinking noise—one of those hmm types of epiphany sounds. I asked her what she was thinking about. She shook her head and said, "I have no idea what I'm reading. What the hell do these billboards mean?"

I looked over at the billboards—the ones that (in the dot-com heyday) cost in excess of $5 thousand a day and make you wait on a list to even have the honor of paying that much.

Marketing so personal it clicks…Way fast…Did you get any lately…Sync is everything…Put in code, get out IBM…

I flew over the situation from a 30-thousand-foot level to think about how those signs would look to people who weren't in the Internet space. It was terrifying. I would probably think I had landed in Prague 100 years ago, or on a Martian landscape. It would be completely foreign, with little connection to what I was about. Then I looked around me: SUVs filled with young twenty-somethings on their way to pitch VCs for startup cash, a truck pulling a narrow trailer billboard with dot-com companies advertised on both sides, and a truck with revolving billboards on three sides. As we neared 3Com Park, I saw a barge billboard in the Bay dot-com keeping pace with the torturously slow traffic. I opened the sunroof and saw a blimp floating overhead, plastered with the latest dot-com advertisement. I turned up the radio, tuned to KQED (the Bay Area's NPR station) to get the traffic report, and noted the dot-com underwriters being listed after each news blurb. I realized I was wearing a dot-com T-shirt I had picked up at a startup party the night before. Even my key chain donned the name of a dot-com. It was so surreal; it made me think of the scene from *Bladerunner* in which advertising encompassed post-apocalyptic LA, and Atari logos (a company that Warner, the movie's maker, had just purchased when the movie debuted) beamed brightly in the bleak city.

As the herds of SUVs passed us by, I asked my friend where she thought all those teams of people were going. She guessed there might be an event at 3Com. I, on the other hand, knew that these vehicles, for the most part, were filled with visionaries armed with the skill sets needed to carry them to the next step. The guys and gals—short hair, goatees, peeper glasses— hang onto the back of the front seats to make heated conversation easier. These people were probably still hashing out their plans for an upcoming meeting. The average time of change for an evolving business plan is only as long as the time it takes a dot-com entrepreneur to get to their next pitch session (if even that long). Often they are making changes to their PowerPoint presentations as they drive or as they sit in the VC's office. They are off to pitch their dreams. Hey, those kids next to us could be the next Yahoo!. They could have been you. All I know is that just thinking about it makes me heady—what a fabulous time and place to be living, where a pen hitting a check could change you from a dreamer to a dot–com success!

"I'm just a frustrated consumer. I have ideas on how to make things better, and so I pursue those ideas instead of waiting for someone else to do it. I don't pursue things I'm not really passionate about."

—STEVE KIRSCH, founder of Mouse Systems, Frame Technology, Infoseek, and Propel

THE CYCLE OF LIFE AND DEATH IN A MODERN WORLD

So how did we get from the invention of the vacuum tube at the beginning of the twentieth century to this unbelievable world of e-commerce? To understand the evolving Internet's future, you must understand its past. To fully comprehend what you're up against is also the ability to know the cyclical evolutions in technology itself. Technology is a strange animal, actually a herd of different species that sometimes run together and benefit each other. At other times, it's a predator waiting to cannibalize the weak stragglers and allow Darwin's theories to take place.

CONTINUED >

The lesson about our current e-volution is that technology doesn't need to be technical. An old idea, such as grocery delivery, can be innovated (notice how I didn't say it could be *profitable*) by a faster way of completing the task of shopping...the Internet.

One of my favorite examples of how an old technology completely evolved into a new industry—and left those who weren't ready broken in its wake—is the silent film industry. Sound changed the entire makeup of an industry, and it changed the world. As we watched in silence as Rudolph Valentino seduced his women in the deserts of far-away places, America's movies gave glamour to life that hadn't been there before. Once sound came into play, a good many actors and actresses were out of jobs because their voices weren't as attractive as their bodies. Music wasn't played live in theaters any longer, and live shows dropped off one by one. Sound allowed us to actually hear what was written across the screen; it made clear communication an evolution. Then new concepts—full-scale musicals with astronomical budgets—came about. These movies built an entirely new industry.

It's also what happened later to Vaudeville when brilliant entrepreneur Philo Farnsworth's TV technology was leveraged by RCA and introduced into homes all over the U.S. Just as we, as a country, had been sharing the same home radio shows while gathered around the Zenith on stormy winter nights to listen to the Green Lantern, we transitioned over to watching those early TV shows that began filling our collective unconscious with pop culture. Live news also began building our culture. The U.S. slowly evolved into a village of assimilated cultures that the future Internet would perpetuate quite nicely. Building this basis of our cultural pop heritage took a hell of a lot of technology and partnerships—both are still an issue in today's Internet market.

CONTINUED >

Technological entrepreneurs continued to play a part in changing our culture and our lives as they began to identify and develop things we only imagined. Each successful technology wove a new thread of evolution into the cloth of our IT history. Some were so successful that they put other industries out of business—look at the vacuum tube versus the semiconductor.

The first written description of the Internet is credited to a series of memos written by MIT's J.C.R. Licklinder describing his vision of a "Galactic Network." It wasn't until 1961, when MIT's Leonard Kleinrock published his theory—the first on the subject—addressing packet switching, that the technology that continues to drive the Internet was jumpstarted. The Cold War continued heating up, and the U.S. budget grew to fight communism and bring about growth in the communications industry. One of those efforts was the Internet—a network of communication that couldn't be destroyed, no matter what the circumstances. By the time AOL came on the scene in 1985, the Internet was well on its way.

The Internet has changed things dramatically for everyone involved. The ability of consumers to find and buy products or locate information online has devastated entire industries. *BAM*s (brick and mortars) are now trying to change their model to *CAM*s (click and mortars) to make sure they don't lose entire markets to companies that can outsell them on the Internet. Many of these traditional companies seek partnerships with Internet companies that can get them on the Internet faster and with a larger presence.

And as we see in our historical technology cycles, many of the technologies we worship today will become a moot point tomorrow. And, as all cycles go, there will be carnage along the way.

WHERE DOT-COM IS GOING

Today I received an e-mail from my friend, Paul Hoffman, associate director of UCLA's Academic Technology Services Department, telling me that Judy Estrin had resigned as CTO of Cisco and had co-founded a company called Packet Design. Because Estrin is a visionary, I believe she is leading the next industry—the technology that will help deliver speed and bandwidth to your Internet connection. Estrin is known as a geek goddess in the industry, and when she does something like leave Cisco and start a new company, everyone in the industry, especially analysts, takes note.

"I like to tell people we're just at the covered-wagon stage of the Internet. The same way we took to get from covered wagons to where we are today needs to happen. That the car is a tool we now take for granted, but at one time, roads needed to be built to drive them on—i.e., bandwidth. We needed ease of use—i.e., the automatic versus the crank. We needed gas stations and stoplights. Those are still the services that will develop on the Net. Then we needed laws."
—JUDY ESTRIN, CEO, Packet Design

I met with Estrin to ask about her thoughts on the Internet and its future. "I do believe that the Internet is simply a different medium, and because it is a different medium it allows information to flow in a different time span than other media. The whole idea of e-commerce on the Web and the reason it is such a powerful tool is because time is so compressed—you don't have to go look in a store. You don't have to happen to get a catalog once a week in the mail, and then happen to make a call and order by phone. The difference is that the information is there all the time, whenever you want it, and the cycle between the buyer seeing the information and actually being able to purchase it is compressed. You have to be cognizant that the Internet changes lots of things, so you have to rethink the way you reach your consumers and the way you keep them.

"For instance, it's much easier [for a consumer] to be fickle on the Net than it is in your local store or a catalog," says Estrin of the importance of *stickiness*. "The benefit is moving around, and it's easier to lose customers if the experience isn't what you want. You have to be very realistic about what the Net changes and what the Net doesn't change. What I'm seeing as a problem for lots of companies is that they think the Net changes *everything*—meaning they suddenly think economics change because of the Internet. I don't believe there's a *new economy*. The rules of economics still exist today, which is ultimately if you don't make a profit, money has to come from somewhere. There are cycles in economics; business ethics and fundamentals don't change the fact that, if you don't take care of your customers, they won't come back. And so, if you are an Amazon.com or a BarnesandNoble.com, it doesn't matter that those books still need to be warehoused somewhere and the books still have to get to the consumer somehow.

Many believe the future of the Internet will bear little resemblance to what it is today. These differences will include the way it is delivered to your various appliances—yes, I said *appliances*. Many believe the next wave of dot-com will even include your refrigerator. Whatever it looks like, it's nearly certain there will be a need for commerce delivered via the cable or wireless signals going into your house to manage a server. And then there are those technologies that will enable your Internet use wherever you are.

Companies on the bleeding edge are now working on products to make Net access available to their customers any time, anywhere. Internet companies that have a real business with genuine revenue models—relatively few, considering the market—are moving toward a day when they can be accessed whatever the circumstances. Estrin believes that accessibility is an absolute in the future of the Internet.

"As we look forward, I think one of the changes coming will be that we'll end up in a world where the bandwidth is much more ubiquitous, so you can start doing things differently, like really seeing more rich media on the Net," says

Estrin. "The world changes from being about PCs to being appliances, so it's not just 'How do I provide information so someone from a laptop can access me?' but 'How can I make sure I'm appealing to the pager, the cell phone, the PC, and the set-top box? Where does it make sense for me to play?' "

"Once you get over the beginning and the hype part of the market, and you settle into the long term, people have to think what is different and what needs to remain the same and where their core competencies are," says Estrin of what we're now seeing in the market. "There's bandwidth, there's appliances, and the third major change is what mobility means to the services provided. How does the increase in the amount of wireless and mobile devices matter to my business? Does a mobile user—might be on a cell phone, in a car, on a plane—look the same from a laptop, or is there something different I want to do to keep that consumer?"

THE NEED TO BLEED

How do you know it's your time to start a company? How do you know that you want it bad enough? From every entrepreneur I've interviewed, I've heard the same story about *needing* to become an entrepreneur—to work long hours, beg for money, and create something of value. They describe it like some alien eating its way through their stomachs—something they know will eventually (and painfully) chew its way out.

"We're looking for entrepreneurs who have the courage, even in this raw form, to reassess themselves, their business, and their market on a regular basis and make adjustments to the plan based on that information."

—CAROL SANDS, founder and managing member of The Angels' Forum and The Halo Fund

Joe Kraus, co-founder of Excite@Home, is no different. His company, founded when he and five friends left Stanford, was something his entire team was determined to carry through.

"It wasn't that it was predetermined or thought out," says Kraus of the beginnings of Excite. "It was all about not wanting to work for anybody else, combined with a desire to do something in the technology field because all of my friends were technologists. Basically the six of us felt, 'Wouldn't it be fun for us to do something together?' And you've got to realize that when you're at school at Stanford, there's a huge amount of role modeling around you—Silicon Valley has these role models who don't go into large companies, they go into garages and start something on their own.

"So we decided to get together at Rosita's in Redwood City [February 28, 1993] and bring some ideas to the table—see if we could do something together. It wasn't a 'Hey, I see a need.' We got together and had terrible ideas, like applications for the Newton, automatic translation software—really bad ideas," says Kraus, thinking back on all the directions they could have taken. "So, at the end of the meal we were really depressed. So we looked over at Graham Spencer, the chief technical brain and really great at spotting trends, who realized that we hadn't seen the Web at this point, but all of us had been on the Net for four years, but just with command lines and Internet tools. His observation was that more and more information was coming online and the tools for searching for it were bad. Let's build technology to search through large databases of text, because there seems to be more and more of it coming online. We came up with our slogan, which was 'Unencumbered by reality.' It was the notion that we didn't know we could fail, so therefore, we were going to succeed. So we just plowed ahead from there. We just hoped there was a market opportunity—it was a little bit of the *Field of Dreams* situation. I thought it was a good insight on Graham's part."

WHY ARE YOU HERE?

The evolution of the Internet has brought about many changes, including the reason you have chosen to read this book. You want to be a dot-com millionaire. You want to change the way someone buys, learns, or uses a product or service. You want to make something easier, so easy that herds of people will flock to your website to purchase what you are only thinking of as a concept at this moment. One thing is crystal clear to you at this moment: You will be one of the survivors in the next round of fallout and consolidation of Internet startups.

I constantly run into your brethren: bright people with great dot-com ideas. The devil is in the details of implementation. Oh yeah, and in that little detail of making sure you really do have a viable business. People send me about 10 business plans a week to comment on. Mostly, if they are unsolicited, I click them through to the trash. Delete. Delete. Delete. From time to time, I open up a couple and take a peek. The entrepreneurs want to know whether I see a future in their business, whether I know of any technologies hovering on the horizon that might kill them. Do I know of any partners who would complement them? Most of the plans are really heinous, and it's obvious, to me at least, that the entrepreneur didn't think anything through or prepare a company plan based on solid fundamentals.

Why do so many bad ideas find their way into business plan format? Because people don't understand what it takes to make an Internet business float. They don't think past buying the URL and making a marketing plan where, in a perfect world, viral marketing (as in it spreads like a virus, no real dollars needed) will take them all the way to IPO. It's called "all sizzle and no steak." Most don't even have their financials planned out for a year. Others have numbers five years out and look like they had a team of polished fiction writers working on them. This may sound harsh, but my opinions about this kind of thing are a bit less critical than the VC you'll be sending your plan to—a VC who has given his or her admin strict orders to trash all plans that don't come with several personal introductions.

Perhaps more than a third of the world's venture capital comes from Silicon Valley, but we're not the only ones doling out cash. There are plenty of money sources, and there's bound to be someone out there who will make the perfect "smart money" partner for you. First, you'll need a company with a revenue model that pans out. One that makes sense to everyone involved. Socks-dot-whatever just doesn't fly anymore. Next, you'll need to groom your business plan and your team, and then put things in place before your hunt for the ultimate cash. So many people go to a money source without any of this in place. And they will die while trying to figure out why no one returns their calls.

The most destructive thing you can do is accept money from friends and family—those who will buy into something because they love you and think you'll take good care of their money. If you take this money, it makes you lazy. You won't get the feedback from professionals who know what's happening in your business sector and why your business may not be a good idea. So, rule one: Don't accept your parent's retirement fund. Go off on your own and build a viable business with money from VCs and angels who will validate your concept. Then, find others who will help you build it.

RU B2B? UNDERSTANDING THE DOT-COM VOCABULARY

Get used to it: You're going to see a lot of letters replacing words, and numbers connecting them. We're running on Internet time now. No time to say entire words.

So what does it mean to be ruled by a new vocabulary? Well, it could really screw you in a meeting if you don't know what you're talking about. What does all this B2B, B2B2C, slam BAM thank you CAM CAM, yadda, yadda, mean to you? Is it important that you know what these terms mean and how to use them? I'd say it's part of the skill set you'll be building as an entrepreneur.

"I truly believe that buzzwords are made up for lack of reality."
—ROYAL P. FARROS, CEO and chairman of the board, iPrint.com

I was in a meeting last year with venture capitalist Christine Comaford, founder of Artemis Ventures (`www.ArtemisVentures.com`). She was listening to a brick-and-mortar company that wanted to go click. (See the *Newsweek* article link on my site, `www.SallyRichards.com`, if you want a blow-by-blow description of the meeting.) They had $10 million in revenues (we'll call this revs from here on out) from their mortar business and were showing some ways to leverage their already existing clients with click technology. Things were rolling along swimmingly until she asked them about their marcom plans. The team, who had been cool, suave, and collected until that time, short-circuited. "Marcom?" the CEO asked as if Christine had spoken in tongues.

"They're just wicked green," said Comaford after the team left. "They haven't been in our world, they've been in the world of leasing. They've got a good technology and a good team for now, so if the due diligence checks out and the marketplace is actually $3 trillion, yeah, I can get excited about that."

These guys pitching were fortunate because they had a solid business idea, so it wasn't important that they didn't know everything. But you can see how not understanding the lingo can make you look like a dot-com idiot in this landscape.

You'll notice nuances in articles and business plans; when you see it, you'll know that the people who made it either know what they are doing, or they made it purely by accident. One of these nuances is the capitalization of the letters in the type of business. For instance, in "B2B," a big 'B' means a *Big* business: Panasonic, Sony, Sun. These would be considered a big-B play. A lowercase 'b,' or 'sb,' indicates small business.

So let's give it a go and cover the essential bases that you'll be hearing a lot about. What follows is a guide to the language of dot-coms. Honey, if you're going to live in France, for god's sake, learn French!

B2C: Business to Consumer

Come on everyone, make an 'L' with your right hand and stick it to your forehead. Ever since the last market *adjustment*, you don't see the VCs climbing over each other to fund the next Yahoo!. B2C is what Amazon is—where the business has direct contact with the consumer. Although there are some winners in this field, they are few and far between.

B2B: Business to Business

This is the winner in receiving the dollars as of late—well, sort of. All the B2Cs switched to a B2B model, and now there's a total glut of them in the market. A B2B model simply means doing business with other businesses. Let's say you have a killer app (application) that allows companies to transfer data to their customers at a 50 percent higher speed rate. The B2 your B licenses your killer app to become an intricate part of their technology. And they pay you for the license. It becomes your revenue model. This is the strong B2B play. If you are Akamai or Propel, you are an intricate, hardcore B2B in the dot-com world.

B2B2C: Business to Business to Consumer

This is the business model that occurred because VCs were scared of the straight B2C play. It's losing its luster quickly. Let's say you're a website offering large corporations a service that allows all of their employees free online banking. Okay, so let's say your clients are companies like Oracle and Cisco who have intranets offering your services via a subscription price they pay to you to make these services available to their employees. The bottom line? The company would pay you per subscriber (or however you work out the deal), and you have income via the business and aren't paid directly by the consumer.

P2P: PEER TO PEER

ICQ is a great example of peer to peer without a centralized source. It's the latest, greatest Internet play, and all the investors are looking for the Holy Grail of P2P companies to invest in. This model allows individual computer users to exchange instant e-mail messages with others, no matter what platform or ISP they are using.

"P2P is super exciting as a technology model, but as an investment, you have to be careful. It's not obvious how some P2P companies are going to make money. There is no centralization, so there's no way to leverage centralization to generate revenue. We're not talking about Napster here; we're talking about pure peer-to-peer models. In a way it is similar to the problems faced in open-source software: If you're giving the stuff away for free, you can get great market share but not much revenue. One of the companies we invested in, not peer to peer at all, is called SendMail. They grew out of a free piece of software called SendMail, which helps route e-mail for most of the world's servers. They still maintain the free version on SendMail to maintain market share, but they make money by selling a corporate version and offering support. A key criteria for the success of a P2P company is thinking through how to generate revenue off of market share success, and also to be ready for competition. A challenge for these companies is that barriers to entry may be quite low; a P2P company that invents some clever architecture has a leg up, but that's all they'll have—a leg up. They'll have to continue to innovate, build new products, and keep looking over their shoulder. As an investment, the attraction is less in the idea of peer to peer as much as the scalability of the technical and business model, and the quality of the management of the company."

—IAN PATRICK SOBIESKI, Ph.D., managing director, Band of Angels Fund, LP

REVS: REVENUE MODELS

Revenue models, herein called revs, are what the VCs are interested in most of all. When they ask you that question, there's no hiding behind the acronym that may have gotten you in the door. You must state how—and how far into the future—your business plans to collect revenue.

THE BANNER ADVERTISING MODEL

Most B2C companies rely on banner advertising (or sponsorships) to feed one of their revenue models. Banner ads are sold to your advertising clients. You are paid on the *click-through* (when a visitor to your site actually clicks the banner to visit the advertiser's site). This was the original rev model for portal sites, until they saw their *burnrate* (how fast you go through startup cash) was slowly killing them and they had to come up with something substantial to bring in revs. Some companies have deals with banks that, if your click-through gives them a client, then you get a percentage of the business that is done. Others only pay a flat rate. Again, it depends on the deal you've drawn up.

THE CONTENT MODEL

In the Valley (and this is where the trends are set), the word is that content is dead, and you shouldn't expect to sustain a business with it unless you're doing B2B content deals (such as iSyndicate, Fatbrain, and AskJeeves). The days of expecting people to pay for content are over. Even popular sites like Napster—which doesn't generate content, but delivers it—are feeling the ramifications of brokering "free" content.

THE LICENSING MODEL

Now this is a fabulous business. Let's say you have *proprietary technology* (a patent already in place) where it disrupts the way that business is already done (a *disruptive technology*). We'll say, for the sake of argument, that you have a killer app that gives your licensee the ability to instantly contact three credit auditors and receive complete credit reports within three minutes. This kind of technology would be useful to car manufacturers, such as GM, that sell cars directly from their site (a good example of a BAM going click).

The people I admire most in this e-conomy are the hard-core doers—that brings to mind Guy Kawasaki, the evangelist who played a big role in making Apple visible. His new claim to fame is being CEO of Garage.com. I consider Guy an optimist—a person who knows a good idea. He is also a realist. So, in this e-crappy e-conomy we're having with B2C and the slowing of the boom, I asked him what is the best advice for new entrepreneurs going into this frigid economy.

"No guts, no glory," he says. "The Internet/New Economy is just beginning. There's more to lose by standing on the sideline than by jumping in."

I suggest you make this your mantra.

ADJUSTING YOUR PLAN FOR SHIFTING MARKETS

It used to be that, in the good ol' days of the Internet (roughly speaking, less than two years ago), you could actually obtain venture capital or angel money with just a good URL. Now, with so many people in the space and the market segments saturated, how many online book and CD stores do we really need? More important, how many can the market support?

It used to be called "market affirmation" when you saw competition move in. It used to be comforting for an investor to see that there was a market and that your product could be faster and more efficient than what was out there. Now it's such a threat to have competitors in the same market space that you rarely find anyone who wants to invest where competitors are built-in. What I'm saying with the term "built-in" is that you go into the market knowing someone else is already in the space and has ramped up to where you plan to be in six months to a year. These competitors have already received millions in funding and are already going full speed in building their brand. So why would an investor give you money to build an online bookstore when Amazon.com already exists? Why, indeed.

This is where proprietary technology comes in. What if you could deliver the same level of service, the same discounts, but not have the inventory issues Amazon is dealing with? Would you have a product? I'd say yes. I would say that with the growing popularity of e-books—and a popular PDA product (that may be a plug-and-play extension to an existing technology like a Palm, for instance; or maybe it's a peripheral that can print and bind an entire book of paperback-size pages in three minutes flat) to deliver the content to the reader—your company would probably take a big bite out of the market of traditional printed books. I would say that, if you could meet the needs in this market, not only do you have a product that might replace Amazon. Jeff Bezos may even be smart enough to buy your technology and make his life easier (although I'd make a cash deal instead of stock on that one).

DON'T BASE YOUR PLAN ON YESTERDAY'S SUCCESS

Investors are like wolves (well, most investors at least). There are those few who will break away from the pack and invest in risky ventures that they sniff out every once in awhile. Now it would be rare to fund a Martha Stewart kind of company based on the name of one person. Well, except for an interesting site I saw pop up recently. O.J. Simpson has a site at www.askOJ.com where, for nine bucks and some change, you can join and hear O.J. talk live on a simulcast about stuff that wasn't uncovered at the trial. You can even ask him your own questions. Man, I thought I had seen it all. It's actually got a great UI (user interface) from what I can see without actually joining. My guess is that it was probably funded with family and friends' money and not by a VC. I could be wrong; stranger things have been funded by Sand Hill Road VCs.

Everyone and their brother in Hollywood wants to start up a website built around their stardom. Sometimes it works (especially if there's pornography involved), sometimes it doesn't. For instance, I was advising a company that had a branding interest, a big name star whose popularity they hope will bring people to the site. The star is actually a proven commodity in their industry, and the portal to other services makes sense. I fell in love with the company when I first saw the potential. But, as usual, when you fall in love, things begin to pop up that make you question your love. It may take you years in real life, but in dot-com time, it may only take a few minutes.

Just to test the waters and see if I wanted to get involved with the company, I made some introductions into the inner sanctum for the CEO to pitch to a few VCs I respect and felt would give me some good feedback. He went in that day to give his pitch, and I made sure I was there so I could get the response firsthand (CEOs tend to sugarcoat what happens at these meetings).

Let's take a look at the hardcore attributes of this company before we go any further. There is no proprietary technology (patentable code). There is no disruptive technology (like eBay was when it first came out, and you were able to participate in auctions online). There is just a star, a brand, no team (except the CEO) around the star, a few pages of the site to demo, and a portal idea for other services and products. Although I see value in this star's brand—this star has millions of sales of associated with a product—I can't see a sustainable rev model unless there's at least many, many million in advertising and other services or products poured into this site. The days of pouring a hundred million into a site for branding before the rev model plays is not a rev model investors are willing to hang their hats on these days.

Back to the meeting I set up. The CEO pitched, answered some questions with unbridled enthusiasm, and then stepped out. I spoke candidly with the investors. They hadn't bought it. They felt it was a licensing strategy. They didn't think it would sustain a business. When I connected this CEO with investors with Hollywood money, they reiterated the Valley's investors' thoughts—*it's a licensing play. It won't sustain a dot-com that is a never-ending, hungry beast that eats money like people eat breakfast.*

Just a few moments ago, I talked again to the company's CEO, a seasoned marketer who has built a dot-com brand in the past. I reiterated that perhaps he needed to go directly to the people who were currently making money on the star and get them to invest—they might *get it*, where others don't see the value. He's already met with two of those companies' venture arms that know the value of the star, but he hasn't heard "Let's do a deal!" from them yet.

"Surprisingly, [incoming business plans] haven't changed that much [since April, 2000]. There's just fewer of them that say, 'We'll get a lot of eyeballs by selling dollar bills for ninety cents and figure out a business model later.'"
—GUY KAWASAKI, CEO, Garage.com

His company was recently offered a million-plus by a firm on the East Coast. I said, "Take it!" He said he's waiting for the big bucks, but the firms he's pitching aren't responding favorably. "Take the money," I advised again several weeks later. Now he comes back—"I have made the deal that will turn everything around!" So now this CEO has signed a deal, worth several million with a major portal, in an *advertising swap*. He allows them to use content from this star, and they give him banners. He was so excited. "BFD," (forgive my crass acronym) I replied. But then, we reviewed. According to the contract with the portal, things need to start only months from now. The CEO is currently working with a firm that has built the infrastructure—and I have a gut feeling it's not going to be as robust as it needs to be to support heavy hits if this thing takes off. The site has no employees who aren't virtual, and no headquarters—just this star and this CEO running a business out of his house.

"A friend of mine told me about Computer Select, a CD-ROM that contained 300 or 400 computer publications archives and it was all searchable. He said, 'Try this disk. It'll change your life.' And the more I used it, the more I became dependent on it. I thought 'Wouldn't it be great if we could share this knowledge with not only the few people who buy this CD-ROM, but with anyone using the Internet?' It seemed like a natural vehicle for this kind of information."
—STEVE KIRSCH, founder of Infoseek, Mouse Systems, Frame Technology, and Propel

I tell him to take the million-plus offer to build the company, get an office, some people on staff—a CTO, a content editor, a secretary—lease some equipment, and get an office. The worst thing that could happen with this portal deal? He could get tremendous click-throughs and the site could crash, or it could be a bomb if there's no *stickiness* (a reason for people to stay). People could visit once and never come back again. If this happens, he will have to put a tremendous amount of money into talking those same people into coming back; but that kind of campaign isn't effective unless you're giving away $10 thousand a day. Internet users are particular. If they see something is crap, they're only a click away from leaving your site—and all this usually happens in less than eight seconds.

Meanwhile, the CEO turns the East Coast money down again, although the *term sheet* (a contract laying out the terms for the money you are taking) is still on the table. He is still visiting Silicon Valley investors—they don't want him. I try to help him restructure his rev model to make it more appealing, but he is dead-set on doing things his way. I like this guy. He's bright, tenacious, enthusiastic. But he's also blinded by the love for his original idea. Remember when you first fell in love with the jerk of whom your friends said, "Dump him, he's no good for you"? You shook your head and kept dating him until you found out firsthand what your friends were trying to tell you. Remember how you thought you could change the way he was, and how you could change your friends' minds about him? Not gonna happen. Sometimes you should at least keep an open mind to what your friends are saying.

The term sheet for the million-plus is getting old. And he keeps pointing at this big deal he made with the portal when he talks with investors. "Big deal," they reply. It's not cash— it's not like a portal's venture arm is investing in this company. "It's *only* banners," they tell him. (It's like watching the 300-pound guy with sweat stains under his arms pitching his wares to a table of supermodels at last call. This can't be good for anyone.) Meanwhile his airtime begins soon and the days are counting down. Money likes money; if investors see that he has a firm giving him *something*, even if it is only a million-plus—they will begin to believe. They may even invest. But carrying around this contract with a portal won't get him Jack. Everyone has one, it's only banner space. BFD. But still, I can't look away. It's like passing a car crash. Deep down inside there's a little piece of entrepreneur in all of us who keeps rooting for these guys, even if they only keep the dream alive until the next pitch session. I'm rooting for this guy. I hope he does come around and pulls a rabbit out of his ass.

DOES THE WORLD NEED YOUR PRODUCT OR SERVICE?

It's not enough to be an entrepreneur who wants to create and build. You also must have a service or a product that's needed. In your case, Ms. or Mr. Dot-Com Entrepreneur, you need a product that people already desire, and you need it to be easily accessible on the Internet. And you need it to pay off. You need to know the pain to create a painkiller. Sometimes that product or service can be something you already do—something you already have a competency in and a reputation for doing well—and something that is transferable to the Internet.

One dynamic duo who has managed to pull this off is legendary pollster Dick Morris, CEO of Vote.com, and co-founder Eileen McGann. Morris is well known in the field of polling, and he has a mission. So when he looked at the Internet as an extension of what he already was doing, the team knew they had a winner.

"Decide this is something you want to do, including knocking on doors, failing, and all the other things that go along with entrepreneurialism. What is it that makes your company unique? We should all have a sense of that, no matter what we're doing—a crystal-clear selling proposition. Hone in on it and show it to all of your friends, show it to all of your prospective employees, show it to investors, and find people to help you. Go back and forth to get that unique selling proposition into shape so that you're comfortable that it's unique, and make sure it's needed. With these two things—*this is what I'm doing* and *I've got something unique*—then cash flows from investors into revenue models that work."
—WILLIAM LOHSE, serial entrepreneur, CEO, and founder of SmartAge.com

"I think Vote.com is really an extension of what I used to do in politics," says Morris. "In politics, I was always focused on polling and what people thought about issues. It's really a constant dialog with voters. I think the main thing entrepreneurially—the business part of it—is really being on the cutting edge of an entire next generation of the Internet.

"There's a wonderful song by Cat Stevens, "Father and Son." A line in it says, 'From the moment I could talk, I was ordered to listen.' That's kind of where we all are with the medium. It's an interactive medium, and what's good about it is that we can talk, yet all the political websites are all fixed on the idea of our [users] listening instead of talking. They clip news articles and information, and we're supposed to read them and be interested and impressed.

"But the whole concept of being able to speak—which is at the core of the Internet—really, there's no political manifestation of that," says Morris of a niche market he decided to grab. His site draws revenues from organizations, companies, and political parties for the polling information Vote.com collects. On any given day, you can go to Vote.com and vote on any number of questions that give you an opportunity to voice your opinion en masse. In Dick Morris' perfect world, no one will ever be accosted by an aggressive ditz with a clipboard outside of Safeway when all you really want is a six-pack and to get home for the game.

"There's a change coming in our politics, which is that the episodic, intermittent, infrequent consultation that goes on in our democracy every four years when we get to elect a president, and every two years when we get to vote for a congress representative or a senator, that those punctuation marks in our democracy are going to become very much overshadowed by the daily consultation that's going on through the Internet," says Morris. "Thomas Jefferson's vision of global direct democracy, in which he wanted citizens to be able to govern themselves without intermediaries and representatives—which was totally impossible in his time—is now logistically, completely possible. I believe Jefferson would have loved the Internet because it makes global town meetings possible.

"If you were to go ahead ten or twenty years and look at what our politics are going to look like on a very local level—where people are worried about a gambling casino or a highway—we'll be focused on the environmental policies of the IMF or the World Bank. The Internet is going to give people an opportunity to vote on a constant and continuous basis and make their views felt in a way that they couldn't possibly do it through letter writing or phone calls or more traditional picnics of passing on your point of view. Vote.com is really a precursor of what I see as a major movement to reshape the whole way our politics is conducted and the way we are governed."

I think Morris is correct. During the 2000 presidential election, we heard plenty about the possibilities of voting online for our candidates. With all the screw-ups in Florida and around the country during this election, something has to happen to bring stability and authenticity to the voting process. It may be a few years down the road before the government reaches these standards and decides how to implement such a huge project, but change is coming.

"I think the key thing about being an entrepreneur is a metaphor. It's as if we live in a city, and every inch of that city is developed. There's no vacant land, there are no air rights, everything is built to the maximum density. And if you want to build a little more, you have to work within the context of what's already there. It's like we all got a notice in the e-mail that said in five years we all had to vacate the city, and all of us have to move to this open vacant land, and we have to recreate this city on this vacant land. That's what the Internet is—it's taking the entire structure and saying, 'If you're an ad agency in the old world, you'll have to become one in the new world. If you're an accounting agency in the old world, you're going to have to become one in the new world. If you're a political party in the old world, you'll have to become one in the new world.' The real estate in that new city is really person-hours online, and the more person-hours online you can command, the more real estate you can own in that new city. And you may have to hold on to it for a little while, and you might have to find a way to support yourself while you're doing that, but the point is that, eventually, you'll be a landlord in that new real estate."

—DICK MORRIS, CEO, Vote.com

SUMMARY

History repeats itself over and over. You may have a fabulous idea, but the time you've taken to execute it could cost you your company. Technology moves like a boulder rolling down the mountain of infinity, crushing everything that isn't quick enough on its feet to shift over another foot or two. Each generation of technology has its own vocabulary, rules, needs, demands, and heroes. If you intend to be one of the survivors— the dot-com successes—study and understand the past, and set your sights on where you want to be when the next wave hits. You'll either have a surfboard, or you won't.

CHAPTER 2

DIALING FOR DOLLARS
The Ins and Outs of Using Other People's Money

Everyone works in the Valley, or at least works *it*. Whatever *it* means is an individual endeavor. The people I'm talking about are working their cash, using their skills to leverage a good deal, or trying to launch a startup. This is the Land of Opportunity, or at least of opportunists. You have millions of people walking around the Valley (and in communities around the world where venture money is thick) with unique goals, and sometimes when they meet up with someone like-minded, there's an opportunity to partner. The odds it works out? Probably the same as shooting craps in Vegas. Some say a bit slimmer.

Personally, I have to tell you, the people who seem like they're having the most fun in this new economy are the angels and venture capitalists. The people who've already made their money and are recycling their millions and billions to make yet more cash. VCs (venture capitalists) and angels are always on the lookout for an entrepreneur who can sell them on the next big thing. These are the most jaded people walking among us— they've seen everything and know of everyone who's been burnt. They know the *dark side* of dot-com. On the other hand, they're still dreamers and optimists—these people really believe in *you* when they put their gold pieces on the table. You can really feel proud of yourself when you and your team seduce a big firm or angel group into giving you a great term sheet—you rock! It's like the feeling you'd get if you took Elle McPherson or Antonio Banderas to your 20-year high school reunion, except better.

Many of the veteran investors in the field are able to scent out a good deal like a hound on the hunt. They know how to shake out the BS from a plan, how to finesse their questions delicately and still rip your plan apart, layer by layer with razor-sharp accuracy. Many of the wisest of them have been in the industry as long as semiconductors have, some longer, and they made their money early on. There are others who made their cash from the desktop computer and software era. Now there's the young breed that's made its money within the last 10 years from the Internet and all of the services it requires.

ANGEL OR VC?

Okay, people throw these words around a lot and have no clue what the real difference is. Many people start out as *angels*, those using their own money to fund promising business ideas. Some decide to bring their friends in—and as long as those friends participate in directly choosing the companies the group invests in, then you have a flock of angels, but angels nonetheless. *VCs* spend other people's money (otherwise known as OPM). Many times, an angel will build a group and then start a fund that accepts money from outside investors who don't have a say in what the fund invests in (thus, they are spending OPM). For lack of a better term, I call those types *angel capitalists*. Others would call them venture capitalists. It used to be that angels provided more mentoring and venture capitalists were harder to get in and see. Today, angels—really good angels—are just as difficult to make appointments to see, and they spend just as much time doing their *due diligence*, a process where entrepreneurs and technologies are thoroughly checked out before an investment is made. VCs are also now giving their companies lots of mentoring. There are also *venture catalysts*—those who introduce others to their VC and angel friends and, when the deal is sealed, either get a cut of the money garnered or stock in the funded company—sometimes both. Many venture catalysts, if their name lends credibility, are also given a seat on the startup's advisory board.

Okay, so how does knowing the definitions of these investors help you now? Is one type better to choose over the other? Before the correction in the market, you could be choosy about whom you took money from. Now you just take it when it's on the table.

Angels used to be the people you received your seed money or early rounds from; now they're funding later rounds and bridge rounds. VCs and venture arms (corporate funds) used to be the people you took your later rounds from; now they're funding early rounds. These days, you hope for the best on the terms of taking the money and move forward to the next round.

MANNERS, PLEASE

There is a great deal of etiquette that goes into playing this game of funding. Whenever you're pitching a VC or angel, group or individual, you should always find out what they have funded in the past. You can tell a lot about the angel or VC investments and its willingness to look at a deal by its website. You can also track down information, such as an investor's portfolio companies, as easily as looking at its online portfolio (if you're dealing with a firm or group). Websites will often describe what kinds of deals they're willing to look at or whether they're even willing to take a look-see at unsolicited business plans at all.

You also want to tactfully choose a targeted few VCs or angels to pitch rather than blanket the entire industry with your business plan in a hit-or-miss style. Locate people who understand your market segment and have helped build strong companies in your sector (although avoid the ones who have funded direct competition).

Nothing annoys investors more than to get a business plan completely outside of their realm of interest. So it's best to find the right investor before e-mailing your plan. It's just as important to know some information when you're talking to someone in person. So, before you even begin pitching someone at a cocktail party—and only do so with an invitation of, "Oh, so what are you working on?"—ask them some casual questions about what their company does.

"The entrepreneurs that drive me away from investing are individuals who have major attitudes and come up to me at a conference and say, 'I sent you 20 e-mails and called your office, and you are so rude that you never return my phone calls. I just can't believe that you have such disrespect for me.' And that happens all of the time. What they don't understand is that when they talk to the receptionist and the receptionist tells them that they are not going to have their messages returned, but they can send an e-mail or leave a voice-mail, but I may not respond—they don't believe it. I may read the message, I may choose to respond or not to respond. The truth is I may or may not hear or see a message because I have other people clearing them for me. Just because someone sent me something doesn't mean I have a moral obligation to read it or to respond to it. So to start a relationship off with a major guilt trip doesn't work for me."

—CAROL SANDS, founder and managing member of The Angels' Forum and The Halo Fund

TO TELL OR NOT TO TELL— IT'S YOUR PREROGATIVE

So, how much are you willing to tell someone without a non-disclosure agreement? We're all pretty paranoid in the business. Why? Because for every good idea someone has, there are maybe 100 other people who have the same sliver of a plan involving a similar concept or technology. Maybe they have friends who can help them ramp up quicker, maybe they have an entire team of gurus in place to help them implement the technology. Maybe, just maybe, they went to the same VC you sent your plan to today, and perhaps that VC funded them and as soon as they open your plan they're going to forward it on to the company. Maybe some VCs and angels take an all's-fair-in-love-and-war approach to business.

Guess what? You will rarely find anyone who will sign an NDA in this business with perhaps the exception of private angels. This is what happened in Hollywood with scripts a number of years ago when the studios began to refuse to look at unsolicited scripts without the writer signing a release that frees them of all liability if they have a similar movie that eventually makes it to the screen. Now, you can't get a screenplay into a production house without having a referral from a recognized agent or attorney.

"The entrepreneur has to ask themself, 'Why do I need a nondisclosure?'" asks Stuart Davidson, managing director of Labrador Ventures II, III, and IV (www.Labrador.com); venture partner, Draper Fisher Jurvetson Funds V and VI; and advisory board member of Utah Ventures.

"One of the reasons might be because their lawyer told them to get it. What I always say when people ask me is 'no.' Sometimes the conversation stops—that's the risk I'm taking. Maybe I'm missing the next Apple Computer or something," Davidson says of the risk of turning down NDAs. "But the entrepreneur needs to ask themself, 'Why do I need an NDA, and what am I trying to protect?' To me, if there are some things that are so proprietary that they don't want to tell the investors, then they should not tell them. They should make some little black boxes and say, 'We have a business and it has a certain amount of return related in this area. But our business model or our technology is so proprietary that we don't want to talk about that stuff right now. If we get into further due diligence, maybe under nondisclosure you can review our patents.' That kind of discussion is received well by investors.

"They may, for patenting reasons, need to maintain a close circle with the information, or they may leak it too much and run the risk of having some information fall into the public domain. What I see a lot of in the creative domain is, 'Somebody's going to steal my idea, and I don't want to tell you my idea unless I have you tied up in NDA knots.' That usually tells me that the person has done nothing else except make up some idea, and just because they had some great idea in the shower they think success is assured. They've forgotten that you then need to put people, money, and plans around that idea and move it forward. Often I try to point to that, and the better entrepreneurs go away, figure it out, and come back. I think people forget that the idea is important, but it's only two percent of the effort."

Would a VC or angel tell you if they had invested, or were already interested, in a company that wasn't currently identified on their website portfolio? What if they were in direct competition with your company? Would they wait until you went into your song and dance to get more information to pass on to their company?

"I would tell the presenting entrepreneur beforehand, but someone else may not," says Davidson. "A tip for the entrepreneur is to come in and say, 'Hey look, we're going into the generic description of the space. I checked your website, and I didn't see anything, but do you have any companies that do X?' And get that straight before you even show up for the meeting. I think it's a good way of bringing up the confidentiality issue and will show a certain seasoned sense to the investor that the entrepreneur understands you're not going to sign an NDA. Also that you understand what the issues are and have checked out our website and are checking us out before you end up in a position that's tough."

Tom Bevilacqua, chief strategic investor officer for E*TRADE and general partner for E*TRADE Venture Capital also has an opinion about NDAs. "I say we probably see twenty-five to thirty percent or so of the folks we talk to who initially ask us to sign some kind of nondisclosure agreement," says Bevilacqua. "Our response is, as investors, that we do not sign a nondisclosure agreement up front when we're learning about a company. We ask the founder to block out the information that's sensitive and not to share it with us. We have an initial look to see if going forward makes sense. If we're going to delve down into some proprietary algorithms, or we're going down to a level where we're turning over something that is truly proprietary, then we will sign a nondisclosure, but only if we get down to the second level."

Do you have much to worry about when you do submit a business plan? I attend a lot of parties and there are a lot of suits (investors) out there who really dig those bragging rights when they've screwed over an entrepreneur, so I know they exist. They are usually young and tend to be avoided by ethical investors.

"If you really did that to a large degree, the word would get out. I'm sure it would interfere with your reputation and the degree of integrity you operate with," says Bevilacqua about sharing the business plans that come in with their portfolio companies. "If somebody were to voluntarily provide us with some information that was extremely proprietary, if anything, we'd send it back to them and say, 'This is extremely proprietary. You shouldn't give this to us.' You just can't take advantage of folks that way."

Mark Radcliffe, partner at Gray Cary Ware & Freidenrich (www.GrayCary.com) and co-author of *Internet Law and Business Handbook* (www.LaderaPress.com), has some definite rules about proprietary information for the startups that he advises.

"Legally, to protect your trade secrets, you need to take reasonable steps to keep them in confidence," Radcliffe says about the basics of protecting your company. "That means you get a written confidentiality agreement. However, in raising money you have to be more flexible. The truth of the matter is that no venture capitalist will sign a confidentiality agreement, so you're put in a position where you have to decide what your goal is. Your goal is to raise money, but the realities of the marketplace are that people will not sign confidentiality agreements. What you have to do is have a layered plan about revealing various information about your company. You start from the philosophy that it's going to be a step approach to make sure you can trust them with your information. So you're going to give them enough up front to interest them but information that is not proprietary. At some point you'll have to start disclosing more proprietary information, so as you become more confident in the venture capitalist, you can be more open with them.

"The first question out of your mouth should be, 'Here's my elevator speech about my company; have you invested in any competitors?' I've had venture capitalists say [at that point], 'We've already made our bet in that space, thank you very much.' Unfortunately, some people will just sit there and listen and listen and listen, and later on you'll discover that they have a portfolio company that's a direct competitor," warns Radcliffe. "One of the things you should find out is the reputation of the venture firm you're dealing with, but also find out about the particular reputation of the venture capitalist you're working with. Information like that gets around really quickly. Most venture capitalists take the position of 'Look, our reputation is what we live and die by, and we're not going to put our reputation on the line by talking about your company.' That's a fine thing to say, but I tell my companies that they shouldn't put information that's proprietary into their executive summary. It's the rare company that will succeed based on what's in its PowerPoint presentation. There may be companies like that, but in my experience in working with companies for almost twenty years, such companies are rare. Even if the business described in the PowerPoint is the one that gets to market, there's an awful lot of work that goes into implementation to make it successful. So merely having an idea is not enough, it's just the beginning of the road.

"Hopefully, you've taken a look at your intellectual property rights and taken appropriate steps to protect them. If your core asset is something that's patentable, you've filed a patent. You can put a little fear in someone disclosing information if you've filed a patent and there's a patent pending. Patents in the United States patents are secret for the term of their prosecution—eighteen to twenty-four months, or even longer, so they won't know what's patented.

"Most of my clients get through the entire time with a venture capitalist without signing a nondisclosure. That's just the reality of the marketplace," Radcliffe says about the facts of NDAs. "There may be some really hard technologies where you can get them to sign a nondisclosure, or there may be reasons to have them sign something for patent reasons. Virtually every company I work for does the whole venture capital process (including due diligence) without any formal nondisclosure agreement in place. That's the golden rule: The guy with the gold makes the rule."

STANDING UP UNDER SCRUTINY

Many kinds of due diligence are done, from bringing in top-notch visionaries, technologists, and scientists to test out the company's potential, to bringing in a private investigator to check out the members of the team. E*TRADE's venture funds go one step further by bringing their entrepreneurs face to face with the market and any of the disappointments it may hold. "We don't routinely hire an investigator to check into the backgrounds of the team only because most of the people have been referred to us from sources we know, although we do reference checks," says Tom Bevilacqua, chief strategic investor officer for E*TRADE and general partner for E*TRADE Venture Capital.

"Let's say it's a company preparing a new product. I think the more important due diligence is going out and talking to potential new customers. These may be customers that are one to two years down the road, or even three," says Bevilacqua of the amount of time-forward research that needs to be put in place to test companies out.

"You'd want to go out to these customers and find out what they think the product requirements or specs should be or need to be, or what they're going to look for in making a buy or licensing decision," Bevilacqua says. "That's the level I think is most important is going out to the ultimate user or consumers and figuring out how they are going to evaluate the decision to use or not use the product. What I think is more important, if it's a product company, is to go out and talk to the customer. One of the luxuries we have at E*TRADE is that we're going in and looking at companies we can add unique value to—that usually means we may very well be a likely user or somehow involved with the type of product they're offering. So when we evaluate the company, we're able to make some very valuable input to the company at the same time as far as where they need to build in order to go after this e-commerce market. That's really important and done by personal interviews, by bringing the young company out to meet prospective customers, by phone interviews, that kind of thing.

"Usually the business has some sort of financial model for the company, so we start with their assumptions. Then we'll go back and reconstruct our own business model using what we know," says Bevilacqua. "Let's say a company is some kind of consumer company, and they're assuming some sort of consumer rates, and we know from our own matrix that the type of conversation rates they're projecting are way too high. We'll overlay our thinking onto theirs and rebuild their plan from the ground up."

BE HONEST

Due diligence is something that you'll need to address honestly when it comes up. Before anyone gives you any cash, you're going to go through hell and back proving out your technology, your concepts, why you, personally, are worthy of the investment. There are no free continental breakfasts left in Silicon Valley; you have to work for your dough now. And no matter what, you should address with great candor the issues that will come up. If you sideline a fact that due diligence will uncover, you're risking your funding, as well as your reputation.

It's not as easy now as it was before April 2000 to get funding. The coffers of VCs and angel groups are heavily guarded, and they have to really defend their investment decisions before the checks are cut. That means that you'll not only need a great business plan to get in the door, a fabulous dog-and-pony pitch, and proven out technology—you'll also need to be drop-dead honest about everything.

"For me, the best policy is to bring things up front," says Stuart Davidson, managing director of Labrador Ventures II, III, and IV (www.Labrador.com); venture partner, Draper Fisher Jurvetson Funds V and VI; and advisory board member of Utah Ventures. "Let's say the entrepreneur has had a failed business in the past. Instead of trying to finesse it in a resume, the person can say, 'Hey, I ran this business and it failed.' And the next question is going to be 'Why did it fail?' And some people say, 'I had no idea what I was doing.' And I like that, I can see what they learned and where they've come from. The fewer surprises you can give investors, the happier they are. A lot of what the process is, is removing risk, and in the early stage, investors take the most risk."

One of the things you should also disclose is whether there may be problems ahead for the company. Actually, saying this will make you mighty unattractive to any investor because it means their money might be used to fight lawsuits instead of build the company, so you should figure all this stuff out before going to them. In the end it will come out, and not taking care of these things before searching for funding is a big mistake. Many investors don't even look at a company unless a patent is pending or has already been assigned.

"There are a couple of problems you see pretty consistently with startup companies, particularly ones that haven't had legal counseling from the beginning," says Mark Radcliffe, partner at Gray Cary Ware & Freidenrich (www.GrayCary.com) and co-author of *Internet Law and Business Handbook* (www.LaderaPress.com). "Another one of the problems is not getting all the rights in the company from people who have left. Maybe you have six founders and one of them decides he doesn't want to go with the group; he goes and gets employed somewhere else. Did he contribute to the technology? What kind of risks are you running if you don't have a [patent] assignment?"

DIVINE AWARENESS

Sometimes angels can be the best help for your company, especially if you're really green and have no clue about the business side of your business. Angels can help you find people who will bring you help—but only if you allow them to. Some angels prefer to be involved (that's where the term smart money comes in) and others want nothing at all except updates and results. As an entrepreneur, you should find the best money for the place you're at in the life of your company. There is this myth that most entrepreneurs believe that angels, by the sake of title alone, are both easier to obtain money from and will always be willing to drop everything to help you.

Most of the angels I know are as tough as any VCs, and some are actually tougher. After all, it is their own money they're investing. With groups of angels, it's easier to find the help you need because there are more people involved. Usually someone will know someone who can help you, and their money is usually the first money in the pot. Many angel groups are going the way of venture capitalists with venture funds and have a double angel/VC role (using OPM to build their venture funds).

One of the more exclusive angel groups in Silicon Valley is The Angels' Forum, a group of 20-plus angels handpicked by Carol Sands, founder and managing member of The Angels' Forum and The Halo Fund, for their skills in various technologies and industries. Its investments include Cubus Corporation, CyberBills.com, Digital Interiors, eAcumen.com, eCode.com, ELetter.com, HardwareStreet.com, OnRadio, PeopleScape, and StockMaster.

How is Sands' group introduced to new deals? "Any business plan that comes in over the transom [unsolicited or without a referral] has less of a chance to get any kind of visibility than if it is introduced or hand delivered by someone we know and trust," says Sands of the process. "If somebody takes the time and energy to introduce me to an entrepreneurial team, then I know they have some connection and that there is some reason and some passion why someone is doing so. By definition, that makes it a more desirable business plan than one that is being thrown into any mailbox the entrepreneur can find. Item number one is, if you really want someone to invest in you, you need the benefit of a third party reference. That third party reference can be your accounting firm, it can be your law firm, it can be friends, family... I just need somebody I know to say, 'I have passion around this. Pay attention to it.' That's kind of the rude reality of life."

The Angels' Forum has a website that does accept business plans. "And we do review them on occasion," says Sands. "And every once in a while there's a little gem out there, and there is something about the technology and the way they're talking about it that makes me say, 'Tell me more about it.' It might be something about the technology that is something so very new, or how they're applying a technology to a very new market, that makes it sound interesting. *Looking at* and *investing in* are two very different things. I only invest in companies that have people associated with them who I believe have the ability, the capacity, the passion, and the skill set to return a gigantic return on my investment."

ON BEING AN ATTRACTIVE ENTREPRENEUR

Finding entrepreneurs who have a strong will for the business, but sense enough to listen to solid advice from people who've been where they are, can be tough.

"With some entrepreneurs, if they're inexperienced and uncoachable, it can be fatal," warns Carol Sands, founder and managing member of The Angels' Forum and The Halo Fund. "So one of the things we're looking for is coachability. Lying is a big issue, and that happens more often than I'd like to admit.

Someone will say, 'Yes I have an agreement with XYZ company,' and then we ask 'Can we see it?' and they say 'No,' and we ask why, and they say, 'Well, I don't have the piece of paper.' We try and give them the benefit of the doubt and say, 'Well okay, when you get back to the office, fax it.' They don't and, by then, it becomes obvious they don't have it. Lying is a big one. That basically says, 'I can't trust you.'"

One of the paces Sands' group puts the teams through is one of endurance. "There are times when we will purposefully stress a team of people to see how the team will respond. The reason we do that is because we are nothing compared to the stress of running a company. And this goes back to my basic premise that what you always, always invest in is people and the ability of that team to deliver. If a team cracks at a point of stress in front of a group of angels during a presentation, what are they going to do when they can't make payroll? The arrogance level is one of the things we look for, and it's an interesting balance. We need the entrepreneur arrogant enough so they can get up and do battle with the world to create a place for themselves and their company. You need some ego actively in place, but if the ego is so large and so out of control that it can't accept new information, then it's going to lose touch with reality. Then it becomes ineffective and actually starts causing trouble for the company and for the entrepreneur rather than solving problems. It's a very delicate balance. We do look for that appropriate level of ego to tie into that coachability. A gigantic part of being an entrepreneur is seeking information and reformulating the business model based on that new information."

One of the things you, an entrepreneur, must remember is that you must have a compelling reason for anyone to invest in your company. The most compelling reason for an investor should be return on their money. Remember, this money is not some source of free funding—the people who are potentially funding you will expect big returns.

"[A startup] starts with a very basic concept" says Sands. "If you are going to ask for other people's money to be involved with you and your passion, there needs to be a mechanism that allows them to be paid back and then be rewarded for having taken the risk. You'd be surprised by how many business plans don't have a clue about how to make money. And once the team has figured out how to make revenue, they still haven't figured out how to make profit, and business must have profit.

"We had a slight suspension of the rules for a very short period of time in the Internet world when we temporarily forgot about profit. Actually, The Angels' Forum did not forget this rule. In order to make it worth an investor's time and energy, there has to be a reasonable return on investment. And in order to get my money, there has to be an extraordinary amount of return on my investment in order to make it worthwhile. The first part you need to understand is that, though the technology is a way to generate all of this, I am never, ever investing in the technology. I'm investing in people who have the ability to execute a plan that will generate profit—and the more the better."

One of the most important things, after a compelling presentation about how you plan to give the investor big returns, is that you can attract other people and have the passion to execute quickly.

"We're looking for entrepreneurs who can attract other team members, because no business that will create the types of returns we're looking for will be able to execute with two or three people," says Sands. "The companies that we bring in will hopefully be able to attract hundreds and then literally thousands of people in later points in the companies' lives. Do they have what it takes to attract a team around them so they can execute? Do they have the courage in this raw form to reassess themselves, their business, and their market on a regular basis and make adjustment to the plan based on that information? Do they have the courage to ask, 'Am I the right person for this position today?' or 'Is there someone else who can do this better?' And do they have the ability to make it all happen in a timely way? There's talk about a window in terms of open-and-shut opportunities—it's really not the right analogy—the right analogy is the door that is coming down like in *Indiana Jones*, when the door moves very quickly from being open to starting to close.

Only the courageous will be the last one or the first one through the unknown to the other side. And that requires a great deal of personal courage."

TAKE THE MONEY AND RUN (TO THE BANK)

One of the toughest things to do is get to work after you've received your first round of funding. If you're able to hit the ground running with your plan and people in place, then you know the money will go as fast as your company can implement the steps to your growth. What that means is that you'll need more money soon. By the time you get your ducks in a row, manage to get into as many offices as you can, go through due diligence, and find a term sheet, you'll be needing money again. All this time, you'll be on the phone or on the way to or from investors' offices.

"When you're in the funding mode, get it done as quickly as you can, and then quickly get your eyes back on the ball, which is creating value for yourself and your shareholders," says Carol Sands, founder and managing member of The Angels' Forum and The Halo Fund. "And if there is a mechanism that allows you to decrease the amount of time that you personally have to spend on fundraising, do it. I'm always amused by entrepreneurs who are in the final stages of fundraising, and at the final stages—especially if you are a good company—there are typically more people interested in investing in you than you originally said you were going to accept. You say you're going to raise a million and then all of a sudden there's a million and a half on the table saying, 'Take me, take me, take me.' The real difference between an experienced entrepreneur and an inexperienced entrepreneur is that the inexperienced entrepreneur will say, 'No, I told you it was only going to be a million dollars, and it's only going to be a million dollars,' and cut off the investors. Which really upsets everyone because you've broken the primary rule of business, which is *always take cash*. And once you scale somebody back, it's really difficult to go back to them and say 'Hey, I'm running out of money, remember that money you wanted to give me and I wouldn't take? Well, I'll take it now.' Well, the terms aren't going to be the same and the punishment for that is that you lose even more of your money.

"The experienced entrepreneur will take the extra money—won't spend it, will just hang on to it. But they'll take it. There'll be something that comes along when they need that extra money. And if nothing else, it allows them to go a little bit further before the next round of financing comes around and they'll have a stronger value proposition to show. Take the money."

KNOW THY INVESTOR

There is smart money and there is dumb money—and some entrepreneurs are just so slaphappy to be receiving *any* money at all that they take it and don't bother to find out what comes with it. Is the person you're taking money from well connected? You're banking on their Rolodex to help you draw more money; you should know what they will be able to do for you other than adding some payroll cash to your till.

It's often not the big things but the little things that will bite you in the ass when choosing an investor. For instance, what kind of character does this person have? How and when do they expect you to grow? Are they expecting you to replace your executive team when the company outgrows your experience? How many other investments do they have, and what have they done for their companies? Ask if you may contact their portfolio companies (investments) entrepreneurs to get the 411 on their style.

I'd be wary of those venture brokerage companies that invite non-qualified investors to functions where they solicit funds from attendees. There are a lot of groups, or wannabe groups, out there that are not following Securities and Exchange Commission (SEC) guidelines. These groups usually have not been qualified to take the money once it's been brought to the table. Even though it may look legit, you could find yourself in deep SEC trouble. If it's too easy to get into a group, there may be a reason for it. Doing some due diligence with these groups could keep your company out of hot water with the SEC.

Much of your success will build on the people who invest in you. Who are these people, anyway? It doesn't take much to find individuals of high wealth—hell, people dumber than door-nails inherit fortunes all the time. On the other hand, many unethical people have also been known to invest money in unsuspecting companies.

"You are known by the company you keep," says Carol Sands, founder and managing member of The Angels' Forum and The Halo Fund. "If you don't know the reputation of whom you are accepting money, that can be dangerous. There are times when the investors you are doing business with don't have a reputation because they're new investors. That's okay. That's better than a bad reputation. Ask people in the industry, 'What do you know about them?' I'm personally more inter-ested in their reputation from a co-investor point of view. Do they have relationships with other investors who will co-invest with them, or are they a one-trick pony?

"There are investors out there who, for whatever reason, are known for stealing technology," warns Sands. "They literally drive the companies to a point of failure and steal the technol-ogy because the company doesn't have the means to go forward. They basically start up a new company, put a whole new team around it, and try to act like it's all theirs. It happens all the time. There are also investors out there investing because they want a job, so they will put a huge amount of money into a company. In return, what they want is a position with the company. Typ-ically these individuals are not well suited to be part of the team. Some people invest and then turn around and recommend their consulting services. That doesn't make them bad or good, but if you didn't know this was going to happen ahead of time, it can be very, very awkward because sometimes they're not your first choice for a consultant. You need to know why they're making the investment. Are there hidden agendas? You can find out some of these answers by asking point blank; others you'll only find out by asking others they have invested in.

"The truth of the matter is that angel investing is something you're going to do because it grabs your passion," says Sands about why she personally invests. "It's very difficult to predict what will catch your attention. The process of what grabs an investor's attention is that you're solving a problem you're personally interested in. There are some businesses that are just so elegant in their simplicity that it's clear to everyone involved that they're going to make great gobs of money. So, when you hit one of those, you're natural inclination is to invest, but those are often the ones you have to do the most due diligence on."

In some cases having an investor with the wrong reputation could be detrimental and shut down your ability to garner any smart money down the line. One of the first things an investor does when they open your business plan is to go right to the list of investors, board members, and advisors.

I recently ran into a company in which one of the investors had made a deal with the company to put his relative on the board (where that relative would be receiving a piece of the company). I saw the name on the board and asked aloud, during a meeting with the CEO and others, "What value does this person bring to the table?" They explained that he came with the deal. They also seemed positive that he would be able to pull some strings in the industry he was in (one I was very familiar with). I was very frank and told them that those kinds of strings don't get pulled without going through many channels, none of which I thought he had the power to control. He would bring no added value to the deal, and he would be given stock for nothing. I had been psyched on the company—a company that could have received much smarter money because they are in a killer space. But once I found out they had made the poor decision to bring someone with no value on board simply because he was "attached" to the investor, I knew that it wouldn't be their last mistake. I wondered how that decision-making process would proliferate in the company's future. I knew if I brought this deal to any other investors they would have a difficult time not laughing their asses off about the reasoning behind the decision to put the person on the board. They also told me they were in negotiations with an investor who had a reputation for scaring reputable investors from the table. Although I'm rooting for them—I'm jazzed about the product and the people involved are genuinely passionate about the company—I know they're in for a difficult time.

The key to bringing anyone into the fold of your company is that they need to add value. Once you start bringing everyone and their neighbor into the deal, you're road kill. You dilute your stock when you start sharing it with just anyone, and your potential investors will not respect you for your ability (or not) to make smart decisions.

Is Your Angel Involved?

I've met a lot of entrepreneurs who were pre-funding. Then, all of a sudden, they get a check for five million, and they're sitting there with their three partners not having a clue about what to do with the check that's starting to make them sweat. What should they do first? After they sober up, literally, they throw away the champagne bottles and begin to plan. They talk and decide where they should get office space. (And if you're in Silicon Valley, because of the tight space, in addition to the honor of paying high rent, you often give stock to your landlord. Although, because of the recent fallout and consolidation, space is freeing up in the Valley and in San Francisco, so I think the days of issuing stock to landlords are just about over.)

Find people? Bring a headhunter on board? Concentrate on R&D (research and development)? Cater a $4.5-million-dollar startup party? Hunt down a celebrity for branding? How should they spend that money, and how do they know if they have a good deal? The great thing about having angels participating on your team is that they can help you out with the stuff they've gone through before.

"There are some angels who are investing their own money who have not read the business plan, who have done absolutely zero due diligence, have not met the entrepreneur, have not even become involved," says Carol Sands, founder and managing member of The Angels' Forum and The Halo Fund, about how many angel investors typically invest. "Most of the time, they don't know what the company does and may not even know the name of the company. You get what you pay for. Those kinds of angels are okay if what you really need is money. But most of the time, when you're early stage, you need some involvement. Some angels will actually invest the time and might even meet with the entrepreneur, but they don't have follow-up. Other investors have status in the Valley and meet the entre-preneur and make the investment. These people have impressive names to add to the investor and board list, but a large portion of those types of investors never show up for the board meet-ings and don't respond to phone calls or e-mails. Their only involvement is on paper.

"The higher-level angels are the ones who read through business plans, get involved with the development of the con-cept, accept board of director responsibilities, and actively par-ticipate in the process to help facilitate meetings and clarify business ideas," explains Sands. "I call it *involved money*. Smart money can still be uninvolved. For instance, a guy who sees a good business plan and can bring $200 thousand to $500 thou-sand into the deal, make a few phone calls, and get his friends to also invest—that's smart money. That person may not be involved with the company from that day forward. The key issue for me is that the more involved an experienced business angel is, the higher the success probabilities of the company and the speed at which the company can ramp up.

"I see bad behavior all the time," says Sands of entrepreneurial behavior she has experienced. "You may go into the deal intend-ing from the beginning to be involved, but a lot of entrepreneurs treat this as if it's the end of the relationship, because once they have your money, they don't have to listen to you anymore. If that's the entrepreneur's expectation, and that is their behavior, it may or may not be okay with you as an investor. But most entrepreneurs clearly communicate during this due diligence phase what they would like the relationship to be.

"One of the biggest assets entrepreneurs gain from experienced angels is guidance through turbulent times or decisions," explains Sands of the benefits an angel can offer. "You may need to get an equipment lease for your entrepreneur. For the most part, an experienced businessperson has been through this process multiple times and knows that it isn't the rate you're looking at, it's a whole relationship, and to never go into any legal document assuming that things are going to be perfect. The whole purpose of having a legal document is because you are working under the assumption that things aren't going to be perfect and there's going to be a problem. The legal document provides you with a path or rule about how that not-perfect solution will be handled. It's all those ifs that make the difference from one lease to another. An experienced businessperson will know these things. What if you say, 'Don't go for this one because this company has these kind of features hidden in their documents. Go for this one because if things should go bad, this is the one who will work with us during that time,' and the entrepreneur says, 'No, I'm not going to listen to you, I'm going to go with this.'? It's not a fatal mistake; it's one of those mistakes that could end up slowing them down because of problems coming up later."

No matter what your level as an entrepreneur, everyone can benefit from a mentor. If you're not willing or able to learn, you're in the wrong business. "If you look at being an entrepreneur as a coaching type of experience, even in the pros—basketball, soccer, baseball—you still always have a coach standing on the side because they can see the whole picture. It's the same thing between an experienced entrepreneur and an active entrepreneur. If they're not willing to accept the coaching, then the amount of problems and the speed at which they can solve those problems slows down. So, it doesn't say whether or not they will be successful or not successful, it's just the pain level this will happen."

GOOD DEAL FLOW

For most investors, companies come to them by referral only. Other groups do a hit-or-miss, "Let's see what they've got" approach and will meet with anyone. That's not necessarily a good thing. One of the groups known for its exclusivity is the Band of Angels, a group that has become legendary in the Valley.

"We've always had great deal flow," says Ian Patrick Sobieski, Ph.D., managing director, Band of Angels Fund, LP, a group that has a good deal of Silicon Valley's royalty as members. This group of investors has only invested in two unsolicited deals in the last two years (out of thousands of proposals). This gives you an idea about the power of an introduction.

"And our deals have always been good," says Sobieski, "but good deals can dip in this economy. We have a lot of deals that are coming back down. As I always say, we're the first step on the way up and the last step on the way down the success ladder. It's because shakeout in the market has caused a lot of companies that would normally have been on the upper trajectory to change course. And those go back down to big funds, to medium funds, to small funds, to angel groups; and we're both a small fund and an angel group."

Just before a company's death rattle, the Band of Angels may see a business plan come by asking for a *bridge round*, a round of money that is often needed to make immediate payroll, or cover overdue bills to keep a company up and running. "Many are probably on their way out of business," says Sobieski. "So in addition to our good, normal deal flow, we're seeing companies coming down the pipeline that have payroll, are out of cash, and in dire straits. Seen a lot of those."

VC and angel groups often have good deal flow because of the number and variety of companies that are in the space. Many times, VCs and angels see a flurry of the same types of deals come across their desks all at once. Once a trend hits, it hits hard, and it wears itself out until another trend hits. Sometimes companies that have been funded and are getting a foothold in the market may not have an opportunity to get another round of funding because the type of business they are have fallen out of favor. We saw this happen with B2C. For instance, there are now a lot of B2C companies hounding investors for bridge loans on their way down the tubes. They will eventually succumb to the market and, in most cases, die 20 people at a time as companies issue pink slips and juggle debt until they succumb to the inevitable.

"We always see seasonal changes in the kinds of deals we get. There are fads in the startup business as in everything else," says Sobieski. "We saw the content plays, the e-plays, calendaring companies, search companies, auction companies. They come and go. Peer-to-peer companies are all the new rage now, so now everyone has some kind of new P2P company. I always say, you have to be really careful, because there are about a million me-too companies, and by the time you read about the trend, it's definitely too late to get in with the early movers. Sometimes you can still get in on the smart ones. Entrepreneurs sometimes read something in the back pages of a magazine and feel that they're the only ones who read it and that they're getting in on a trend."

"[Fundraising] was difficult. We got turned down a lot [with FrameMaker]. People make judgment calls all the time on new ideas. Some people see merit in your ideas, others don't. And you can learn from the people who don't by understanding why people see your idea as not promising. I remember the story of Palm Pilot—they got turned down by everyone. It's not like you get a 'Yes!' immediately. You get 'Give us more information, give us more information.' And you'll be working with a number of different people, and then eventually someone will say 'Yes, we want to fund this,' and give you an absurdly low evaluation. You're celebrating in one sense, but you're not celebrating in the other sense. Funding is not like an instant gratification."

—STEVE KIRSCH, founder of Mouse Systems, Frame Technology, Infoseek, and Propel

Working with Venture Funds

Many green entrepreneurs don't think about going the way of the venture arms, although it's a very smart way to go. Some corporations invest in complementary technology, products, or services to their own; others wish to diversify and invest in a little of everything. Your job is to investigate the venture funds—most have a Web page within the company's website under "Investor Relations," usually titled "Venture Fund," "Investments," or "Portfolio Companies." For others, you will have to call and obtain more information about them before submitting your proposal.

The great thing about having a venture fund invest in you is that it most often means the possibility of a buyout if your technology is complementary to a company. It also means they have close ties with investment bankers and other investors who would also be able to help complete funding rounds.

One of the Valley's aggressive venture arms is funded by Adobe Systems. Dr. John E. Warnock, co-founder and CTO of Adobe Systems and head of Adobe Ventures, heads up the company's venture fund. Warnock has been through the Valley's cycles and its moody technology trends. He is also one of a handful of CEOs who have managed to hold on to the reins of the companies they started. Adobe's venture arm has funded such companies as Sendmail Inc.; Tumbleweed Communications Corp. (TMWD); Netscape/America Online (AOL); Siebel Systems, Inc. (SEBL); eCircles, Inc.; Shutterfly.com, Inc.; CoVia Technologies, Inc.; MediaBridge Technologies, Inc.; NetClerk, Inc.; Vignette, Inc. (VIGN); and Salon.com (SALN).

"In every one of those cases [portfolio company investments], there was a market need and a fundamental value proposition," says Warnock. Whether it is dot-com or a network company, Warnock feels that a good proposition remains the same in any sector or time.

"What we're expecting from companies really hasn't changed," says Warnock of the 2000 crash. "April actually made no difference whatsoever. I think generally, in the Valley, people are being a little more cautious relative to seeing a clear path to profitability in the various companies that they're talking to. The deal flow has not changed substantially. There are still as many people trying to start companies, but the climate is a little different than it was before April. In evaluating companies, I don't think we've changed at all. We've always been pretty hard-nosed about it."

What does Warnock expect from a company when they walk in the door? "When someone walks in the door and gives you a pitch, I think there are a number of questions you have to have in the back of your mind. One is, what is your fundamental value proposition, and how will this company make the world a better place? If it really doesn't have that fundamental business proposition, then it's really hard for us to invest in it. There are a lot of companies that have features—they don't have companies. They come in with an idea that would be a great feature in a product, but not a company. When you're looking for companies, you're looking for a core idea—a core idea with the potential of being manifested in a number of different products and markets around that core idea. A lot of companies don't have that, they have a twist on something and that's all it is."

"We also look for the idea of having a sustainable competitive advantage. This is extremely important. An idea that can be knocked off by bigger companies and doesn't have intellectual property protection, or doesn't have something where the new company can sustain an advantage under an attack from a larger company, then we almost never invest because it's so easy. Even though you're first in the space, a larger company can come in and outspend you and bury you. So I think an important part of starting a new company is having something sustainable and not just saying, 'We have an advantage because we're first.' At least, in our analysis, it just doesn't cut it unless there's a way to stay technologically ahead, stay ahead by patent or intellectual property protection."

–DR. JOHN E. WARNOCK, co-founder and CTO of Adobe Systems and head of Adobe Ventures

Strategic partnerships are very important to a startup. If you can get other companies to believe in your product or service, then it will be easier for an investor to believe in you. "Most people come to Adobe to get a relationship," says Warnock. "We were allowed to invest in Netscape. Netscape didn't need our money; they wanted the association and the stamp of approval that an Adobe investment would give them. And a lot of the companies that come to us are not necessarily in search of the money, but in search of the relationship. I think that does carry a lot of credibility with other investors and other companies. If you only come with a bunch of VCs in your investment port-folio—unless perhaps it's Kleiner-Perkins—it doesn't carry the kind of weight that having a strong, ongoing, profitable com-pany has to an investor."

As with many of the old-school technologists who came into the business needing to make a profit on a solid business propo-sition, Warnock's future vision of the Internet seems to have a great deal to do with core business beliefs. One of the ways Warnock measures Internet companies is by how they've changed his business and how he can relate to their core values.

"I think in Adobe's case, for instance, the Internet has allowed us to restructure the company in a way that probably five years ago would have been impractical," says Warnock of the changes Adobe's infrastructure has gone through. "Two years ago we went through a functional organization and made everything centralized. The network has really allowed us to do this with incredible efficiency. In the past, we had these geographic head-quarters that were out in Scotland, Europe, and Japan. These headquarters were sort of mini-businesses, and we eliminated all that so all of the financial reporting goes to San Jose now, and all of the payments go out of San Jose. And this is enormously efficient in terms of being able to track and monitor your busi-ness and seeing how your business is doing.

"The other thing is that we use the Internet to communicate out to the field and out to all of the international organizations in an incredibly efficient manner," says Warnock. "Adobe really runs paperless. All of our communications are electronic. And this has brought an efficiency that we've never had before in the operation of the company. I think that every company is now discovering that they can restructure themselves using the Internet as a core capability within the company, and that is bringing efficiencies and productivity that I think are the main reason the U.S. economy is so strong. So the technology is enabling modes of communication that allow us to be more productive, save money, and be more efficient and timely with product services, with change, with all of the things that drive a business to growth. That's the primary value proposition behind the Internet; the extent that companies can exploit that primary value proposition, as long as that happens, it will be thriving. For us, the Internet has changed the way we do business in a primary way— we couldn't live without it. We couldn't operate the company as efficiently as we did without it. I think it has become an integral part of business life, if not everyday life. I know my buying habits are very, very different than they were three or four years ago in the way that I look for products, in the way I locate products, in the way I buy products.

"I see huge, huge fallout and consolidation ahead, and I think it's already started to happen. There are some really good examples— people thought there was a business in putting your photographs on an Internet site, and there were five that did it. It's not clear that there is space enough for several, or even if there is space for one. We'll have to see how that all plays out."

E*TRADE: ADDING VALUE TO ITS COMPANIES

E*TRADE's venture fund is one of the strongest I've seen yet as far as its ability to add value to its companies. Tom Bevilacqua, chief strategic investment officer for E*TRADE Group, Inc. and managing general partner for E*TRADE Venture Capital, is a native Californian who has seen the ups and downs in this Valley. Having been an attorney at various firms for nearly 20 years, Bevilacqua took the offer to head up E*TRADE's venture fund two years ago. "Just by virtue of being associated with the E*TRADE brand, our deal flow is phenomenal," says Bevilacqua. The group gets about 30 to 50 screened business plans a week and meets with three to five startups a day. "It's a real challenge to manage the inflow of what you see so that you can focus on areas where you can be the most effective. We're a completely unique, different type of fund than anything else out there. One of the challenges is getting the word out about how we're unique and why we're different. Most people, when they hear the name E*TRADE in connection with the venture fund, assume that we're a corporate strategic investor, like an Intel or a Cisco or an Oracle. We're not. We are a pure financial investor and only invest to make returns, just like a Kleiner-Perkins or a Benchmark Capital.

"We look just like an independent venture fund in terms of what our focus is, and that's important because, for most corporate investors, it's a strategic investment of the corporation. That's because most corporate venture funds are trying to make an investment in a young company and trying to pull some strategic benefit back to themselves. And we've completely flipped that model around and have said, 'We're only going to invest in a young company that we think we have some proprietary knowledge that we can put into to make that company more valuable and, thereby, increase the overall returns on our capital.' From a financial investor standpoint, I think we're a very attractive fund because we have this unique ability to put value into a company and immediately propel our value, which is something our investors are looking for."

E*TRADE, a public company, now has two investment funds, each with outside investors. Each fund is represented by about 25 percent E*TRADE cash, with totals of $100 million for the first fund and approximately $250 million for the second fund. The funds' investors are a mixture of financial investors, large insurance companies, family foundations, and strategic corporate investors.

"I think most important to the entrepreneurs and the founders of these companies, we are a true value-added investor—we're entirely about adding more than value," says Bevilacqua. "We're only going into situations where we think we can bring something unique and powerful to the company we're going into. That's our whole investment philosophy. One of the things about E*TRADE is that we have a company with over three thousand employees who have various skill sets. We just invested in a company in the network security area, so we pulled in some people from our security group who, in their case, were experiencing a particular set of demands that this company seemed to solve. So, it was the perfect match of their skill set with the company. We'll do that from time to time. It's a huge resource we have that simply isn't available to most funds. We'll be very proactive in helping this company mold their services around the needs of a very large e-commerce company like ourselves. I think the odds are high that we'll also use the product."

"In our case, we're extremely hands-on, particularly when a company is in pre-product launch mode. It's not uncommon for us to be onsite with a company once a week. We're paying close attention for two reasons. One reason is to make sure things are going as projected, and also because we are this extremely value-added investor by nature. The only way I know to add the value is in person and on a continual basis. So if the company is designing out their specs for their product mode and we want to provide the overlay of what a large commerce would expect from that product or service, we're onsite to help them."

—TOM BEVILACQUA, chief strategic investment officer for E*TRADE Group, Inc. and managing general partner for E*TRADE Venture Capital

BRANDED MONEY

One of the unique ways E*TRADE is adding value to its portfolio companies is by allowing them access to the database of marketing analysis it has gathered about the Internet market. Three of E*TRADE's portfolio companies include Digital Island, Critical Path, and WebVan.

"All of the recognition studies show that we have one of the strongest brands on the Web. It's actually three times stronger than any of our competitors," says Tom Bevilacqua, chief strategic investor officer for E*TRADE and general partner for E*TRADE Venture Capital. "We know the effectiveness of different media, and we know what kinds of media yield what kind of customer. Basically, those are the types of matrix we track, and we make those available to the companies we go into. If you are a company that has a branding exercise and we fund you, what we will do is sit down and go over the draft of your media marketing plan and basically give you our experience about the effectiveness of different media. We know how messages work across different types of media, what kinds of spending levels make sense, how many times to approach a customer—that is all very proprietary-type knowledge that we're putting in the hands of the companies we fund to give them a leg up on the competition. E*TRADE has gotten to be one of the largest e-commerce companies over the last four or five years through a constant trial-and-error process. Part of what we're trying to do is take our own learning experience and give it to the companies we fund to put them on a straight line rather than a trial-and-error, zig-zaggy process to the outcome.

"Primarily we're aiming at the infrastructure that supports the delivery of e-commerce services, which cuts across many vertical segments," says Bevilacqua of their investments. "We happen to have a particular skill set in the financial service segment, to which, for the companies that we go into where financial services is a key vertical, we have a lot of value to add. Like most investors right now, we're probably less focused on consumer-oriented e-commerce companies; although, that being said, we're not ruling it out entirely. If we see something compelling that has a huge market in front of it, and it's distinctive—just because it's in a consumer area doesn't mean that we won't go after it."

Each venture arm brings a different value to its portfolio companies. Although finding investors may be tough, an entrepreneur's best bet is to find the investors willing to add the most value to your company. Taking the first venture fund's money that offers it to you could be a dire mistake. The demographics say most of you haven't been married, but taking the wrong money could be as painful and expensive as the worst divorce. Difficulties and disagreements with your investors early on could mean rough roads ahead. Pay attention to red flags. Initially identifying and clarifying differences in the relationship with your potential investor could save you a lot of pain down the line. Look at the relationship as a marriage—your company being the child. You and your team are one parent, the investors the other. So remember to always do what's right for the company, including finding that perfect mate. Remember, in a perfect world you'll be connected with that mate until the child is grown and on its own. Choose wisely. They have tons of money and hot attorneys—you will most probably lose if it goes into a legal battle. So make sure that marriage works before the conception takes place. This is my version of practicing safe funding.

"I think the most important thing by far—all these years I've had of counseling entrepreneurs and the way they go to find funding—is to make sure you're going to a funding source that will stick with you through the good times and bad," advises Bevilacqua. "Not just one that will fund you to the minute your sector gets some trouble and then chop you off at the knees. Look for those who will weather the storm with you. Look for the fund or investors who will be able to help you—the capital is great, but capital is fungible; you look for someone who can really help you. Don't necessarily get caught up in the brand name. Sometimes it's not the biggest brand name fund or company that's going to help you. Look at the individuals, look at the skill sets, look at how they're internally organized to see if they can indeed really help you. That alone—having financial backers that provide something other than capital that can really help you—helps insulate you against potential failure."

LOOKING FOR ALL THE RIGHT STUFF AT AUTODESK

One venture arm, headed by one of the most high-profile women in technology, is Autodesk's. CEO Carol Bartz, who can spot an entrepreneur worth investing in a mile away, heads the venture. Her recent investments include Buzzsaw.com and RedSpark, Inc.

"The people who come here are a total snapshot of the Valley," says Bartz. "We're doing a lot of things at Autodesk around the Internet, so we're interested in mobile and Internet infrastructure technologies—anything that helps us understand how to move this world of design to new platforms. We're looking for smart people with good ideas. We look at technology that is accessible; I believe the wave of the future is open accessibility and how simple the technology is to use. I think technologies can be very complex underneath, but if you're going to expand in any market, people need to be able to get it.

"In B2C, you're seeing people go back to brands they know and understand," says Bartz of an upcoming trend. "They want the Web to vary, but if I buy from the Gap online, I know what I'm buying. If I buy from Clothes.com—what is it? [Brand recognition's] what we intend to bring to the market and that's what we look for [in investments], not that they already have a brand—but who are they and how do they fit with our company? We've started investing in companies, and we've done acquisitions all along the way, but it's all about how you can't move fast enough internally. You can't do everything. I don't want to re-create credit transaction processing, I want to be able to sell my product on the Web. I don't need to redesign the infrastructure. You don't necessarily need to invest in those companies; you can partner with them. It's a combination of what you do best, what I do best. What do I join around me and what services do I need to make it all work? So I try to invest in products and services that make my portfolio great and my company stronger."

What are the qualities that score points with Bartz when she looks at a new company? "If you have some reasonable excitement about the possibilities and some good folks to join with you. I think the smart VCs are looking for entrepreneurs who have thought about their market and have people to support them, because the biggest problem right now in the Valley is finding people. You can have some of the best ideas, but without a team to execute it, you're going to have a difficult time; although, if you go to a good VC and they like the idea, they may introduce you to some people for your team. If you've done your market homework, have passion and proof of concept, I think you'll get money."

GETTING TO HEAVEN THROUGH THE GARAGE.COM DOOR

Guy Kawasaki is the evangelist who brought Apple to fruition. Since that time, he has become a legend according to the measures put forth here in the Valley. He's written books about starting companies and branding, and now he has startup boot camps. He brings in experts from all over the world to share their experiences with green entrepreneurs. His company, Garage.com, is a venture capital investment bank that helps high tech startups raise money from VCs, corporate investors, and angels. Once a startup is chosen, they are posted online in Garage's heaven where subscribing investors can check them out.

Garage.com is a company with an excellent reputation. Kawasaki is having a blast. He has surrounded himself with a stunning group of executives who share his vision. One of these people is Bill Joos, vice president of Business Development. Joos' job? He helps make the companies that Garage.com selects to be their clients more attractive to the company's member investors, who will, in turn, fund those companies. Sometimes he is challenged when it comes to making a promising sow's ear into a silk purse.

"I have a horse track analogy—you have to have a valid race-track, and I view that as the market. You have to have a wonderful business idea, which is the horse, and smart bettors bet on jockeys. So one of the things we're looking for is a combination of racetrack, horse, and jockey," says Joos. "We're also seeing companies early enough where they may not have all of their jockeys in place, so we have to be able to evaluate an opportunity and see what they would be like with an additional one or two key members that they may not have. So, while we do occasionally see and support a one-person startup, the reality is that they will need to have a portion of their team in place, not necessarily all. You have to be realistic—hiring management and getting funding is the chicken and the egg scenario.

"We are generally the last money in the deal, not the first money. What we fundamentally do is seek out those companies that we feel have the greatest chance of success. Once we have evaluated them and accepted them as a client, we then present that opportunity to our group of eclectic investors—the angels, VCs, and corporations. And some combination of those will express an interest in the company. Garage.com itself will make an investment, but generally, we're the last ones in the deal. So part of our business model is, in fact, to acquire equity positions in the companies we've supported. Usually our business model has changed a little bit, but the vast majority of what we do is find the first "professional" money the companies have raised. They generally will have received the *three-Fs money*—fools, friends, and family. Sometimes that money is an 'A' round, in which case we'd be investing in their 'B' round."

There is generally a seed round, and an 'A,' 'B,' and 'C' round. Sometimes, when a company first starts out, the executive team puts up a small amount of their own money, or three-F money, to cover the expenses of lawyer fees to incorporate and secure patents. This round is generally called a seed round, or an 'A' round. Then a mezzanine round may follow before a company is ready to file for its IPO.

"Our investors' money is usually their first professional money," says Joos. "Sometimes friends, fools, and family money is done on warrants or terms and conditions of the first round. So 'A,' 'B' and 'C' is a little misleading—think of it as their first external money, no matter what it's labeled.

"However, having said all that, we are now seeing a trend with our clients that have been satisfied in what we've done for them, where we're assisting them in subsequent rounds, as well. It's really more common than to call it the exception, but it really isn't our mainstream business."

VIRTUAL INVESTING

There are several groups that will bring you on board to help you get funded. One such group is OffRoadCapital.com, which is making such a stir because of its live "pitch session" presentations to its investors via the Internet. The company is using the Internet to all of its advantages and is one of the coolest online venture brokers. Just because some of these venture brokerage groups are online doesn't make them any easier to get in and see. These companies are still very selective about the dot-coms they select to present to their virtual members. You must put your best foot forward with these companies, as well.

TERMS OF ENDEARMENT, OR AT LEAST OF THE CONTRACT

Terms are a tricky thing—and many times the entrepreneurs are in way over their heads. There can be pages and pages of terms involved in an offering. Many of these terms are even difficult for an expert to evaluate. My advice? Get a top-tier attorney who will be able to take those terms and bend them every which way before returning them to begin negotiations. Many firms will be dead-set on keeping their terms in place, but some—especially if you're hot—can be persuaded. Although, in a bad investing environment, you may take whatever money is on the table no matter the terms. You do what you can to make the company work. Ten percent of a functioning company is still better than 80 percent of nothing.

"We would never, ever invest in a company for anything other than preferred stock," says Tom Bevilacqua, chief strategic investment officer for E*TRADE Group, Inc. and managing general partner for E*TRADE Venture Capital. "We're always going to insist upon a liquidation preference. Meaning, in the context of a sale, or merger, the investors get their capital back first and then there's some sort of an allocation of the sale price above and beyond the capital. You always expect to get your capital back first, because we're putting in our hard money as opposed to stock options, etc., and [we also insist upon] the ongoing right of first refusal. So, no matter what percentage we put into the company initially, we have the ability as long as we put up our money to maintain that percentage going forward."

"I think VCs have funded many, many bad ideas. What I'm hearing now is that the top Sand Hill VCs want to do fewer deals. It used to be that you'd have to have $50 million in your revenue line, and now they're saying a billion. So they're looking for the next Cisco. It's kind of funny, because there's more money, but I think they're just keeping it right now. Eventually it'll burn a hole in their pockets. There are really too many companies, but I think it's getting harder [to get funded], and they're getting more discriminating."
—MARLEEN McDANIEL, chairman and CEO of Women.com

Bevilacqua believes that there are several things that must be in place—correctly in place—before funding happens.

"We prefer to see a company already structured as a C corp, not as a partnership, not as an LLC, not as an S corp. Although as part of the funding process, you can terminate the S corporation fairly easily. If they have something that is proprietary technology, that they have taken steps to protect the IP (intellectual property) rights, whether it's patent filing, copyright notices, or trademark filings. And basically, that they have defendable position with respect to their IP where we don't have to go through a major IP audit that could spell some problems. We like to fund startups involved with a quality law firm that knows the startup and technology worlds—there are terrific law firms and accounting firms that focus on other areas; it takes some very unique skill sets to protect IP rights."

RULES AND LEGALITIES

There are a couple of problems seen pretty consistently with startup companies, particularly ones that haven't had legal counseling from the beginning. One very common problem is the issuing of stock from people who do not qualify under the SEC rules to issue stock. That can range anywhere from trivial to very important, depending on the number of shares that were issued and how difficult it is undo it.

"There are a number of questions you can ask a lawyer. If they look like a deer in the headlights when you ask them, 'Should I be a 505 or a 506 exemption?' and they are clueless, you're dealing with the wrong law firm. You need to find someone who lives and breathes this as a living, not Uncle Joe, the divorce lawyer, who says, 'Gee, I can incorporate you in Delaware and save you some money.' That may be true, but if he doesn't know when the company should be a 504, 505, or 506—you can pay me now, or you can pay me later. The ugliest deals that we see are the ones where they have started down the wrong path and have raised money under the wrong circumstances—an investor wants to see that they will be able to focus on your team and the business opportunity."

—BILL JOOS, vice president of Business Development, Garage.com

When it comes to capital, there are plenty of ways to screw up your opportunities of ever receiving any. There are SEC rules, and those of VCs and angels, that need to be followed to a 'T.' Basically, they don't want to have their legal department spending a whole lot of time on mistakes you've made in forming the company and the stock that's already issued. Most of these mistakes are made early on, and screwing up can cost you time and opportunity.

"The security law problems can be the most serious because they take the most effort to overcome," warns Mark Radcliffe, partner at Gray Cary Ware & Freidenrich (www.GrayCary.com) and co-author of *Internet Law and Business Handbook* (www.LaderaPress.com). "People need to remember that the securities laws are basically meant to protect widows and orphans, so they are rather strict and kind of clumsy. I think people would consider them rather odd, particularly in the hyper atmosphere of the Valley. The truth of the matter is that they were designed to protect people who are relatively unsophisticated; and whether or not the person is sophisticated, the laws apply to everyone. You need to really pay attention to securities law issues. Generally, what happens is that investors get preferred stock and your founders get common stock. Employees joining after the founders get options to purchase common stock, and occasionally you'll give warrants to purchase preferred stock or common stock to banks or other institutions," explains Radcliffe about the basics of issuing stock for a startup.

"First of all, the venture capital industry is relatively mature in the sense that investors have a certain way of doing things, and so this is the way they do things. It may not be a very good reason, but it's true," says Radcliffe. "You can offer preferred stock at up to ten times the value of common stock because of the difference in rights between the common and preferred. In other words, at the time of issuing common stock at ten cents a share, you can issue preferred stock at up to one dollar a share. The reason you want to issue stock in that manner is so you can keep the price of your common stock low and use it for options as an incentive to your engineers, while giving up a relatively smaller part of the company when you were selling investors preferred stock at a higher price. Preferred stockholders get a bunch of rights with their preferred stock that are discussed in the term sheet. Typically, there are rights to preferences in bankruptcy or a merger context ['double dipping,' which is called participating preferred] and anti-dilution protection. In the current environment, where there are a lot of down rounds, anti-dilution provisions are very important. Other rights include right of first refusal to purchase in new rounds of investment, and the ability to control certain corporate actions, like mergers. The investors will get preferred stock, options are for employees that come on after the founders, and board members normally receive options to purchase common stock. Board members will generally get options instead of common stock. They generally prefer options rather than stock because, if you receive stock, it's taxed like income and it's illiquid; you can't sell it off to pay your taxes, so you have income but no cash to pay the taxes on it. If options are granted under a stock options program, they have other beneficial tax treatment."

Go out and get a professional to do this stuff for you. I only mention the terms in this book to make you aware of how many places you can, and will, screw up if you don't.

"We're very careful not to talk about legal advice with our clients, except for what makes a standard deal look like a standard deal," says Joos. His company takes on startups and matches them with capital via its member investors. "The first thing we do with our clients is tell them to get extraordinarily smart professional advice," says Joos. Sometimes it doesn't work out quite the way it was supposed to with attorneys.

"One of our clients out of New York was dealing with a very prestigious firm in New York. This law firm knew everything there possibly was to know about Wall Street law, but come to find out, they knew very little about private placement investment. They weren't giving bad advice, just partial advice.

"We'll have entrepreneurs who have sold common stock to investors before a good lawyer has helped them—and frankly, that's just insane," says Joos of a common error he sees companies come to him with. "Investors get preferred stock. Common stock is for employees. There's lots of reasons why that's done. But a lawyer who is not tuned in to it may give advice that seems common sense, but it's counterintuitive to what Silicon Valley investors are looking for. If you have to explain that Aunt Martha gets stock options if the moon is high, and Uncle Charlie because of something else, every time they have to hear that they say, 'Why should I have to listen to this when there are so many companies that are clean and standard?' So sometimes the things someone has done to shortcut the process exclude them from consideration because the investor says, 'I don't care how you did that— all I know is, that's not a standard deal. If your capitalization table is dirty and it gets in the way of me being able to focus on you and your idea, why should I invest in you?' One of the things I think we do successfully is convey the early need for true professional assistance to make sure that you launch the ship right, because if you don't have the time to do it right, you may not have the opportunity to do it over."

STOCK OPTIONS FOR EMPLOYEES

Normally, once you get funded, you'll bring a director of human resources in to handle all of the details about explaining how your stock options packages go. Until then, here's a quick overview.

"There are several important concepts about options: the term of the option, when you can exercise, when you vest and then the exercise price," says Mark Radcliffe, partner at Gray Cary Ware & Freidenrich (www.GrayCary.com) and co-author of *Internet Law and Business Handbook* (www.LaderaPress.com). "The term of the option is how long the option lasts; however, if you're an employee, and you decide to leave the company, in many cases your right to exercise the option will end very soon after you leave the company. Vesting arrangements with employees tend to be a fixed four-year vesting period, with a six-month to one-year *cliff* before options start vesting. The idea is that you don't want people hopping from company to company picking up options. In addition, if you hire somebody and they don't work out, you don't want them taking options with them.

"The answer to when you exercise the option will depend on a number of factors. One will be your financial situation— when you need the money. Another factor is if the company has gone public. Exercising options in a company that's not public generally doesn't make sense, because it is very difficult to resell the stock (it has no public market). On the other hand, by exercising options before the company goes public, you can start a holding period to make your shares tradable under Rule 144. Even if they are not otherwise registered, the stock gets better capital gains tax treatment for non-qualified options. Generally, people exercise their options on a liquidity event such as a public offering, or wait until the stock is at a high value after going public. Virtually everyone in the company will be locked up for six months after the public offering, because the underwriters who are going to be supporting the stock in the market don't want to have a lot of stock from employees sold and make their job more expensive.

"Generally underwriters want to provide a smooth curve for the first six months," says Radcliffe of the IPO process. "It's generally a condition by the major venture investors that everyone who has significant shareholdings, frequently described as one-percent shareholders, have to have a lockup in place, and the option plan frequently includes such a limitation as a condition of getting the options. And when you go public, the underwriters may impose even more dramatic limitations, which is that nobody in the company can sell for six months, and make that a condition of the offering."

SUMMARY

Well, you've heard it from the experts. The main gist of this chapter is that you shouldn't take money from just any Joe Blow investor. Take your time and find the right one for your company's needs. Check out everyone who wants to be a part of your company and evaluate the value they'll add. And don't do this alone. And be honest; when it comes down to it, your reputation is the only thing you own lock, stock, and barrel. Get advice from people who are experts at starting up companies so you don't screw it up. It may cost money to do so, but it'll cost more in time to ramp up later. I just got a call from an entrepreneur I met a few months ago. The first thing he said was, "We'll, we're all set to go. My friend, the attorney, just set us up as a limited partnership." I cringed and sent him a copy of this chapter.

CHAPTER 3

COME PLAY WITH ME
Building a Killer Exec Team

Once you have an idea and you start to figure out that, "Hey, maybe I have a dot-com here," there is the next step—a very important one. You may be able to engage people with your totally compelling story and talk of a trillion-dollar market, but the truth is in the results. Maybe people will nod their heads eagerly with tongues lolling like a big St. Bernard as you tell them about your concept, but will they leave their killer jobs to come play with you? That, my dear reader, is the million-dollar question.

So, how will you respond at the next startup party or networking event when someone asks you, "That sounds killer, dude, who's on your team?" Will you answer, "Well..."—shuffle your feet, look down at floor—"I really haven't gotten to that yet." Or will you say, confidently, "I've just wrapped up the prototype, and I've got my feelers out,"—smile, nod—"Do you happen to know anyone who does (describe open exec positions) and would want to come over to a promising startup?"

Well, that's all fine and dandy, but what will you say when
they ask the next question, "What's it pay?" That's when most of
the *oomph* goes out of recruiting conversations unless an investment in your startup has already been made.

Okay, let's use the other extreme. Say you meet someone at
a party, you tell them your compelling story, and they take a
quantum leap and buy your dream lock, stock, and no cash. This
is a meeting you will tell your PR people to proliferate when
telling your founding story to the press. The story will live in
infamy: the night you and Biff met at Guy Kawasaki's Startup
Boot Camp mixer and began sketching out on a napkin the
technology you would deploy to finally launch your dot-com.

Remember, you may get lucky at last call in a bar, but do you
ever end up marrying your "last call" guy or gal? A networking
party is about the same caliber of risk, especially when you can't
find any investors to give you money because you can't develop
the technology enough to entice them. It's a Catch-22 in the
worst way. There you are, trolling around the no-host bar looking for the best candidate to put into your CTO position before
you run out of savings next week. Desperate is as desperate does.
Just as it is in that desperate moment of last call at 1:44 AM
(you're probably not going to be passing out any engagement
rings under those circumstances), don't promise anyone a job
until you've checked them out and had a few more meetings.

And until you can trust someone and put them under a nondisclosure, it may behoove you to stay fairly general about the
details of your proprietary technology. Tell them just enough
to tantalize them, but try not to be too paranoid about the
whole thing.

Last week I spoke to an entrepreneur who had met with a
potential CTO. Instead of an interview, what transpired was theft
of a concept. The CTO loved the idea of the disruptive technology, took the idea, and ran with it. The CTO had built a team
within the month, had a working demo, and pitched the entrepreneur's original idea to the VC as his own. During the pitch,
the VC had suggested that he introduce the CTO to a CEO
with a similar idea, in case they might be able to partner their

efforts. Although the VC did not mention any names for the suggested partnering, his idea was met with the CTO's great apprehension. Had the CTO not pitched to the VC who was a personal friend of the CEO, the CEO may never have found out what was going on.

As it was, the CEO did find out, and his attorney sent a letter of cease and desist. But these types of things are difficult to prove, especially when the concept is hot and the technology to create it doesn't need to have much patented software to carry it through.

You'll have to tell potential team members about your technology, but tell your story in layers. And the more you can trust someone (perhaps trust assured with an NDA), the deeper you can go. Remember that you have proprietary technology to protect. Like you read in Chapter 2, no VC or angel will sign an NDA, but you can protect yourself by getting other entrepreneurs or potential team members to sign them.

I recently asked Guy Kawasaki if it was ever too early to start telling people about a new dot-com idea.

"Not really," advises Kawasaki. "I'm not paranoid. Very few ideas are stolen and then implemented. The key is not a good idea that's kept secret. The key is a good idea that's implemented well."

KNOCK, KNOCK. WHO'S THERE?

Okay, back to due diligence. Let's say you find someone who doesn't come to you with a high recommendation from someone you know. What could happen if you choose the wrong person to join your team? Well, because there are contracts involved, it could end up a nightmare (and in some cases, end up in the national news).

As you can see from the following press release from Venturewire.com, due diligence is necessary. But how deep do you go?

PRESS RELEASE

OAKLAND, Calif.—Business-to-business software firm Luna Information Systems said it appointed co-founder Mark Christiansen to the position of interim CEO. This follows the departure of former CEO Farid Khoujinian, who resigned after a report found he had misrepresented his academic credentials. Mr. Khoujinian served as CEO for three years. An executive search firm was hired to find a permanent replacement. Luna is backed by Altos Ventures, Discovery Ventures, H & Q Venture Associates, and Interprise Technology Partners.

I had a horror story occur not too long ago. I was approached by someone I work with from time to time. He passed along a business plan to me, and it looked like a great idea, But the space was crowded at that time (pre–April, 2000). I passed it on to an influential angel who gave it some consideration. The team looked well structured and had some recognizable names, but I didn't know *how* recognizable.

I was having a conversation with the person who had given me the plan when she casually mentioned that one of the exec team members had served time. *Served time!* It was time served for a felony committed at a company he had been employed by. Yikes! Had I known this, I would have passed on this information with the business plan. As it was, I made a quick call to tell the angel reviewing the plan. Someone in his circle had already seen the name and made the connection. Granted, it had happened some years earlier, but the group was not willing to take that kind of chance with someone who would be so close to the funds. Needless to say, the angel passed on the company rather than confront it with the information.

I learned from that incident a very important lesson about due diligence, and one I feel is worthy of passing on to you. Choose your team well and check them out thoroughly. If somebody's had a bad break, don't put them on the executive team, or be open with the VC and hope to receive honest feedback in return. When doing due diligence, there are more reasons for someone to turn you down than to sign a check over to you. It's up to you if you want to give them more reasons to say, "No," than "Yes."

CREDIBILITY GOES A LONG, LONG WAY

"The first few hires are always a specialized thing, and the venture capitalists are always involved," says Sid Valluri, vice president and general manager of FutureStep.com, Korn/Ferry's online recruiting service. "You need some really strong influences to get them to come over, because those are the people who are taking the biggest leap of faith. Once you have a CFO/CEO and other executive members, then their credibility will bring in other people." Korn/Ferry is often looked to for bringing executive team members aboard startups. Valluri's candidates are looking for a fair market wage and an attractive stock package. "In case the company does take off, it is definitely an important part of the package," says Valluri, who is straight-up about wages being competitive. "You also have to offer a stock package that will pay off a couple of million if the company does fly. It would be surprising to get senior level people without a generous stock option package unless you're paying a lot of cash. Let's say you're making $100 thousand and somebody offers you $130 or $140 thousand. Well, it does improve your quality of life, but taking you from there to $200 thousand does not do quite as much as giving you a stock option package that can make you a couple of million.

"After the you're-finished-paying-the-bills kind of money, the getting-rich money is where you actually get their attention," advises Valluri. "Now the bigger thing people are looking for is the opportunity to have an impact. One thing this whole startup craze has done is allowed people to occupy positions and have influence where, in the past, they've had to climb up a very long ladder. That's the attraction of this whole entrepreneur thing. You've created the company, and you're going to be the boss. No one is going to give you that at another company. Because of the scarcity of good talent and the risk associated with some of these startups, one of the ways you really get people is to give them opportunities that would usually take fifteen or twenty years to get to. If you take a CTO from one company and try and migrate him to another company, one CTO is pretty much the same as another CTO position. There's some differences for industry and size, but it's roughly the same job. So you had to offer them something that's really attractive. For instance, in Korn/Ferry CTO searches, I've seen them mix the job and say, 'Not only will you be CTO, but you will also have influence on marketing.' Now this person has a chance to expand their experience, expand their horizons beyond what a traditional job description would have allowed them. And it's companies that are innovative in what we call the 'psychic rewards' they offer people, instead of just the financial rewards, that are more successful in attracting and retaining people these days."

RECRUITING EXECS AND NETWORKING

You're not going to miraculously find every executive by some twist of fate. It's good to rely on networking through associates and networking activities. But if you have the cash, you should use a recruiter to get that slot filled as soon as possible. "Whether you're a founder of a company or a venture capitalist, everyone can benefit from networking," says Daphne Albert, founder of ABA Associates (www.abaassociates.com), a San Francisco Bay Area recruiting firm specializing in executive-level management. "The importance of networking cannot be overstated. It's the most effective, direct, fastest, cheapest means of finding people. Networking is great, but it's unrealistic to think you can do large-scale hiring that way. You're not always going to be guaranteed the exact qualification you're seeking for a specific role. Opportunity does not always walk through the door, you have to be proactive, and networking is the most efficient way to meet people. A lot of startups are not recruiting for specific jobs, so if someone walks through the door who has a really impressive background, they will sometimes create a position for that person, just keeping in mind where they're going to be in the future."

When putting your feelers out, you'll find your team members all over the place—from sitting in the hotel bar after Garage.com's conference to people you've known your entire life. It's not *where* you find your executive team members—it's who they are and what they can bring to your company.

"It is *so* who you know," says Kurt Ludwigsen, president and CEO of Contest.com. "I've kept relationships a lot longer than some people. My CFO went to kindergarten with me. Did we plan on building a company all these years? Of course not. We lost touch maybe ten times over the last thirty-some-odd years. The fact of the matter is, she was one of the main people on the finance side of the Sierra Club, and when it came time, I called her up and said, 'Hello, we haven't spoken in a while, I'm doing this—pick up your bags and follow me.' And she did. Over half the employees here I've known for over ten years. Employee retention is not a problem here. We have had zero turnover, and I don't foresee any. We're a pretty tight-knit group."

As we go through life, we build relationships in the different phases in our careers. We tend to let some of them go, but the relationships we keep, we usually keep for a reason. Those are the key people who may be a good resource when you're building your team. Look through your own Rolodex for the skill sets you need before you go any further. Even if the people you know don't have the skill sets you need, they may know someone who can give a good reference. A great reference from someone you know usually beats the hell out of a headhunter grabbing someone's resume off of the transom. Headhunters are helpful, but only if they've already thoroughly prescreened the applicant and can verify that they are qualified and serious about the job.

FINDING THE IDEAL TEAM

Finding the ideal team is the thing most VCs fantasize about on their way to the office every morning. Usually they find a team that needs work, and within its roughest form, identify the beginnings of a strong foundation. It's like when you find a lover who is a diamond in the rough. He has great potential, and you try to picture him with new peeper glasses, well-creased khakis, sans sideburns, and a few pounds slimmer. It may take some convincing, or coercing, to get them on board with your program, but it could work out. The big difference? Well, if you're a VC, you better break it to the team quickly that they'll need some tweaking. Time is money, and if your CTO is a scientist who doesn't know much about infrastructure, that's something you can't change in Internet time.

"Bring in experienced people—people who have done it before—as opposed to your buddies from college. Surround yourself with advisors who will give you objective advice, advisors you trust."
—STEVE KIRSCH, founder of Mouse Systems, Frame Technology, Infoseek, and Propel

So what kinds of team members should you bring to the table as an early-stage company? Ideas about working with an entire team and putting people in place to keep an eye on them via the board of directors, or replacing members of the team, run the gamut. Sometimes a VC will use up the creativity and energy of the existing team to the point that they have to be replaced by a more experienced team to take the company the rest of the way; others will replace team members right off the bat. Investor philosophies vary from company to company. All you can do is do your best and hope it's good enough. And if it's not good enough, have the best judgment to do what it takes to get your company off the ground. Most investors will have a clause in their funding contracts that gives them the right to replace team members if they're not performing to a satisfactory level.

PUTTING THE 'C' IN CEO

Finding the ideal CEO is urgent in your mission to start up. If you're the inventor, you should set your ego aside and look for someone who has management experience. Being the CEO means that you have to be the motivator, the instigator, and the proliferator. The CEO is the cog that keeps the other cogs moving. One of the things a CEO will need to do is raise cash. A venture capitalist doesn't want to hear your CFO or your marketing guy talk—they want to hear what the CEO's about, that's the message—directly from the soul of the company. Oh yeah, the CEO will also need to be the soul of the company.

If you have an idea for the company, but you're not much of a people person, step back and put someone else in the role. Make yourself another title like Chief Engineering Imagineer or something. Often, if a VC likes your company but doesn't feel that you have the experience to head a company, they will make the investment contingent on your replacement. Sometimes that kills a deal; sometimes it makes a stronger company. Don't let the company suffer because you have an ego.

"What entrepreneurs will sometimes find is that the team should probably be altered if they run into a situation where there are deficiencies, but the business is so compelling that it should continue. We need to know everything that is right and wrong, because we need to help make the company a more fundable opportunity so it will be much more successful. That doesn't mean fix deficiencies to make it fundable, it means fix the deficiencies to make it a successful company. Entrepreneurs are extremely candid with us. For that reason, we've added a human capital department. Filling out a managing team and getting some people in the company is very important at this stage. I can build a case that human capital is harder to find than real capital right now."

—BILL JOOS, vice president of business development, Garage.com

Marleen McDaniel, chair and chief executive officer of Women.com, recalls her first meeting with Ellen Pack, that company's founder, senior vice president, and general manager.

"When I met Ellen Pack, she was funding the company with her own money," says McDaniel. "We met through Anita Borg's network [www.Systers.org], and I don't quite know—and I ought to ask her one of these days—if she thought I was going to help fund the company. Well, I wasn't prepared to fund the company at that time, but I was prepared to help her find the money. I believe in funding companies with other people's money, and I would advise this to almost anyone—it allows you to play with a fuller deck than if you were worried about your own money. Unless you're a billionaire, that is. I didn't know her before she found me on the Systers' network. She made a luncheon date with me and got me interested in what she was doing and put me on her advisory board. She gave me her business plan, and I started giving her advice," says McDaniel, who had helped launch Sun Microsystems, 3Com Corporation, and Crescendo Communications.

"I gave her some feedback on her plan to build a little company with one to two million in revenues—she thought she'd only have to raise $750 thousand. The plan changed, and now we've raised $175 million and counting. In '94, we were called Women's Forum on CompuServe. They thought it was cool because they thought women could help them build their numbers. If I went back to the time when I was raising money, I didn't even know how we were going to make money. Let me remind you how early it was—there was no advertising out there, I don't even believe that the subscription model was that good. When I raised that money I didn't have a job, I wasn't getting paid—it was Ellen's plan and my motivation was to help her.

"The investors were not intrigued, but they basically thought we'd figure it out, and we have," says McDaniel. "We were the first Internet company to sell a sponsorship—we sold that in '95 to Levi Strauss. We were early and one of the first websites of any kind back then that had any brand recognition."

While going out and pitching the company, McDaniel got a bite from one of the VCs who found the idea a worthy risk. The only catch? She'd have to replace Ellen Pack, the company's CEO.

"Now I know that all you do is raise funds when you're a CEO," says McDaniel. "Had I known, the advice I would have given to Ellen back then is that it doesn't matter if you are a private or public company—raising money is your job and you cannot delegate it. Ellen lost her job to me when she delegated raising money to me, not when Eldorado gave us the ultimatum [for McDaniel to replace Pack]."

It's common practice in the world of venture funding to make changes in the executive teams before funding is solid. It's not the end of the world. It may hurt, you may pout or be bitter for a while, but this too shall pass. After all, they can't take the title "founder" away from you. As the saying goes, it's only business. No one is going to replace you because you're 45 and don't personify the dot-com image. They're going to replace you because you don't have enough experience. Look at it like this: let's say you have the "opportunity" to give someone $1 million and wait and wait and wait until they found a way to make the company profitable and could give you your money back. Would you want some bright-eyed entrepreneur with a good idea, or someone who has done it before? I believe that if you look objectively at this scenario, you'll know why VCs have to do what they sometimes do. If it's all about the company for you, you'll make the sacrifice. If it's all about you, you'll go from VC to VC looking for funding until you've missed your market window.

"When we go into a company early on and there's a CEO and we see that that person will need to be replaced, we don't mince words or hide behind it," says Tom Bevilacqua, E*TRADE's chief strategic investment officer of E*TRADE Group, Inc. and managing general partner of E*TRADE Venture Capital. "We talk to the founders up front. Then we build it into the term sheet that will say we are going into an agreement that will result in a search with a mutually agreeable search firm to find a CEO to take the company to the next level of growth. We try and identify that very early on so we can talk with the company. One thing that we try to avoid is one of those stories you hear where a venture firm goes into a company three months after funding and decides to oust the management team or the

CEO. There may be some legitimate reasons for doing that, but often you wonder, 'Would they be facing this if they'd had the conversation before they funded the company?'"

WHAT MAKES A GREAT CEO?

There are all kinds of ideas about what makes a great CEO, especially from an investor's standpoint. Some like 'em green; others prefer those with a long line of startups behind them.

"Ideally you'll see the long-term CEO—the driver of the organization—in place, with relevant industry experience and strong leadership skills," says Tom Bevilacqua, chief strategic investment officer for E*TRADE Group, Inc. and managing general partner for E*TRADE Venture Capital. "You look for that person, and you look at people overall in the team who have the ability to bring similarly skilled, like-minded people back into their company. In this labor market, where highly skilled folks are in huge demand, the ability of a strong leader to recruit in a team is a huge hallmark to look for. Nothing terribly unique there; it's a recruiting skill set that's important.

"If someone has been a CEO somewhere else before, that's great. You're hitting on all cylinders at that point. But the likelihood of that early on is not great," says Bevilacqua. "So often what you're looking for is someone who has run a business unit or has been a project leader—basically has had some management leadership skills, as well as experience in the business area. If you are so fortunate to get someone who has been the CEO of a large company, or a unit president of a large company, sometimes that person's transition is really difficult, and sometimes it poses its own obstacles. Ideally, you'd find someone who has been the CEO of a number of other startups on a serial basis, who has grown the startups to a level of liquidity, or a more experienced CEO in that industry has taken over and then is looking for a new startup."

RAISING MONEY IS JOB #1

As the CEO, fundraising for your company will be your number one job. And what a job it will be!

"[Fundraising] is the hardest job I've ever had, and I was selling the Internet when no one knew what it was and no one wanted to buy it," says Kurt Ludwigsen, president and CEO of Contest.com, and former sales executive for Match.com. "It's tough for a couple of reasons. One is the market conditions right now. VCs are holding on to their money even tighter than they used to. Number two, the frustrating thing is that it's my first time around. There are a lot of people who are on their second time around, and those are the people getting the money because they've already done it. I've proven myself, but I haven't proven myself for running a company, I've proven myself to run divisions but not to run it myself. That's difficult because I don't have as many contacts, my Rolodex is not as large as a lot of these guys."

"There's one more component that we look for—whether or not the CEO has experience or no experience. We look for passion and the drive to make something happen. Many times we'll get a company where the CEO has been a CEO for forty-seven different companies and this is another one—they're not in tune with the technology and they don't have a passion about it. I try to avoid those companies because having someone who can articulate the passions behind their proposition is important."

—DR. JOHN E. WARNOCK, co-founder and CTO of Adobe Systems and head of Adobe Ventures

As a green entrepreneur CEO, you'll be facing all kinds of problems when you look at the competition. You'll see that many of the CEOs you're up against for the VC's money are serial entrepreneurs. These are the people who've been there, done that, built relationships with their initial investors, and are spending time golfing (never underestimate the power of an afternoon on the links) with them.

"You take a Marc Andreesen, for instance. He comes out with Netscape and everything goes well, and he comes out with Loudcloud, and he gets $50 million," says Ludwigsen. "The truth of the matter is that VCs are putting their money in *you*, they're not putting their money into the company. A time comes when the VCs want their money in the company and not you. That's when you see all these CEOs stepping aside and new people coming in. Basically, they'll say it's for this or that reason, but the truth of the matter is they'll say, 'You know what? You've had your time, we need to see the growth now.' If the company gets to the point when it gets too large and I'm hindering the process, I will be the first one to step aside. I'm not dumb—I have shares in the company, too. If someone can increase the value better than I can, who am I to say no?

"I have two dependents at home, but I have 11 here—who also took pay cuts to work for Contest.com," says Ludwigsen of the environment he faces between rounds. "I am not responsible *for*, but I'm responsible *to* everyone who works here. And when it comes down to it, there's only one guy raising money. I came out of a funding pitch once and one of the guys asked me, 'How'd you do?' and I said, 'I give myself a B.' He looked back at me and said, 'It's really more like pass/fail, it's not an A, B, C thing.' If you get a B all the time, no one is going to be impressed."

"The average life expectancy of a CEO in the Valley is 2.4 years. I think you go into these things understanding that there are very few people who start a company, take it to mid-size, and get it to large-size. That seems to be pretty rare. There are guys who are historically good at starting up companies, but when it gets past the startup stage they are no longer good. A lot of them realize this and get out of the company at that point. Then there are a lot of CEOs without much experience running a company. But I love to bet on people. Even if a CEO is green, I'd rather go with the passion than say, 'Oh gee, he's green. We need to find a seasoned veteran.' I think it's better to find the passion and sort of prop the people around him that have the business expertise than it is to bring in someone who is old and jaded about business. I'd rather gamble on a young person and give them enough rope until they make a serious mistake or clearly demonstrate that they're not going to grow with the job."

DR. JOHN E. WARNOCK, co-founder and CTO of Adobe Systems and head of Adobe Ventures

For many CEOs, fundraising is a test of endurance. I mean, what happens when you don't come back to the office loaded down with gold pieces? Once you've already received rounds and have a compelling passion—one where you know you could continue to grow and succeed if you could just convince someone—it becomes even more of a challenge to make sure someone finally does sign a check over to you.

"I don't believe in PowerPoint presentations. I believe in sitting across from the person and looking them right in the eye. The first part is, I sit down and tell them what we do—it takes me about two minutes," says Ludwigsen of his job as CEO and chief money guy. "Either they're in or they're out at that point. After two minutes, if they don't buy into the concept, it doesn't matter what I have to say. It's two things—the concept and the revenue projections. Those are the only two things that matter. Where we get grilled is on the revenue projections—and that's what VCs do. And everything we do is based in reality, so we're very confident that we know what we're pitching. With the successes I've had they've known they wanted to invest in the first two minutes. You look at pitching like this—with every 'No,' I'm just that much closer to a 'Yes.' It's hard. I get depressed. You have to separate it and take it from a business standpoint, not personally. But the truth is, I truly feel bad for the people who turn us down. I'm very gracious in accepting defeat. I feel bad [for the VCs who reject Contest.com]. One day they're going to pick up the newspaper, and they're going to see the success that we've become, and they're going to have to answer to someone who says, 'Gee, I wish I would have had the opportunity to invest in them.' And the VC will say, 'I actually did have the opportunity to invest in them, and I turned them down.'"

WHAT MAKES A GREAT CFO?

Basically, your VC or angel will be looking for proven experience in most cases. But what about the person who will be taking the checks to the bank? What does it take to be a CFO?

"In the early stages, the focus isn't necessarily on a CFO," says Tom Bevilacqua, E*TRADE's chief strategic investment officer for E*TRADE Group, Inc. and managing general partner for E*TRADE Venture Capital. "We're looking for somebody with a basic controller skill set who is able to manage the finances and set the company's budget. You're looking for someone who can keep the books straight for audits. The ability to interact with Wall Street analysts—well, that's not relevant at this stage. What about the ability to help present the company? Sure, it's helpful, but then again, if the company has a strong CEO who can present with the head of marketing or head of business development, the company can do quite well without the CFO. When a company ultimately gets larger and is in the public markets, the CFO is providing a financial backdrop to all of the investor presentations, but that isn't really isn't the case for a young company. Ideally, you'll find someone who has come out of a large accounting firm that has dealt with small companies before."

WHAT MAKES A GREAT CTO?

What about a CTO—what do investors like to see in the chief technical officer before they lay down the greenbacks?

"Ideally you're looking for someone who has come out of a background where they know a lot of other folks and will be able to reach out and recruit onto their development team, says Tom Bevilacqua, chief strategic investment officer for E*TRADE Group, Inc. and managing general partner for E*TRADE Venture Capital.

"You're clearly looking to match up a skill set that parallels whatever technology your company is working with. Once that's the case, what you're looking for is that CTO's ability to go off and recruit a team, get that team in place, and manage that development project. He or she may not have a lot of actual management as opposed to pure development experience, and there are distinct differences in managing an organization that's built to an outcome as opposed to developing it yourself. You're looking for a management and leadership skill set."

KEEPING TRADE SECRETS SECRET

While looking to build your company, there are a lot of technicalities you have to keep in mind. Why? Because it might land you in court.

Often enough, new companies are started because someone at an established company saw a better way of doing something and broke off to start their own company. If this is the way your startup began—and especially if you took some people from the old company with you—it could be a big red flag to investors, especially if you're working on the same technology you left at that company. And all this will come out at the time of due diligence.

"One thing that's very common in Silicon Valley is that a group of people break off from a larger company to build a smaller company that may compete against the larger company in certain areas," says Mark Radcliffe, partner at Gray Cary Ware & Freidenrich (www.GrayCary.com) and co-author of *Internet Law and Business Handbook* (www.LaderaPress.com). "What happens in that situation is that you have to make sure they don't take any technical information along with them. Make sure that, when they're sitting around thinking about what they're going to do, they do it in a way that can be documented in not using the equipment of the original company. If they did, the original company has some rights because they were using their equipment on their time. What you need to do if you're going to be leaving your company is get an attorney as soon as possible and make sure [technology] doesn't fall within the scope of your obligations to your old employer. You may have done everything right, but if you can't document it, you're going to spend a lot of time, money, and effort proving it in court. I keep saying 'don't do it if you can't prove it,' because if you do and get into a fight it's going to be very exhausting. Sometimes startups fail because they get entangled in litigation, lose focus and their market window, and they just kind of slag down because so much of their attention is focused on the lawsuit."

Radcliffe suggests that you leave a company in a way that doesn't irritate your old employer. "That may or may not be possible, but you certainly want to be as accommodating as you can. If they're working on a project and they're two weeks away from completion, let your people complete it, and then make sure they don't bring any confidential documents over with them. Also make sure you don't use any confidential information when you're hiring, like saying, 'Joe used to earn $75 thousand.'

"Obviously you have that information, and sometimes it's hard not to use it. Maybe it's not confidential. Maybe it's been disclosed. Maybe the other party hasn't taken the necessary steps to keep it a trade secret. What you need to do is get with your attorney and structure it in a way to avoid a lawsuit. In a lawsuit like this, you could easily crank through $50 thousand to $100 thousand in legal fees a month. That's pretty impressive for a startup; and besides, investors are not going to come into a young company where there's a potential of more money going out to the lawyers than into building the company."

So what happens when a company does decide to bring suit against your new little startup? "The burden of proof is on the company trying to enforce the rights," says Radcliffe. "They have to prove there is a misappropriation of trade secrets, a wrongful taking. And the trade secrets have to be something that they've taken reasonable steps to maintain in confidence. Depending on the laws of the state; for instance, in California it has to be reasonable economic value, either positive or negative."

What this *positive* or *negative* experience learned at your last employer refers to is if you obtained information that a technology was a dead end and not to go there. Let's say the company went through a number of steps to prove out the technology, and all the while you learned what didn't work. That is still knowledge that you learned to help you develop something that did finally work. "There are a number of hot buttons. Sometimes people do stupid things," warns Radcliffe. "Let's say your old company has five man-years invested in a project—say it's a software product—and you go out and a month later, *Wow!* You have a piece of CAD software that does the same thing. No one is going to believe—starting with your former employer and the courts—that it took you one month to develop it when it actually took five man-years of effort. A lot of this is just common sense—you shouldn't steal stuff from your former employer. That doesn't mean you can't take your inherent knowledge of the industry. So if you're a semiconductor designer, you can go to your next company and design another semiconductor, but you can't basically design the same design you made at your last place."

DON'T BURN BRIDGES

Many people don't leave their jobs on good terms; sometimes it's just time to move on. Good managers and CEOs want what's best for their people, no matter what the sacrifice. In those cases, it's best to seek advice and well wishes from your former boss. By being open about your new plans, you never know what opportunities may arise.

"For me personally, I think my biggest jump forward was that I called Carol Bartz, my former boss, as a courtesy," says Lisa Henderson, CEO of LevelEdge.com. At that time, she had already left Autodesk and had worked on several other projects. But she had left originally on good terms and had even helped start up Buzzsaw, one of Autodesk's spin-offs. "I called her and said, 'Carol, you might be hearing about me.' Of course, I had huge dreams," laughs Henderson as she looks back. "'I've started a little company. I'd love to come in and tell you what I'm doing.' Carol was fantastic. She said, 'Come in and talk with me tomorrow.' In reality, she's never free, and her schedule is jam-packed, but she made room for me. I went in and presented the idea to her. I only got a few slides into the presentation—Carol is one of those people who evaluates what you're saying and processes it quickly—and Carol said, 'I really love the idea. I'm interested in the idea, and not only that, but let me make a few phone calls for you.' So, here's my former boss—someone extremely well respected in the Silicon Valley—and she's making a few phone calls to introduce me to the venture community. That really helped with the process, and I think it's even more important with today's market where I've heard some CEOs say it takes up to five recommendations to one VC before they even return one phone call."

SUMMARY

What do you call one entrepreneur? Unfunded. What do you call two entrepreneurs? A potential investment. What do you call three entrepreneurs? A team (and much closer to fundability than two entrepreneurs). Building a team around your concept that can carry the vision through is key to your success. Exhaust all of your resources to make a team worthy of the closest scrutiny by venture capitalists. Build a kick-ass team, and you'll find yourself moving at Internet speed; build a weak team, and you'll find yourself just another piece of dot-com carnage on the Internet Superhighway. You get out what you put in.

CHAPTER 4

THE PITCH IS BACK
Selling Yourself and Your Company

S o you're finally invited into the inner-sanctum, a mahogany-walled room containing a large, square table that probably cost as much as a Java programmer makes in a month. Serious looking guys in Armani suits sit around the table. They stop talking long enough for you, your CTO, and CFO to hook up your laptop to their monitor and ready your PowerPoint presentation. All eyes are upon you as your team members take their seats, and only you are left standing. Everyone waits for you to click through the canned presentation that you've been giving, albeit somewhat improved after each one, for the last four months.

Could it be that even *you're* tired of what's about to come out of your mouth? Will these guys buy what you're about to say anymore than the last group who turned you down?

The truth about this presentation you're about to give? Although you may have passion for your company and its mission, you and your team may be living in an optimistic vacuum. This is not a circle jerk where the object is for you and your team to work yourselves into a frenzy of self-gratification over your service or product. Your job is to excite those *other* people whose job it is to protect the money they're handing out. Let's face it, it's easier for them to say *no* than *yes*. A *yes* could cost them their job, at the very least their reputation until they invest in a winner. A *no* is easy, especially if they see that no one else has invested in your company. Especially since they see your incorporation date was six months ago. Why haven't you been able to generate any interest in that time? That's the only thing in the forefront of their minds as they listen to you pitch. That and the fact that your head is shaved and your tie is too loud.

Many times when leaving a presentation, after having been grilled for 40 minutes about the hardcore facts about your company, you don't have much time to get honest feedback. Honest feedback is not as readily available as a listening ear. It's not a VC's or angel's job to give you feedback; giving feedback may put them in an uncomfortable position, considering that constructive criticism is often met with defensive argument. I hear angels and VCs complain all the time about how, after hearing a pitch and giving a team a *No*, they are practically stalked by the entrepreneur to tell them how they can fix things so they can turn it around to a *Yes*. Guess what? They've done you a big enough favor by just letting you pitch. There are companies that charge many thousands of dollars for the fine-tune feedback you're asking for. If you want it, go out and pay for it, but don't expect to get it for bugging someone.

So all you can do is the best you can do and hope for a favorable outcome. But remember that the market has gotten a lot tighter, and the great dot-com companies with solid revenue models are few and far between. These VCs have expectations of you that even you're probably not aware of.

So how do you get your pitch into shape and make sure you have a winner before you give your pitch to the next VC board? The answer? Spend some of that friends-and-family seed money on getting a good coach—they're out there if you look hard enough. And I'm not talking about some Toastmasters trainer; I'm talking about someone with a track record who can manage to help their client garner startup cash. And, by all means, get references. You're going to be paying cash for this transaction of services, so don't be shy about getting the numbers of other CEOs they've helped. This is no time to be meek. Did I mention to check references? Okay, so you probably get the gist that there are a lot of shysters out there ready to take your hard-earned startup cash for "coaching" services.

So where do you begin? Many firms and angel groups are associated with people or agencies that offer professional services such as business plan writers, technologists, lawyers, and pitch coaches, so don't be timid. Call your "dream" investor's office and ask an assistant if they can recommend someone. All you can get is a "We don't know anyone." Nothing ventured, nothing gained. Often, after your coaching is completed, they may even be interested in taking stock in your company in exchange for introductions. After all, if your dream investor recommended the coach, chances are they can probably get you some face2face time to beg for money.

This business is harsh, and it beats the weary to their knees. You have to be strong and surround yourself with people who will get you to the starting line. Kim Marinucci, founder and CEO of WinningPitch.com, is one of those people sought by entrepreneurs who are open to direction. Guys, it's kind of like that asking-for-directions thing. If you can put your foolish pride aside for this process, you'll have it made.

Marinucci began her career in pitching as an organizational development, team building, conflict resolution, and internal communication coach five years ago. "The biggest thing in my background that led to this career was how to structure a message to get through bias and create a space for listening. One of my clients was working in a startup, and soon I was being referred to others." As of that first startup client two years ago, Marinucci handles startups exclusively.

This year she helped several women CEOs formulate and refine their pitches through working with the Forum for Women Entrepreneurs (FWE.org) and the National Association of Women Business owners prepare for Springboard2000 (www.springboard2000.org), a showcase of 26 women-owned technology companies. The event the women trained for was the mother of all pitch sessions; it took place before an audience of more than 400 VCs and angels. Reported signings of investments between the companies were more than $210 million!

FWE is a unique organization that will help you build your skill set as an entrepreneur if you allow them to. There are plenty of women who get involved with the organization and succeed in their startup endeavors, yet there are others who pooh-pooh the mentorship provided because they don't want to hear the harsh realities a seasoned coach brings to the table. It's that whole thing about being open to listening and willing to take good advice. I've seen these CEO's who thought they could do it faster on their own. If you're going to join FWE, you should be intelligent enough to absorb all of the information provided to you—it may be hard to apply, but this organization has proven itself in so many ways regarding the successful companies it has helped to fruition.

"The idea behind the organization is that if you can address specific issues, we can change how little money is going to women-run organizations with a woman CEO," says Denise Brosseau, CEO and co-founder of the Forum for Women Entrepreneurs. "Currently that statistic is five percent. We want to get that to fifty percent. We address that issue by doing three things. We create a knowledge base among women of all walks of life who have or are creating high-tech or life-science businesses on the venture funding process. So we demystify the venture funding process and give them education on the funding issues, the legal issues, the accounting issues, how to write a business plan, how to build strategic partnerships, how to negotiate a term sheet, how to think big. And we work very hard to help develop their networks, and our networking is both on and off line. And we have a very strong e-mail list where our members can ask critical questions and get back answers from other members at the touch of a button. We try to bring them into educational programs and also bring them in front of other people, such as our Springboard event."

WHY USE A PITCHING COACH?

One of the things hiring a pitching coach gives you is a sounding board. A good coach will listen to your pitch and give you objective feedback. Sometimes, if you use a pro, you'll find out just an initial consultation will be more insight than you've ever received. It may even be enough to turn things around for you. This is valuable because, up to this time, perhaps only your friends, family, or team members have heard the pitch—maybe dozens of times—and would they really know a good pitch if they heard one? Did they even use the Internet before they invested in your company?

It will also give you a fresh perspective on whether or not your revenue model makes sense to someone who could potentially have the power to recommend your company to an investor. This is the real deal. Many pitch coaches who work with startups are also tied in with angel groups and venture capitalists, so you could very well be pitching for real money during your practice spiel.

Kim Marinucci, founder of WinningPitch.com, often suggests people reshape their companies to solve the real problem behind the market need. "Recently," says Marinucci, "I was coaching a B2C company. What ended up happening was they totally changed their business plan. When I hear a pitch, I tell people 'I'm kind of like your lawyer. I'm going to challenge you with every question that comes into my head, so just fight back. When you get in the room with people who aren't necessarily on your side, you have to be ready for those questions.' There's also a time when I might say, 'I just don't buy your business model. It's too expensive to go after what you're after. It just doesn't make sense to me.' But, then I say 'Push back, I'm ready!' Now, after this whole B2C business that's gone on in the market, some of my clients are going to change their businesses to appeal to investors. It's harder, but people are really trying to make it fit."

READY, SET, GO!

Put yourself in their shoes for a few minutes. Actually, let's look at the worst-case scenario where you end up with a venture virgin. You're a venture capitalist (well, actually you're an associate who has just finished your MBA at Stanford) and you've received a business plan that looks interesting. You are so green, this is a plan that looks like what all of your mentors at the firm are telling you to look out for. So you give them a call and ask them to come in. It's your decision whether these people get past you—the gatekeeper—for the rest of the group to look at.

The group of three guys and a woman looks to you to clearly be part of the hip dot-com movement. The guys are dressed in creased khakis, black T-shirts, and sports coats with a high sheen. The woman has jet-black hair and a nose piercing; she is wearing an all-black suit. She is the CTO and looks very much in charge of what's going on with the laptop. You're sitting down in the meeting room with them, and they're looking around for the phone jack. She asks you if they will be able to plug their computer into the one closest to her. "Is it safe?" *Safe?* "You know, a phone jack I can plug into?" she asks, clarifying her question. You have no clue. This is the first time, other than your interview, you've been inside the room. You excuse yourself and ask the secretary. She says there's an outlet on the other wall they can use. You go back in and let them know.

You can tell they've done this a few times before; they're pretty succinct in their method. They have a large flat-screen display hooked up to their laptop, and now they begin what your associates call *the pitch*. The very first pitch out of business school that you've seen. You have the power to make or break this company. They seem like they have it together, and you hope this will be a company one of the partners will congratulate you for finding.

This scenario is a good one to keep in mind. Assume you are talking to someone who has knowledge of what a good investment looks like, but doesn't have the wherewithal to get past the technology—they just know a good business model when they see it. Don't get caught up in the minutiae or you will lose them. Then again, you might be talking to one of the seasoned analysts at the company. The point is, you never know who you're talking to, so start with the bare bones and build it up when you get questions.

GET TO THE DAMN GIST ALREADY!

"The most common mistake people make is speaking at a level that is so abstract that people don't understand them, especially when they're using acronyms that aren't common knowledge," says Kim Marinucci, founder of WinningPitch.com. People understand what an ASP is, but sometimes they are so close to it and have been living and breathing it for so long that they can't back away and give a broader view. Then it becomes difficult for them to see the most important thing about their company, the thing that will help people *get it* right away. They lose perspective. They may also have a bag full of statistics that are compelling, but they don't have time to tell every single one, so which one do they use?"

I was in a pitch session the other day that made my toes curl—and that's a tough thing to do when you're wearing pointy heels! This company had an Australian moderator—great sense of humor and delivery, but a bit difficult to understand at times. When she came to the slide in her presentation that explained who the five team members were, she pontificated on each of their backgrounds, reading with the slide, which seemed as if it was in 9-point type (I couldn't read it, and I was at one of the front tables). It was excruciating. What had been a fairly decent presentation droned on and became painful. The eyes of everyone in the room glazed over. I was tired and saw that others were not inspired to hang and mingle with the companies—they wanted out and were ready to bolt. It was late in the evening and it was time to go home. And it hadn't helped that the presentation before hers had gone over by 15 minutes.

Too bad the companies weren't better honed, and too bad the host let the one company go on past their time to knock everyone else into overtime. Minutes can seemingly turn into hours and kill enthusiasm to write checks. This is the stuff of lost opportunities.

"We've never had anyone break down in tears, but we did have one person who was presenting a business plan that didn't make any sense. It was internally inconsistent. I happened to have our entire team in the room—about twelve or thirteen of us—and we started, not in an aggressive way, to pick apart what he was presenting. He folded up his laptop computer, said he wasn't going to 'sit in a room and be insulted to this degree,' and stormed out. All we were doing was asking questions about why things didn't add up."

—TOM BEVILACQUA, chief strategic investment officer for E*TRADE Group, Inc., and managing general partner for E*TRADE Venture Capital

FIRST DATE

Think of pitching as a first date. What do you want to know about that person before you invest more time in them? Probably the same things—well, not *exactly* the same things—an investor wants to know about a company. Basically, they want to get a warm fuzzy and a genuine feeling that they want to spend more time with you. Again, put yourself in their shoes once. What, if nothing else, do you want to convey? You want them to know you are competent. So, be sharp! A quick checklist about first dates with investors follows:

- First of all, be ready to see a VC. If you don't have a team or a fleshed-out concept with some real numbers behind you, don't bother making the appointment.

- Dress like a professional. Steve Jobs can get away with wearing jeans, but you don't have his money in your bank account.

- Cut the acronyms.

- Cut the fluff.

- Be confident about your core competency—what is your competency, anyway?

- What is the need/problem, and how do you solve it?

- Who is your competition? (And don't ever say there is none—that is the lamest thing anyone could ever say.)

- Don't be arrogant about your space—they probably know more about it than you do.

- Be genuine.

- Be honest.

- Be entertaining.

- Open your ears and listen. Don't try and fill moments of silence with nervous chatter—wait for them to respond and really listen to their questions and concerns.

- Be clear on what it is you're presenting.

Companies who want to do the exact same thing you do
have probably pitched your audience at least three times. They
are probably listing—in their inner dialogue—the competitors
you don't even know about because you've had your head
buried in the business. Maybe, if they like you, they'll give you
a heads-up, or even suggest a partnership. After all, none of these
guys sign NDAs. I've seen it happen. I've seen it work to a great
advantage for both companies involved.

They also want to know if you already have partners. My
best advice: be *very* honest. I've seen these things blow up if an
entrepreneur is bluffing. I remember the afternoon well. A room
full of people and an entrepreneur pitching the group of investors
starts naming partners. Well, the person who heads up the division at one of the companies mentioned by the entrepreneur is
sitting in front of his face. The division head asks, "How far
along are you on that deal?" The people sitting in the room
snickered, because they know who the man is and why he's asking. The entrepreneur says they "have a deal in the works, and
we're waiting for the finalized paperwork."

Why hadn't the entrepreneur recognized the investor?
Because the entrepreneur's business plan had been rejected in a
different form on three separate occasions from the company.
Unlike the rules of metaphysics, visualizing a deal does not make
it so. The investor stood up and introduced himself and shook
his head. "You have just made an ass out of yourself, young
man," he said, collecting his cell phone and packing up to leave.
It was clear he would not be coming back to this group. The
entrepreneur, who had been feeling quite cocky only moments
before, wearing an expensive suit and a healthy tan, went white
and looked like he was about to throw up. Actually, fainting
about then would have been a good plan. Instead, he continued
painfully on until the pitch came to an awkward halt and another
team was brought on.

Awkward silence? Yeah, you could say that. Many of the people
in that audience also belonged to other angel and VC groups.
Just as scripts in Hollywood get a thing called *coverage,* where
other studios hear about scripts and how good or bad they are,
so goes the Valley and the deals that could have been.

TELL THE RIGHT STORY

After you get the whole truth thing down, the thing you have to worry most about is pitching the concept with the right story. Kim Marinucci, founder of WinningPitch.com, says that the challenge of conveying a story tops her list of problems with pitches.

"That's when an outsider's help is needed the most, someone who will come in and tell the truth. For example, a friend of mine and one of her colleagues from the Stanford MBA program just started a company and asked for help. They knew that people were interested, but were not sure if people were giving them feedback about how it's *really* going. 'We have a sense that they're being polite,' they told me. They didn't have any money to hire me at the time, so I said, 'Come by for an hour, and I'll just give feedback.' They gave their story, and I said, 'You're solving the wrong problem. According to you, stress is the problem. This is not the problem. The problem is the fragmented market.' "Sometimes your target is important, but in this case, they were spending too much time on statistics of how stressed women are and what they do about it, blah, blah, blah. But this wasn't the problem to solve. I find that there are different layers to the problem, and often people are starting too high, too generalized."

"Either you don't know how to tell your story, or you need to change the way you're telling it. Maybe you have a bad story and you need to adjust that by adjusting either your strategy, your market, or your people. Maybe you haven't knocked on enough doors and you need to try other avenues. For example, Palm had a great plan and a great vision, but their timing was poor. So for them, it was a matter of not knocking on enough doors. You have to listen to why people are turning you down. Sometimes they're right and sometimes they're wrong—you have to make that assessment yourself. Clearly, as we saw with Palm, even really smart people can all make the same mistakes. But they're the exception rather than the rule. You'd rather be the company where you go in to give a VC presentation and all of the VCs say they want to invest. You don't want to take forever to explain what the business plan is—get to the point, and have data that backs up your claims. One guy wrote me an e-mail last night that said, 'I have a cure for heartburn—I tested it on fifty of my friends.' Well, that's really not sufficient."

—STEVE KIRSCH, founder of Mouse Systems, Frame Technology, Infoseek, and Propel

TELLING THE *REALLY* WRONG STORY

One of my biggest pet peeves is listening to non-technologists blather on about the technology of their company. Often, I ask these people if they have a CTO and they shake their heads, "Not yet, but we're looking. Know anyone?" Well, what I really want to tell them is that the technology they're going on about only exists in their minds. Some people truly believe that, by visualizing it, the technology will just happen. They don't realize that they're talking about something that has been in development for years and might even be looked at as the Holy Grail of that particular industry. Ah, that might explain why such a good idea doesn't exist, yet. Duh.

I highly recommend that you sit down with a technologist and validate your concept before you start pitching your idea.

"There are comparisons to the gold rush and the '49ers being made today. There's some validity there, but, there were no '50ers. I think the way people went about it back in 1849 was the same way they went about it in 1999, where they think, 'Who cares, let's just pack up everything and get out there. Give me a pick. I don't even know how to use a pick, but it doesn't matter because what I've heard is, you just throw it into the ground and boom—up comes gold.' "

—ROYAL P. FARROS, CEO and chairman, iPrint.com

FIELDING e-IDIOTS

One thing that occurs when a green entrepreneur is finally happy with their practiced pitch is that they may not be willing to work on the issues that arise from telling it. For instance, a team was pitching me about a software product that would make good sense on a young teen site. Well, there's no teen site big enough to make a viable business from selling it to them, and these guys were looking for *big* bucks to back their software development. I asked them how much a buyout would have to be to make it worth their while. They named some ridiculous amount, and I scoffed. I named a company that has a killer app, now part of a bigger company, and how much they were originally purchased for. It was a third of what this team wanted. But that's what they thought they had—a mega-killer app.

"I don't know what motivates all these [entrepreneurs]. Are they motivated by the gold rush, or because they have a great idea and they're passionate about it? I think most of them are here because they want to be rock and roll stars. I truly question their sincerity and their viability. I think the VCs have every right to turn down ninety-nine out of one hundred companies. You have to put yourself through all the tests, the viability of your plan. It doesn't have to be perfect, but I hope these people are in it for the right reasons. If not, they may get into a situation where they get into crappy times, and they start going out the window and out of business. I think it's all related, because it ties in with how connected you are to our own human needs, awareness, and value system."

—MARLEEN McDANIEL, chair and CEO of Women.com

I suggested that the team think about licensing the app to teen sites that are part of large portals. They had no idea how licensing worked or how much they could charge for such a service. They did know they still liked the idea of selling their company to a big corporation. I told them that they'd have to show the big corporation they were *something* first, and that licensing the product to some impressive clients (for cash) was the best bet for doing that. They had a quick pow-wow and decided it was still best to build a company around the product. They couldn't see it any other way and went back to the idea of having a huge valuation. They may get into a VC's office, but they probably won't survive the exit strategy part of the pitch.

"Some people handle resistance on the defensive rather than the offensive," says Kim Marinucci, founder of WinningPitch.com, of one of her biggest pet peeves about entrepreneurs. It's my pet peeve, too.

ANTICIPATING AND CONFRONTING RESISTANCE

"When I work with people, I want to know what the number-one objection is," says Kim Marinucci, founder of Winning-Pitch.com, about confronting obstacles. "Although there may be many different ones, there's usually one main one. For instance, online training is a crowded space, so the biggest issue is, *here's another one—how are you different?* Competition is the biggest objection. So if people aren't handling that up front in their elevator pitch, no one is going to be listening after 30 seconds. Having your competition slide as number eight in your presentation is not the way to handle it. Go into it, right there. *Boom.* You're in a position of strength by acknowledging your main objection right away. If I bring out your own internal dialogue and acknowledge it, it's going to wake you up and you're going to be listening. That's the best way to deal with someone's resistance—name it. But people are afraid to be negative or to be too focused on the competition. I find that people can be too Pollyanna about their competition."

Marinucci recently attended a pitching event at which judging panelists, made up of venture capitalists, listened to entrepreneurs pitch. When they are done, the entrepreneurs get helpful hints from the VCs, and who knows—maybe they even get the opportunity to hand an investor their business plan.

"There was a mixer beforehand," says Marinucci, "and this guy came up and said, 'Oh, so you're the coach—give me some coaching.' He told me what he did, and I said, 'I don't understand the problem you're solving.' He told me more about the problem, then I told him, 'I don't know your business well enough yet, but you need a grabber in the opening. Something like, 'How many of you have ever had a problem getting a taxi in San Francisco?' Well, he goes up to pitch and says, 'How many of you have ever had a problem getting a taxi in San Francisco?' Nearly every head in the room went up, and then he made a joke and everyone started laughing. Then he described the problem from the taxi's perspective and from the consumer's perspective and then—*boom!* He went off with all the business details. People thought it was the best presentation that night."

The entrepreneur provided—or rather, Marinucci provided—an emotional connection. It's important to create a human aspect, a need connected to a story—one that connects on nearly a universal basis. A problem and solution that the members of the audience will click right into. Well, depending on the complexity of the product and how much your audience members vary, you may be able to do that flawlessly once in a while. But, there's one in every crowd...

"Afterward, one of the VC panelists said, 'This is one of my pet peeves! I get it!' Then another guy gave him the thumbs down and said, 'I put a lot of thought into this, and I think it's a supply-and-demand issue. If it's raining, there are no cabs, and if it's not raining, there are cabs.' If I was working with him again, I'd tell him to open with, 'How many of you have a problem getting a taxi in San Francisco? What we do is, the next time you need a cab and it's pouring down rain, we'll have it to you in five minutes.' That's what I mean about weaving a story and building in some resistance."

BANDWIDTH THE WIDGET WHACKS AMPS, YA!

Huh? Sometimes listening to a pitch I feel like I'm listening to Andy Kaufman in his "Taxi" role as Latka. What the hell does it mean? Sometimes I ask the entrepreneur if he can help *me* out. "Am I having a brain hemorrhage, receiving a message from a parallel universe during a quantum time shift, or did you really just spiel out a series of words that made absolutely no sense?"

"What we ask the entrepreneur to do, besides taking us through their canned presentation, is to give it to us in one, two, three sentences. What about their company is unique? Why should we invest? What's the overall attractiveness? I'll often ask them to describe the company not to me as an investor, but as a recruiter trying to get someone to join the company."
—**TOM BEVILACQUA, chief strategic investment officer for E*TRADE Group, Inc., and managing general partner for E*TRADE Venture Capital**

They usually take this somewhat good-heartedly, and we move on, the entrepreneur choosing their words more carefully. There are some people at these events who get so excited talking about their technology that they practically start hyperventilating—these are the developers who shouldn't be allowed to see the light of an investor mixer. It's not a pretty sight, and certainly not what I'd call inspiring. These types of people, when thrown into a mix of relatively calm people, will just serve to agitate and alienate their company.

Then there's the extreme entrepreneur who does a massive download on me when I only have five minutes. *Always* assume people only have five minutes. To assume anything else these days is a bit too presumptuous for my schedule, or anyone else who may not care about your company because it's not in their space. Wait for the person to give you subtle hints, such as questions, that they actually *want* to hear more.

"I have to say, in general, most of the people who come to me know that they need to be talking about the business," says Kim Marinucci, founder of WinningPitch.com, about tech talk. "They're savvy enough to say 'I'm a technologist, and it breaks my heart to get away from that, but that's why I need your help.' "

 What are the two top things Guy Kawasaki, CEO and founder of Garage.com, looks for in a presentation?

"Brevity and passion, though not necessarily in that order."

I have to admit I'm a girl geek, and I love to hear the technology details. I hang with physicists who discuss theories about harnessing quantum physics and the endless possibilities of doing so. So start talking about packets and broadband, and I'm completely yours for a couple of hours. But, that's my job—I conceptualize this stuff so people can understand it. I'm hired by huge technology companies to sit down with their developers and talk about how they're helping a licensee build tools. Then I talk to the licensee and one of their clients. Then I build the description of what's been developed and how it can help other companies. I'm a geek and I'm writing for geeks, but I still keep the jargon down. Why? Because I'm writing the description for CTOs who are probably not familiar with their own development technologies, and I have to write to a level that they can wrap their heads around. Problem. Solution. Get it?

Now, if I have to keep the jargon down for CTOs, what does that mean to you? Keep the jargon to an *absolute* minimum.

DANGERS OF ORBITING PLANET ME

Pay attention to your listener's body language and eyes. Are they still with you while you're giving them a tour of Planet Me—taking *their* time to talk about *your* product and how *they* can help *you*? This is truly Self-Centersville. I know I keep bringing up this analogy, but remember the first-date thing? Well, this is the point where your date at the party may leave with someone else if you seem too eager, or too boring, or too desperate. Or too self-involved. The more desperate you are, the more this person is going to look like the cat Pepe LePew is caressing extremely tightly while he professes his love for her.

If the investors have any friends in the room, they will come over, make up an excuse, and pull them away. I do this all the time, and I'm thanked profusely. It's called *running interference*. And you will be avoided like the plague.

Make sure you're checking in mentally all through the pitch to check out your listeners' responses. Sometimes people will even tell you important things if you'd just shut up and listen. Listening will also help you get a grasp of their level on the technology scale. Are they participating? Are they asking questions? Have they folded their arms? Have they walked away?

On the other hand, be careful not to patronize your listener. Personally, I like to get the Full Monty on the technology. I hate it when I have to pull the details of the technology (slowly and painfully) from a technologist. And I *absolutely* hate it when I ask men (funny thing, this never happens when I'm talking to other women technologists) for the full technology story and they dumb it down, assuming I don't understand.

HIDING THE BITERS

There are certain people at your company (and you may be included) who should never see the light of an event. I call these people *biters*. They're like a bad dog—the dog that bites people or rubs up against them in embarrassing ways. Well, this is the *biter*. What do you do with that dog when you're having a party? You lock him in the back bedroom, or leave him at a friend's. You hide the bad dogs. I make this analogy because there are bad dogs in every company.

The other day, I had a strange thing happen when I was at a celebration where many startups were on showcase. I went up to a team all wearing neon-colored dot-com T-shirts that displayed their logo. They seemed very cool, with happy, bright shiny dot-com faces. The group, half men and half women, ranged in age from their early twenties to, I'd say, 40. Okay, so I'm interested. I'm talking, they're talking. We're having a great time. We all have drinks in our hands and the shrimp toast things they're handing out. There's probably about 300 people at the party, ranging from the mayor of a major metropolitan city to the people representing the companies that would make or break this team.

Well, one of the guys on the team was a particular smart ass, and all of a sudden it strikes me that this guy reminds me of a guy I went to high school with; looks like him if you'd put 15 years on him. I said, "You know, you remind me of a guy I went to high school with." And he answers, "You're way older than me, babe," expecting to get some laughs, but his team is mortified.

"Are you always an asshole, or is it my lucky night?" I asked. I turned my back completely on him and continue talking with the team. By then I'm kind of in pissy mode, and my drink is wearing off, but I try and tune in to what a woman on the team is telling me. I said, "Whoa, back up, what did you just say?" She goes on to say that they are the leading provider of the service their site is offering. I happen to know they are not, not by a long shot. So I said, "No way. Leading in what way? Leading me with your statement? What else could be leading about this startup? You just started up."

Well, I thought she was about to cry. I backed off when she explained that she had just started that day. Okay, so I just happened to latch on to the two people who should not have been allowed to see the dance floor that night. It was at that time the CEO came up—a really nice guy who is a veteran in the industry—and politely introduced himself. By that time, the team had lost their luster, so I shook his paw and excused myself. I went on to discover another company that evening that filled me with inspiration to write a story about them. I will never write about that weirdo company (well, except for this) no matter what they do. Why? Because I don't have to.

Update. It's been about four months now since that event. Two weeks ago, I received an e-mail from one of their new PR people telling me about a product release. I asked him to call me so we could chat (there actually had been something I was interested in about the company's technology). He never followed up, via e-mail or phone. Sometimes companies are just systemic in their hiring practices and tend to attract flakes for the sake of getting a body in a chair. One thing is certain: This company will not get a third look from me

Do yourself a favor and make sure your people are informed and polite—people who are offended often will bite back if provoked.

I recently attended one company's technology showcase, and they had let out all of the scientists. I was in heaven because I got to geek out and have some pretty heady conversations about technology. I ended up talking to this middle-aged guy—probably going through a mid-life crisis, and I would bet he owned a red sports car and used some product to keep what hair he had. We got into a heated conversation about packeting (Internet technology), and by that time, most of the attendees had left and evening was upon us. We were relatively unobserved in the courtyard. The next thing I know, he is kissing me. I had just been talking about bandwidth and a complete stranger was kissing me. I pulled away and demanded, "How did *that* get *there?*"

Talk about awkward. I told him that if that was his way of winning a debate, he must be *very* effective with his male associates.

And I walked away. I won't be attending that company's open houses any time soon!

When you're at one of these industry parties, you never know with whom you're talking—I don't even wear a name badge half the time. Some of these people could be worth billions of dollars; others might be just like you. Or maybe someone like me who is looking to make fodder of your follies. So, keep the drinks down to a minimum, keep your e-idiots off the floor, and don't let them wear your dot-com T-shirt in public. There are just some things you can't ever take back—this includes sticking your tongue in someone's mouth. Sometimes I wonder what kind of stress we're putting people under that could make them crack so entirely without shame or notice.

AND THE OSCAR GOES TO...

Telling a compelling story is difficult enough. Sizing up your audience and pulling a new story together, one customized for the audience, is a magician-like thing you will soon learn to do second nature.

"I worked with a dot-com company where the focus was elder care," says Kim Marinucci, founder of WinningPitch.com. "So, *who* cares for elders? The VC audience was mostly males. Are they worrying about this issue? No. One of the lines that we practiced was 'How many of you are looking forward to having your mother-in-law come live with you?' How did we find a way to get their attention? It's not rocket science; you just have to look at who your audience is and what their motivation is."These entrepreneurs have to make the VCs fall in love with their business," explains Marinucci. "Yes, you have to have all the business facts and your ducks in a row to convey why this is a good business. But in the end, it's an emotional decision. *Are we going to go with this one or that one?* We want to be inspired. Investors know they're going to be spending a lot of time with this person and we all want to be turned on in life. Too many entrepreneurs are totally focused on what they're doing and conveying the facts that they forget to build an emotional connection with whoever is on the other side of the table."

The Business of Plans

Business plans are sometimes the big obstacle standing in the way of many entrepreneurs getting off their asses and making a business. I can't tell you how many times I've heard someone ask if I'd write their business plan for them, "because you're the writer." *Paleeeze.* You don't need to be a Hemingway (or a Richards) to write a business plan. I often find that these entrepreneurs have not taken the time to figure out their business model and are stuck because they don't know how the business will make money. I suppose you can pay someone to beat a business model out of you, but if they have to, is your company even ready to have a business plan? And will it be the right one?

"No one really knows if they have a viable dot-com business until they ship it and see. One good test is, 'Would I use this product, service, or company?' If the entrepreneur wouldn't, most likely, no one else will either."
—GUY KAWASAKI, CEO, Garage.com

Green entrepreneurs usually haven't done much research in the market and don't know about competition, market cap, or if there is a real business somewhere in their concept. For example, a friend came to me with just a URL and an idea and said, "Can you find an investor?" I explained to him that, a) he had to have a business model where he could show how the site would make income, and b) he'd need to have a business plan before he could get into pitch anywhere. He was clueless when it came to technology and thought all he had to do was hire some guy in a garage to do a website using FrontPage. "Could you write my business plan?" he asked naïvely.

Asking someone else to write your business plan is plain lazy—and it's part of the Zen of building a company that's a journey only you and your team can take. If you're not passionate about everything about your company, including writing the business plan, you should definitely keep your day job. I've met people who were willing to give me big time points in the company, or lots of cold, hard cash if I would write their plan. That alone worries me about company. I mean, there are even computer programs that format everything and ask all the questions.

There should be nothing stopping you from writing your own business plan. Nothing. Zippo. Nada.

BREVITY IS BEAUTIFUL

An executive summary doesn't need to go into much detail, but it does have to address the business model, and it does have to show that you'll make a profit. If you don't know when you can see a profit, why should an investor write you a check? What would you say if someone said to you, "Hey, I have these great people who want to work with me. We have an idea. We don't know how we're going to pay you back—we don't even know how much money you're supposed to get on your return, but could you cut us a check for $50 thousand?"

To have a business plan is to know that you have thought things out. And on your revenue model page? Well, you'll actually have some numbers that have some basis in reality, and a plan built around the revs, and even a story to push it all through.

"The comments that I get from people after I speak at conferences are that they learned the importance of brevity. You have to have depth, of course, but it doesn't mean you have to tell me about it up front," says Bill Joos, vice president of business development for Garage.com, who participates in the Garage.com's Boot Camp for Startups conferences.

"I joke and say, 'My ability to get you funded is inversely proportional to the length of your plan.' If you spend more than six bucks at Kinko's, you probably can't get funded," says Joos. "What that means is that if the business plan is ninety pages with appendices, charts, and graphs, you wonder, 'Why don't you just go execute, why'd you do all this?' The business plan isn't the end result. The discipline of thinking through business models is important, so I'm not dismissing the need to have done that critical thinking.

"We probably see more money raised with twelve to fifteen PowerPoint slides, a well-written executive summary, and an articulate communicative team than we do with the ninety-page Kinko's spiral-bound plan. While that's good and may help people gel the company in their minds, nobody in the Valley has time to read those things. It's more important that you have the underlying assumptions thought out and the ability to articulate the dream. I can't think of a single circumstance where people are executing against their original business plan anyway. If they're not fast, fluid, and flexible with changing market conditions—for instance, look what's happening to dot-coms—they went from being in vogue to being poison. B2C followed it and we're not done with the cycles yet."

Joos is famous for pulling out a fanned, four-panel, business-card sized business plan at conferences. He got the business plan from a Hawaiian startup that had already received funding. He keeps it in his pocket until the right time, when he pulls it out and blows away entrepreneurs who are getting hernias from carrying around their own business plans.

"The whole point of this executive summary on a four-sided, fan-fold business card is that we're in sort of the MTV generation where you need to make your point," says Joos. "There's a quote that I love—it's been attributed to Mark Twain—and it says, 'I didn't have time to write you a short letter, so I wrote you a long one.' When people are seeing ten thousand to fifteen thousand business plans a year, you need to break through the clutter and have a compelling story that will stop them in their tracks. So we spend a lot of time with our clients on brevity. It's very easy to be verbose. It's extremely difficult to be concise and compelling. My guess is that it took the company a long time to write that four-paneled business plan, as opposed to writing a fifty-page business plan."

Joos sits in on many pitch sessions a day to sort through the hype that may have caught his attention in the submitted business plans.

"I view a business fundraising meeting as the microcosm of a company," says Joos. "If you can't run the meeting, are you going to be able to run a company? It doesn't mean that the meeting has to be heavy handed or overly controlled, but there are all kinds of issues. We will occasionally meet with entrepreneurs, and when they leave the room, we huddle and say, 'There's no way this group can pull off this idea. They're disjointed.

They're not on the same page.' This doesn't mean there isn't room for healthy discourse and differences of opinion, or that they have to look unified in an artificial way, but we ask enough probing questions so we can get past the façade pretty quickly. The fundraising process is a really, really good predictor of how that specific match of a team would function running a business."

HOW TO LEARN THE ROPES

I've seen partnerships, alliances, and other great introductions made at Garage.com boot camps. The conferences allow you to have an opportunity to meet with other entrepreneurs, pitch to venture capitalists in a casual atmosphere (at least they did last year), and hear other people pitch. The first Garage.com conference started out as an experiment to see if it would fly. It was held in a 600-seat auditorium in Mountain View and was instantly sold out. Just to test the waters, the company put up a waiting list and had an additional 900 people sign up for cancellations. Garage.com knew they had a market, and now its sold-out conferences are held around the U.S., as well as in London.

"There are any number of conferences out there, and an entrepreneur in learning mode should try to learn wherever and whenever they can," says Bill Joos, vice president of business development of Garage.com. "There's an insatiable demand to understand how to work at Internet speed and get smart in an area. Being an entrepreneur requires an extraordinarily strong set of skills in the management team. There are security and exchange issues you need to be aware of, there are legal issues, intellectual properties issues, hiring, managing an engineering team, banking, Internet banking, investor banking. The amount that an entrepreneur needs to know covers a lot of disciplines, and it's extraordinary unlikely that a single entrepreneur is going to be smart in all of those disciplines. Boot camp is designed to give people a cross-section view of some of the things that are necessary in areas they may not be aware of."

DON'T COUNT OUT SERENDIPITY

It's important for entrepreneurs to go out in the world to events like Garage.com's boot camp, as well as to reach out to others who they may never run into in the course of their normal networking. You can never do too much networking.

Personally, I network to the extreme. As a hyper-networker, if I see a business card on the floor after a conference, I'll consider it fate and make a call to introduce myself. Sometimes you just have to take a risk and make a call. If you see someone who can help you, try to set up a meeting and begin building a relationship. I'm always timid about jumping right into things. I like to find out what a person is about and where they land on the reliability scale. Then again, sometimes you don't have an opportunity to build a relationship and you need help fast. So many people in Silicon Valley take a risk and ask for help from high-profile people that they rarely return calls, and sometimes they luck out. One such risk was taken by Joe Kraus, senior vice president of content and co-founder of Excite@Home.

"Initially our company was funded by family and friends, and we were able to build our prototype from that. We met our first angel on an airplane. I was with our chief designer, coming back from Arizona where our engineering partners are. On the plane, we were redesigning our logo. A gentleman sat down next to us, and he kind of looked over at what we were doing, and by the time we landed, he had agreed to give us our angel funding. We met with him that next week and the lawyer sent over the paperwork. It was very lucky. I made my pitch, he kicked in some money, and then he got an individual who manages a much larger fund to put in some money, as well."
—KURT LUDWIGSEN, president and CEO of Contest.com

"Small events can end up cascading into a large outcome. That's how our funding was," says Kraus of the company's humble beginnings. "The chain of events is long. We borrowed $15 thousand from our parents and sat down in a garage and set up shop where three of us lived. We did stuff like stole our chairs from Oracle and bought VT100 terminals for $10 out of Stanford's graveyard. We had built a technology that started to look like it was going to work, so the time came to look for funding. My name became—and still is—*Phone Boy*, because my job was to get on the phone every day and try to convince people what we were doing was the greatest thing on earth. I got a book called *Accidental Empires*, written by a guy by the pen name of Bob Cringely. In it, he says, 'Tips for entrepreneurs—Call me, I'm a cheap date.' "

"So I call Cringely, we go to lunch, and I tell him what we're doing," said Kraus. "He says, 'Awesome, I'd like to join the company.' He didn't end up joining the company, but he did end up introducing us to InfoWorld, a magazine where he had a column. At InfoWorld, we showed them a demo of our technology and they said, 'That looks cool,' and gave us our first $100 thousand to use our technology to create an archive of their materials and put it on the Web. We didn't know what our business was going to be at that point, at least they were a paying customer. They said, 'If you do a good job, we'll introduce you to our parent company, IDG, and maybe they'd be interested in investing in the company. We did a good job and we made the presentation to IDG. At the meeting, we met a VC in Boston who said 'I might be interested, but I need a West Coast partner.' So we were introduced to IVP, now Redpoint Ventures, and met Geoff Yang.

"We had also started meeting with other VCs. All the meetings went terribly because we'd show them a demo of this technology, and it was very cool, but the first question was always, 'How do you make money?' We'd say, 'You know, we were hoping that you could help us with that. We know the technology, we know the Internet, we know where this is going, we know we can be big, but we thought you could have some input in that.' That usually ended most meetings on a flat note.

"Geoff Yang had the same question, but he did introduce us to Vinod Khosla over at Kleiner-Perkins. Vinod's first question when he saw the demo was not 'How can you make money?' It was 'Does the technology scale?' Now that was a question that nobody had ever asked us before. We gave him the honest answer, which was 'We don't know. We can't afford a hard drive big enough to let us know whether or not we have a technology that scales. Within 10 minutes of meeting him, he gets on his cell phone and asks his assistant to buy us a $6-thousand hard drive, and he gave it to us. We thought, *Awesome*. It was really through that first hard drive that we put together a financing with Vinod and Geoff Yang for our first $3 million."

DOES YOUR PITCH STACK UP?

You never know to whom or where you will be pitching. This only goes to show you that you should always be ready. Silicon Valley is a surreal place to live. Nearly everyone is involved in technology in Silicon Valley, including Jamis MacNiven, whose title on his business card reads *Just the Pancake Guy*. MacNiven is owner of the world-famous Buck's Restaurant, the wacky restaurant with a suspended dirigible, a miniature Statue of Liberty, and various other cool icons of pulp culture. Buck's also sponsors the Sand Hill Challenger Race Car Derby every year for charity, where Sand Hill Road is closed to all traffic and the Valley's digerati compete in cars of their own creation.

As you can tell by now, MacNiven is no ordinary Pancake Guy, and Buck's is no run-of-the-mill restaurant. It is set in one of California's most exclusive towns—the place where the VCs and angels actually live—Woodside, a heavily wooded mountain town that rises to look over the entire Bay Area. It is as close as many people will actually get to heaven. It is our "90210" (except with higher stakes, and no Tori Spelling). All the rest of the strange drama is fit fodder for a weekly HBO drama. This is where the digerati come to roost and where the players play.

Woodside is so riddled with juicy stories that writers sit here and suck in the atmosphere for their next tell-all blockbuster. Hey, even MacNiven is closing a deal on a movie he's making. For being just off the beaten path, this place is pretty exciting. You can always find a news crew taping or a journalist or writer off in a corner of Buck's looking for their next story. This ought to be the first stop on your list of field trips for the new entrepreneur.

"We had a Stanford anthropologist in here the other day studying the posturing of the male investors and entrepreneurs," says MacNiven. "He commented it was a little like cockfighting, or watching peacocks. What I notice most is the guys who are pitching don't usually end up with the time to eat." If you're going to study this topic, Buck's has got to be the best place to do so. On any given day or night, you can find the Valley's top-tier VCs and angels huddling in booths with entrepreneurs and drawing on scraps of paper to illustrate the revenue models of their up-and-coming startup.

"Buck's is a neutral territory where people can eat and size each other up in a public place," says MacNiven. "I did have a Japanese film crew in here, and they were focused on the Power Breakfast. So they kept saying, 'We want to see the Power Breakfast.' Well, they were going on all around them, but they wanted the food associated with the Power Breakfast. So I brought them some blueberry pancakes, and they did their shoot, packed up their equipment, and left."

MacNiven is so used to the digerati who come in to his hidden-away Woodside restaurant that he doesn't blink an eye when someone worth $3 billion walks through the door. As a matter of fact, he is a restaurateur-turned-human-catalyst. He puts people together who have common interests. He even suggested an introduction while we were sitting in the bar the other day for lunch. It's what he does. We started talking about this book, and he went back to his office and came back with one of the more ridiculous plans he received lately. We had a good laugh at this plan from the Midwest that didn't give a hint about what the company did. He told me I could keep that one because they had sent a stack.

One of the things you get used to if you're a venture capitalist is that having a meeting at Buck's means you will be interrupted. MacNiven enjoys hazing green entrepreneurs with some of good ol' Buck's humor.

"California informality has reached its current level here," he says. "I feel comfortable enough to interrupt people's pitches and say hello, ask them how they're doing. I have to do all this with a straight face, which is sometimes difficult. But if these guys can pitch here, they can pitch anywhere."

To check out Buck's recent goings-on and all the juicy details that go with it, go to www.BucksWoodside.com. For other places you might chance to meet a VC, go to MacArthur Park bar in Palo Alto, The British Banker's Club (in Menlo Park, where I plugged my laptop in most days and evenings while writing this book because my neighbors had construction going on the entire summer). You might also get onto the Stanford campus and find out about alumni activities that you can sneak into.

SUMMARY

I hope I've gotten it through your head that there are a ton of ways to screw up your pitch and business plan. There are also a lot of ways to make it better, and many resources to help you do so. Being an entrepreneur, for most of you, is a new thing; like anything, where there is risk involved (flying a plane, hang gliding, brain surgery), you should take some lessons before venturing out and actually introducing yourself as an entrepreneur. You should also educate the rest of your team and company that they represent you every time they talk about their job. So surround yourself with competent, excited people from the get-go, and you'll go a lot further than you would have gone had you not done so.

CHAPTER 5

E-VOLUTION
Surviving the Fallout and Consolidation

J ust as television and radio markets found themselves danger-
ously repetitive in their spaces, so will Internet companies.
The major companies will have gained stability, such as AOL
has already done with Warner as a media conglomerate, and
soon we will see who will rule the e-world. At the time of this
writing we're only seeing the tip of the iceberg as far as the fallout and consolidation ahead. Without solid revenue models and
partnerships, repetitive companies will disappear. Hopefully,
your company will have gotten in under the wire.

"Be sure to present and build a financial model around your company that
makes sense. Don't make the mistake of saying, 'If we drive a lot of traffic to
our company, we'll monetize it somehow in the future.' Show today—through
matrix that exists in the marketplace right now—how you're going to do that.
If you leave it to 'we'll figure out how we're going to do that later,' the odds of
your getting credibly funded are very, very low."

**—TOM BEVILACQUA, chief strategic investment officer for
E*TRADE Group, Inc., and managing general partner of E*TRADE
Venture Capital**

This chapter is filled with great lessons learned about partnering, revenue models, and common sense from people who've been there. And yes, I have fantasies of my readers sending me thank-you notes (and opportunities to buy friends-and-family stock) in the not-so-distant e-future.

SOME EPITAPHS FROM THE DOT-COM GRAVEYARD

Dot-coms are falling to the wayside in rapid order. It's as though the Ice Age has come and we're in the middle of its coldest winter, watching as the big, well-funded beasts die slowly and the little ones bite the dust before they even have a chance to get their websites up. The stench of dot-com death is everywhere, and the press smells it from miles away. So when a story hits the press that someone in your segment has bit it, it won't be long before you'll be hearing from the VCs that they're full up in their portfolio for "your market."

All you can do is protect yourself by having strong revenue models and prove yourself. One of the biggest mistakes I see entrepreneurs making is not learning from lessons that have devastated others. Research your market and find out why others in your segment crashed—then at least you have something to say when the objections come up about investing in your market.

On Upside's website, at `http://www.upside.com/texis/ mvm/graveyard/index`, is an assortment of dot-com bombs that went down in flames (or on slow, well-maintained BBQs), and some of the famous last quotes the CEOs were caught saying on record. I advise all of you newbies and wannabes to take a tour through the graveyard before you take the plunge. It may fix some of the misplaced arrogance and give you enough of a reality check to have a business plan you can really hang your hat on. The following tombstones were put together by Jeff St. John at Upside. The dot-com body count rises...

"By year-end, we expect…Auctions.com will have more listings than any other auction site or network."
—Tom Finke, president of Auctions.com

RIP
AUCTIONS.COM
Was: Auction services provider
Born: December 1999
Died: Aug. 31, 2000
Burn rate: Unknown

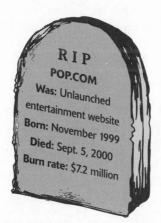

RIP
POP.COM
Was: Unlaunched entertainment website
Born: November 1999
Died: Sept. 5, 2000
Burn rate: $7.2 million

"There was just no market out there, and Paul Allen has just been too good to us.…Who knows, with IPO currency, it might have been different."
—Pop.com backer and Dreamworks SKG partner Jeffrey Katzenberg

"Profit? Are you kidding? We're in Amazon.com mode."
—Stuart Skolman, Reel.com founder

RIP
REEL.COM
Was: Video rental and e-tailing site
Born: April 1997
Died: June 12, 2000
Burn rate: $90 million

BE A SURVIVOR

Okay, so what do you need to know about the future to water-proof your business plan and avoid being part of the bloody carnage on the information superhighway? There are many segments to this new art of *survivability*. They include, but are not limited to

1. A solid revenue model—preferably, you'll have several.

2. Smart funding.

3. Kick-ass partnerships.

4. Fantastic marketing.

5. A smart executive team.

6. Hard-working employees.

7. Conservative spending.

8. A well-executed exit strategy.

One strategy I haven't covered in the other chapters is the wireless issue. If you have the common sense it takes to be an entrepreneur, you'll find in your company all of the key elements I just listed. I've definitely seen an e-volution in the business plans being pitched. It used to be, not so awfully long ago, that companies would only pitch usability only on the Internet. That soon expanded, and venture capitalists were then asking "Can that play on a PDA? Do you have a deal with Palm?" And now it's, "Do you have an Internet appliance partner?" If you want to waterproof your dot-com technology, you better make sure it'll float on all the open channels leading to your core competency.

I can feel it coming, and I know I'm not the only one. Just as radio, TV, and cable came and went in popularity, so will the Internet. I don't mean it's going away, I just mean that it is going to be an everyday, and believe it or not, an intricate part of our lives. It will be as though we've been assimilated by the Borg—resistance won't even be an issue. We'll be there, and we won't even know it. Kind of like when we all stopped eating TV dinners when microwaves came out. Aluminum containers changed to plastic, and we began microwaving our dinners. I can't pinpoint exactly when it happened, it just did. And all of us accepted it.

There are those of you who are praying to the Techno God on a nightly basis for the day when we are all connected by a chip implanted in our brains that runs a digital readout on the inside screen of our retinas. Innately, you believers know that this day will come. But one day, before this happens, there will be a server in our homes that will run all of our Internet appliances. Our refrigerators will know when to order milk and will do so automatically. We'll be able to close our shades and lock our doors at night with our Palm Pilots—ten thousand miles away, we'll be able to appear on our spouses' home office computer screen via the streaming video micro camera in our PDA to say goodnight. It will all be an everyday occurrence.

"I think changes are coming, and as you look forward, we'll end up in a world where the bandwidth is much more ubiquitous," says visionary Judy Estrin, CEO of Packet Design. "So, you can start doing things differently like really seeing more rich media on the Net." The world changes from being about PCs to being appliances, so it's not just, 'How do I provide information so someone from a laptop can access me?', but, 'How can I make sure that I'm appealing to the pager, the cell phone, and the PC and the set-top box? Where does it make sense for me to play?'"

And play you will if you want to survive. Listen to Estrin's advice, and you will make it. If not, I can guarantee you will be part of the post-apocalyptic e-wasteland that will come.

2B OR NOT 2B?

One of the things you should be aware of are the changing fads of the revenue model and the fickleness of the market. I was at a 13-year-old's birthday party in Palo Alto, playing the cool-"aunt" role and keeping the group of girls entertained as they did their own thing and painted pottery in Palo Alto. One of the girls sitting at my table was telling me about her father's company, and she had a real in-depth knowledge of the industry. So I asked, "What does your father's website do?" She looked at me and said "B2C," spitting out the letters like sour milk and shaking her head in disappointment, as if saying *this is what he did with my college fund. I better work on a scholarship strategy.* Whew, she's hardcore Stanford MBA program material, I thought as I painted my clay box.

That's *what it is*—even a 13-year-old girl knows that B2C is dying a slow, painful death. I'm not saying that the B2C companies of yesteryear—those that handed out content and were paid via banner advertising—are over, just that they need stronger rev models to survive the fallout ahead. One of the points I stress is that all of this jargon-bullshit acronym-crap is telling us something. You just have to put your ear close enough to the rail without letting the train decapitate you. No matter what a VC tells you about cutting the acronym stuff, you know that they will, when they have to tell the rest of your group about your company, categorize you. No matter what, you will be categorized by VCs, by the press, by 13-year-old girls. It's the nature of the beast. Ready yourself to overcome the objections.

Currently we're hearing from everyone that B2B is *in*, but is nearly saturated. Although the angels and VCs I know are shaking their heads and saying, "Cut the acronym crap, and just tell me how it works." One of the reasons for this is because many B2Bs are sheep in wolves' clothing. You may have categorized yourself without knowing what you really are.

WEAK PLAYS = DARK DAYS

I was at an entrepreneur conference a few months ago. I sat with a number of entrepreneurs during lunch—all men (not too many women except for reporters and speakers)—and I started asking them about their rev models. I couldn't believe it. I felt like the clock had been wound back, and that I had landed in 1995. Everyone at the table was back in *B2C Land,* where everyone thinks they can sell books directly to consumers at a marginal profit and rule the world.

"Why are people taking the *dot-com* out of their company names? Because of the stigma associated with it. Even at large companies like Adobe, we try and look at the larger picture. We're not riding hype— we're essentially trying to build really fundamental value propositions for customers in the various segments that we serve. You have to ask yourself 'Will my company or service really make people more productive and more efficient in the way businesses work?' What are the measurable results I can take to the companies to show them that they're either going to save money or make money?"

—DR. JOHN E. WARNOCK, co-founder and CTO of Adobe Systems and head of Adobe Ventures

Within a few minutes, and between bites, I learned what everyone's core competencies were. I offered them strong B2B solutions for their business plans. Then I wondered if it was Darwinian—that maybe those entrepreneurs (who will now have decent B2B solutions) were never meant to get out of the gate. Did I screw with e-volution? Perhaps I was only feeding their pipedreams of being the next Steve Case. How could they have gotten this far without studying the space—*their* space? They seemed like smart guys. They had spent nearly $1,000 on a conference at which they would be exposed to some hardcore entrepreneurs who would feed them inspiration, and speakers who would give them some insights. And if it were all based on osmosis, they'd be brilliant dot-com successes by next year. But—and I'm still shaking my head—how could they have gotten this far?

"Since April [2000], in the consumer-oriented B2C, you aren't seeing as many of those [types of companies], so they've fallen out of favor. I think some people are self-selecting out. What I'm seeing is a new sense of mortality by the entrepreneurs. We went through a period that, no matter how light or shallow their business plan was, they'd be able to get funded and become a success. This kind of unbridled optimism and 'nothing can go wrong' attitude has dropped. People now realize both the private and the public business models that make sense. They aren't looking for short term; they're looking for stronger companies."

—TOM BEVILACQUA, chief strategic investment officer for E*TRADE Group, Inc., and managing general partner of E*TRADE Venture Capital

Then it came to me. *Blind ambition.* Usually these are the people who poke their own eyes out with sharpened lead pencils to keep from seeing the truth. These are the entrepreneurs who must suffer. The highways of Silicon Valley are strewn with the sighted who refuse to see. These entrepreneurs only know they have a good idea and the rest be damned—including strategy. If you are one of these e-idiots, change your ways now. People are plotting day and night to take over your market. For every brilliant idea, there are numerous people—with partners, team members and technologies—who are greedily rubbing their hands together and waiting for the perfect moment to make their move. Wake up now, and put some serious meat in that plan, baby.

SHIFTING SANDS IN SILICON VALLEY

So what about this whole B2B thing? I'm not saying that quickly changing your business model from a B2C to a B2B is going to guarantee you a winner. I'm not even saying that it will get you in the door of a VC's office. These shifts are taking place even in established e-companies with cash, branding, expertise, and stamina.

I recently got a call from a CEO of a company that once looked promising—one that I would have bet on. He was the darling of the investors for a while, and then as quickly as success had come, it was gone. His company was promising, but it wasn't making money. He had planned on going out for another round of funding before April 2000. He couldn't even get a bridge loan to make payroll because he couldn't show how he was going to make money. No one is immune, and what doesn't kill you in this market might even make you more resilient.

Let's say you have a company like Beyond.com that made its livelihood (or tried to) from selling software on the Web. Okay, what if everyone decided that this looked like a damn fine distribution model, and your efforts to make a successful B2C software site became diluted? That's what happened to Beyond.com last year as it began its downward spiral. According to *Forbes* (May 1, 2000), Beyond.com burned through $125 million on revs of $117.3 in 1999. Now, Beyond.com has a new rev model: it's going to run e-storefronts for companies that want a Web presence, or at least those who want to hand the responsibility over to someone else to run (why reinvent the wheel, right?). These services include site development, transaction processing, physical and digital fulfillment, customer support, and e-marketing programs.

What do you think about this strategy? This e-case was one of the early hopefuls—an e-company with tons of startup cash, an experienced exec team, and decent branding. In my mind, what Beyond.com wasn't prepared for was a shift, but moved quickly when it came. Here's the deal: This company started out B2C, then shifted to a B2B. What exactly does that mean to its rev model? It was not ramping up revs quickly enough to make it a viable business. Software manufacturers (such as Symantic) offer its software on its own site, as well as on scores of others, in catalogs, and stores (Beyond.com was just one of many). Manufacturers just want to get the product out; they can't offer exclusivity just for the sake of getting more traffic to a website that isn't even their own. So Beyond.com lost market share because of the dilution in the marketplace.

It's the mall scenario all over again. What happens when you have five CD stores in your local mall? We know what happens, and it's not good for anybody—unless you are the manufacturer, or you can buy in the biggest quantity and can offer the biggest discounts. Then you become the big silverback gorilla CD-store of the mall, and you can squeeze your hairy hand around the competition.

Now that Beyond.com is collecting its revenues from other businesses for services, instead of painfully collecting one small consumer Visa purchase at a time, its new lifeline rev model may just end up saving it. Who knows? Maybe Beyond.com will be one of those miraculous turnaround company success stories of next year.

WILL YOU GET E-SCREWED?

What happens if you base nearly all your rev model on another company's service or product? What if you were Priceline.com (PCLN)? You've kept your costs for branding down considerably by bringing aboard a middle-aged actor named William Shatner—who will work for stock and complete adoration—and whom Baby Boomers latched onto and made your site a success. Congratulations! You're branded, you have customers, your stock is decent. Smooth sailing, right? What could possibly happen? Well, on June 29, 2000, the *Wall Street Journal* reported that American Airlines, America West, Continental, Northwest, United, and US Airways plan to create a joint venture in which they offer discounted tickets. So what does this mean? This means that Priceline.com may be heading for rough water.

"There's a great Zen saying: 'Don't get mad at the tiger for being a tiger.' Tigers eat people. Don't take it personally—they're just hungry. Cycles are cycles. April fifteenth happened, and the company is now worth less than it was on April fifteenth, and it will cycle back."

—WILLIAM LOHSE, serial entrepreneur, former CEO, and founder of SmartAge.com

Would you have seen that one coming? I would have said you were crazy. After all, that's kind of like all of the networks getting together to put together a daily listing of shows so they could take advertisers away from *TV Guide*. It's reinventing the wheel. What does this e-incident tell me? Could be that, unless you own the service (like if Priceline.com owned a fleet of planes), your value could be depleted completely when the service decides to undercut you and sell the product itself. In that case, it could mean that everything you've built—all of your e-bidding infrastructure, everything—is useless until you can find another service to offer and can offer it in a competitive format. Basically, bend over, you're about to be royally e-screwed.

Perhaps if Priceline.com had concentrated on selling blocks of travel to businesses at bidding prices, maybe then it could have had a B2B rev model with a client list the airlines would see as attractive. It would have been a buy-out, and that's an exit. Perhaps what Priceline needs is built-in clients, not just a list of cheap people who buy transportation tickets and lodging with apparently no loyalty to brand except the cheapest bid. It's not like they own the list of Southwest's website users who are loyal and repeat buyers for a particular brand.

Today I checked my e-mail, and my subscription to Venturewire.com was in. I read through the June 29, 2000 issue and there were two stories right next to each other—both pertaining to this story:

WIRE STORY

(Venturewire.com, London)—Priceline.com, which enables users to bid for airplane tickets and other goods and services, and General Atlantic Partners said they formed a new company called Priceline.com Europe. The new company expects to begin offering products and services by the fourth quarter of 2000. Dennis Malamatinas, CEO of Burger King, will join Priceline.com Europe as its president and CEO. Timothy G. Brier, co-founder and former executive VP of Priceline.com, has been named chairman of Priceline.com Europe, effective immediately. General Atlantic Partners is providing financial support through its purchase of equity securities in the new company, as well as additional operational and strategic support through its professional staff.

Right below this press piece ran another, posted from New York.

TEXAS PACIFIC IN TICKET VENTURE WITH MAJOR AIRLINES

NEW YORK—Private investment firm Texas Pacific Group and six major airlines have formed a new company that will sell bargain airfares online, according to the *Wall Street Journal*. The site, code-named Purple Demon, has received minority investments from United Airlines, American Airlines, Northwest Airlines, Continental Airlines, US Airways, and America West Airlines and will launch this fall as Hotwire.com, according to the paper. The Purple Demon website says the company has raised $75 million in initial funding with backing from TPG. http://www.purpledemon.com.

A month and a half later (or so) now, I have recently found out that Priceline.com has received in excess of $150 million to regroup from an investor. More recently there was a big story on the news about Priceline.com offering gasoline for bid—a big deal considering the gas prices here in the Valley—and a team of reporters buying their gas online and then trying to actually fill their tanks with Priceline.com gas. Lots of disappointment dampened the enthusiasm of the launch when bad publicity hit about the associated gas stations that didn't honor the Priceline.com purchases.

After the collapse of Priceline's airline sales (about 80 percent of its business at the time), the company concentrated on selling groceries and gasoline. WebHouse Club, a privately held Priceline.com licensee, recently said that in 90 days, the gas and groceries business it provided for Priceline.com would come to an end. To add insult to injury, WebHouse was founded by Priceline founder Jay Walker. He pointed the company's failure toward its inability to raise more capital. Perfect Yardsale, another Priceline.com licensee, also announced it will not be providing Priceline with any further services. Perfect Yardsale provided Priceline with pre-owned product to Priceline users through an online auction technology.

What's all this mean to Priceline and its future? Well not only did all this news hit the fan in relatively short order (in Internet time), but Priceline made the headlines in TV news show "48 Hours." It was a witch hunt. They interviewed some people who were pretty pissed about tickets they had purchased on Priceline. And then they got Shatner admitting that he never used the service because his schedule didn't allow for it. A few days ago, I saw a new Shatner rap commercial where he was hawking car rentals. There's word that the company will get into insurance and credit card sales. Both of these markets are crowded, but whether it's good or bad, they do have a brand name now. Only the future will give us a clue about what will happen with this company. No matter what the outcome, a case study on revenues and branding on Priceline definitely belongs in future Stanford MBA programs.

MotleyFool.com recently had a contest in which members were asked "What if you were CEO of Priceline?" Motley Fool, as much as it pokes fun at others, has little space to jest—I couldn't even get their system to take my suggestion (Motley Fool's UI leaves much to be desired). Stay tuned, folks, we'll see if someone comes up with a solution for the troubled company.

CHOOSING YOUR PARTNERS WISELY

Many startups get e-screwed by giving away their technology or services for the privilege of partnering with a company. So many companies have died making the wrong partnerships. How do you know when you find the right company to partner with?

As any successful dot-com will tell you, partnerships are the essence of building a strong foundation for your budding company. "Partners are a pain because they're self-interested, but you have to realize, no one can do it all. The more peer partners you have, the larger your distribution. Our strategy has been to partner with as many partners as we can. Partnerships are entirely situational—so it's hard to give a systematic approach to making partnerships. Partnerships should flow from one's unique, proven selling proposition—what it is that one has to change the world with."

—WILLIAM LOHSE, serial entrepreneur, former CEO, and founder of SmartAge.com

One technology company came to me and said that it had partnered with a major computer company—and its software had actually been bundled with the computer company's software. The only benefit it received was that they could say they were the computer company's partner. The things wrong with that? They reaped no benefits, they had no other clients, they had no investments, and they were armed and ready to go to investors and other companies touting the computer company's name. Only one thing wrong after I saw that on their business plan—when I asked them how much they were receiving, they said, "Nothing. At least nothing yet," the computer company was going to see how well it worked for them and then maybe work out a deal. I could see where signing a deal like this would be tempting for a startup, but it's hardly worth the effort.

"We were part of a corporation that had a focus on profit—something far different from other Internet companies, that at the time were pretty much free-spending. We'd go out and do partnerships with every major Web property from Yahoo, Excite, AOL, Women.com, and iVillage—we had to do those partnerships in a very cost-efficient manner. We had to look at what was the value we gained from a subscriber, and how much could we afford to pay per subscriber. Then we'd negotiate deals where we would pay a certain amount of money for a guarantee of a certain amount of subscribers joining through that partner. The money we spent generating profit for Match.com was there if we could find cost-effective ways to utilize that money."
—JOHN SPOTTISWOOD, serial entrepreneur, former COO of Bigstep.com, and former president of Match.com

Signing a deal with just anyone isn't good for anyone. Although investors can see why you were tempted to do so, it shows investors that you're not as smart as you think you are. "Above all," says Tom Bevilacqua, chief strategic investment officer for E*TRADE Group, Inc., and managing general partner of E*TRADE Venture Capital, "you should look for partners that you have a real relationship with. Where the people you're interacting with are in a position within their own company to modify their company's behavior to fit you as a partner. If you're getting a level of commitment that is so low or extremely unconnected with the company, you should ask the question, 'How powerful and how strategic is that to the other company?' These are such high level things, and you want to make sure that the company you're dealing with has a reputation for honoring its partnerships.

"I think you should be looking for relationships where your incentive sets are aligned," advises Bevilacqua. "If you go into an arrangement of strategic alliance or partnership, and the incentive sets are not aligned, and one party has the ability to profit at the other's expense, I'd watch out for that because that's probably what's going to happen. The big benefits that you can get depend on the relationships. I'll use an example about companies partnering with E*TRADE—if you are a consumer-oriented company maybe having a financial service product or anything appealing to consumers, we have a consumer base of about three million, highly active online consumers. So from an access point, three million customers is a significant base for any young company to tie into. That's one thing to look for—certain distribution and access to online savvy consumers. You can also look for the channel relationships a company can help provide. If you were to have a partnering arrangement with Cisco that would be extremely powerful because it could open up many doors and access points. It just strikes me that you should know that something is wrong with the partnering relationship if what you're delivering is of value to the other company or to its customers—and you're not benefiting—you've got to be compensated for it."

And what about those banner-based relationships we see so much of? "In the real world you have to ask, 'How valuable are those banners?'" says Bevilacqua. If what you're getting from that other company is not of great value to them, you have to wonder just how wonderful you are to them. And if you're not being perceived as a significant aspect of what that other company is doing or somehow material you're going to be last in the stack and treated that way."

PLAYING THE REV MODEL GAME TO SURVIVE

When Lisa Henderson, CEO of LevelEdge.com, got the great idea of putting a database of high school and college student athletes online for recruiters, she created both a disruptive technology and a technology that could be leveraged for other applications, as well. Henderson, not a newbe to branding or the Internet market, began her career in product development and then went on to become a senior research analyst at Ralston Purina, and then was key in launching BuzzSaw.com, Lucy.com, and HungryMinds.com.

The point of Henderson's story is that, even if you only begin with one revenue model, to survive you must come up with several streams of income to make sure your company is prepared for any of those lines drying up. It all goes back to the good business sense that prevailed before the Internet—what one company all throughout time has relied on one product without diversifying? So, work it, baby—work it for all it's worth.

"It's really a database application that helps high school and junior college students physically break down the economic and geographic barriers they face to obtaining visibility to attend colleges and universities," says Henderson of her company's product. "We have found that out our application as it exists is not only of use to folks involved in the process of recruiting student athletes to colleges and universities, but we've received other interest as well.

"We've received lots of interest from colleges and universities who just want to license our application because they have file cabinets full of kids they're already tracking," says Henderson. "We now have three areas of our business—the first being the management of the process of end to end for students athletes and exposure to colleges and universities. A database application that colleges and universities to license to manage and track kids they're already looking at, and then professional and minor league organizations looking at it as a vehicle for keeping track of the players in the professional ranks. It's been interesting, since we started out with this very specific niche that we were filling and gained enough traction that it created interest and enthusiasm up the line.

"We took a good idea and were able to expand the rev model and make it much larger," says Henderson. "In this particular market everyone wants to talk about revenue—and what's nice for us is that we were able to take a good idea and expand the revenue." Henderson chose to fill her executive team seats with seasoned pros. "My entire executive management team has run profitable businesses their entire careers—we know how to talk about bottom line operating profits and how to get there. It's worked out really well."

THE IMPORTANCE OF REV MODELS IN SURVIVAL

You need to diversify to survive in today's Internet economy. Many of the dot-coms are doing this by leveraging their technology into other formats, whether it be wireless or other delivery methods. iPrint.com decided to diversify its Internet application into a kiosk model. Funny thing, it reminded me of what Nolan Bushnell did for gaming by bringing video games to the masses. Apparently, the time it takes for someone to be waited on by a human sales person to order a custom (business) card is about 30 minutes and the rate of return, because of miscommunications (due to the lack of training in high employee turnover in chain stores) is high.

Royal P. Farros, CEO and chairman of iPrint.com, found a way to make a market transition. Now, OfficeMax and Sir Speedy are using iPrint's self-serve kiosk system. "[The store's customers] are true-blue customers who we wouldn't get anyway. They were going to get this technology whether we provided it or not, it might as well be us. People who were helping to brand iPrint said, 'What are you trying to do, torpedo us? Amazon didn't give away their technology to Barnes and Noble.' The reason is the depth of the technology we have."

"The best way to waterproof your plan is to put a heavy emphasis on technology—what I'm planning on doing is taking that technology into different places."
—ROYAL P. FARROS, CEO and chairman, iPrint.com

"There is no technology, per se, in the classic e-tailing model. For someone to come into our market it would take them years," says Farros about the first-to-market advantage. "iPrint.com is the most sophisticated interactive e-commerce site on the Web today and I'll tell you why I can get away with saying that. Because one, we're not talking about the entertainment world—there's some really great interactive sites out there in the entertainment world. Two, if you look at e-commerce, people aren't creating things, they're just taking orders."

LESSONS LEARNED ON THE ROAD TO SUCCESS

One CEO who has seen a lot of action in his career is William Lohse, who prior to founding SmartAge.com served as president of Ziff-Davis. Lohse was the founding investor in Knowledge Adventure, which later sold to Cendant. He was also founder and CEO of Timeline, a software company later sold to Symantec. Prior to that, he was VP Marketing and Sales at IUS/AccPac Accounting, which was sold to Computer Associates. So Lohse is someone who has been around the block a few times.

After the April 2000 crash, SmartAge decided to pull its IPO and had to go out hunting for funding in a hostile environment. Lohse's company has its work cut out for it. But Lohse seems to have an excellent sense for moving quickly when the ground shakes. And it's shaking now. I recently spoke with Lohse about his company. During that time, he has let go half of his staff and is working with his team to regroup.

His advice for survival is just as valid as it was the day he said it—you have to find an existing market and find a way of serving it.

"Our customers are in the small business market, so we have the luck of the small business market that really doesn't care much about NASDAQ, it cares about a few customers—and hopefully more customers—and getting done what they need to get done. None of our customers are listed on the stock exchange,"—a B2SB play (business to small business), as Lohse calls his strategy, a game plan that seems to be kicking Microsoft's small business arm's ass (you know what I mean).

"We have a lot of competition in this space. There are roughly one-hundred startups that participate in the market. As we look at them, most of them forget about a revenue model. Most of them start out with, 'How do I serve me and bring in traffic?' That's all good and proper, but it doesn't turn into money."

PARTNERING FOR SAFETY

When you can offer your service to a bigger company and keep it from developing its own technology to compete against you— hey, this is not a bad thing. If you choose wisely, who knows you may even get bought up. But, at the very least, it will keep one more competitor, with the budget to bury you, out of the space.

"There's a company in Detroit that we partnered with— we're now sister companies," says Kurt Ludwigsen, president and CEO of Contest.com. "It just made too much sense not to do it. The company, ePrize.net, has quite a bit of money behind them, and they wanted to go head-to-head against Promotions.com. But it had no destination site to put its promotions— that's where we came in. We think together, the two companies are much stronger than Promotions.com is by itself. And for us, this is an additional revenue stream, because we get a piece of the revenue from all of the promotions that are posted on our site. You have to partner. People are trying to build sites all by themselves and garner the traffic—but it's really an uphill battle— and no one has all of the answers. And this is something that was instilled in me by John Spottiswood [former president of Match.com]. If you're not partnering with number one, two, or three, don't bother partnering at all. Go out and find the leader in what you want to do and provide something of benefit from your side, and then go do it together. It's been very beneficial."

Partnering to increase your strength in the marketplace is a great idea, and it sure beats the alternative of getting killed because you couldn't get a healthy distribution for your service or product.

"How do you pick your partners?" asks Lohse. "You pick partners who are bigger because it allows you to distribute what you're doing out there. I also recommend you stay clear on your unique offering. If your unique offering is a current technology—you're in trouble because technology always gets duplicated by somebody else. There has to be something that is customer focused and has a commitment that you've made that no one else has been able to execute."

MAKE IT SIMPLE FOR CONSUMERS

Many of the most stable dot-coms in today's market have found a way to disrupt the way a service or product is delivered in the real world by bringing it to the Internet. Instead of going for the easy concept, these companies created something of value, both in loyalty and technology, and built a strong company around those elements.

How do you know when you have a viable dot-com business? I mean, it takes more than a great URL these days, right?

"A lot more. No one really knows if they have a viable dot-com business until they ship it and see. One good test is, 'Would I use this product or service or company?' If the entrepreneur wouldn't, most likely no one else will either."

—GUY KAWASAKI, founder and CEO, Garage.com

Royal P. Farros, CEO and chairman of iPrint.com, found a way to do this. He is building a company that brings value right to their customers' doors. Before founding iPrint.com in 1996, Royal was co-founder and chairman of the board of T/Maker Company, a Silicon Valley software company named three consecutive years to *Inc.* magazine's List of the Top 500 Fastest Growing Privately Held Companies in America. As one of the Valley's top consumer software companies, T/Maker created such market-leading and award-winning brands as ClickArt,

WriteNow, and PFS:First Publisher. In 1994, T/Maker Company was acquired by Deluxe Corporation. Royal served as an officer of the company, as well as the executive vice president of the newly formed Electronic Direct Group.

Farros learned that a solid market is what you need to run a business. "If you go back to 1994–95, everything before '95 is traditional. You didn't measure yourself in terms of revenues, or customers; you measured yourselves in terms of profits. The business plans all turned around—over the last years [before the crash], you didn't have the time to make a business plan, so you put it on a cocktail napkin. You didn't even have enough time to do that. You just have to get it out there. Is it a good idea? Investors won't even think through it, they just invest. Part of that was because there was so much money coming into the marketplace. There was so much money that investors were literally just shot-gunning at anything that made sense.

"I do a lot of advising," says Farros of his mentor role. "And sometimes it's sad when you see a company going down a path that doesn't make any sense, yet they continue to come back and say, 'Which venture folks do you think would be interested in this?' I say, 'Okay, let me say this again, *no*. You are content, and that's not what people are investing in. The fact that you're *licensing* content is really great, and there are ways that you'll get funded, but not through traditional venture funds.' Then they go out and get angel funding, and that may not be what they want because it's not enough to kick you to the next level."

Margins That Matter

The important thing about offering a product is that the margins have to be worth it. For instance, the margins on books are not that great—especially if you're a retailer and storing them and shipping them from your own warehouse. I think we're watching the aftermath of Amazon finding this out. My feeling about Amazon? I think in Q2 of 2001, we might be seeing Bezos step down to let another CEO from a traditional business background to salvage what's left of the company. At least that's what I'd be asking for if I was on Amazon's board. Learn a valuable lesson from the first round of dot-com fallout we've seen since April: Before you decide on a service or product to offer on your website, you should also figure out how much it's going to cost you to deliver it.

"I keep a back eye on competition, not a forward eye. I have watched the B2B/B2C thing going on—these trends are interesting. And everyone spending $50 million on TV commercials during the Super Bowl—and now they're saying it didn't work. So I spent a little, not $50 million. I fell into the trap of e-commerce, but not for very long. Basically, you have to be fleet of foot enough to experiment, but not get totally sucked in by what other people say. Why did Reel.com go out of business? Because there wasn't enough margin to support the infrastructure. Our site is thirty-five, as far as visitors to our site, and we have racks and racks of servers and big pipes, so I try to keep my eye on our basic business objectives and keep costs appropriate. It's difficult in this business to run profitable, and I'm not alone in saying this."

—MARLEEN MCDANIEL, chairman and chief executive officer of Women.com

---

iPrint.com has proprietary technology that allows people to create, edit, and purchase company items such as business cards, letterhead, etc. It gives complete control over to the customer (primarily the small business owner).

"My business cards cost about $53.99 through iPrint," says Royal P. Farros, CEO and chairman of iPrint.com, about the importance of margins in keeping your company in the black. "If you take that card to any other printer, it's going to be just north of $100. We like to say we're twenty-five to fifty percent less than the traditional quick-print shops. Even if we throw in tax, we're still under that. We're lucky because very few people have commoditized printing because it's very hard to do. Depending on who you sell to, the margin is very high. If you want to negotiate with me on a business card and you want two-hundred fifty, then I say, 'Tell me when you want to buy two million of them, and maybe you'll have some leverage.'

"Small-business margins are among the highest; when you get into providing services. By definition, those are great growth margins. It's when you get into the medium and large business sales—anytime you have a professional buyer involved—that's when margins are the lowest, because you have people beating you up over price. We've been very good to stay away from that market. Our professional quotes are very different because you have professional buyers involved."

CUTTING CORNERS IN THE NICK OF TIME

One of the lessons that the dot-coms learned after seeing companies spend millions on Super Bowl TV spots was you can blow an entire year's budget in no time at all, especially if you're just planning on asking for more. Royal P. Farros, CEO and chairman of iPrint.com, put his team and company to the test when he said, "Let's just pretend the market has hit rock bottom and see ways we can implement a plan that could possibly save the company." This was before April 2000. Holding on to your money and being frugal with your spending is important to a company's survivability in today's (or tomorrow's) market.

 "Developing partnerships was a significant challenge. We had to go back and forth and back and forth on every deal, especially when a company like Yahoo is signing a deal with AutoWeb.com or CarPoint.com and is getting $7 to $10 million dollars over two years. And we're asking for the same amount of exposure, and we're going to pay less than a tenth of that. And we're trying to argue that deal because they're selling cars, and all we're doing is getting a monthly subscription for a dating service. It's still a very challenging thing to do, yet, as you know, there is more space for advertisers on the Web than there are advertisers. You can drive down the price as long as you can convince people that it's the lowest price they're going to get. It took a long time to negotiate favorable partnerships."

—JOHN SPOTTISWOOD, serial entrepreneur, former COO of Bigstep.com, and former president of Match.com

"Pretend this is your money. Are you going to spend this money?" Farros asked his company directors—that was easy for him to say because a good deal of Farros' own money went into building the company in the seed round. Knowing that it might be easier—and trendy—to go for more rounds of cash to fund elaborate branding campaigns than it might be to cut corners and save money, Farros opted to teach the company a lesson in economics.

"That's actually a real trend happening in the Valley," says Farros, "because money is so plentiful, venture money used to be used for investment, you used to do business to get revenues to drive working capital. And now, in the last two years, venture capital is working capital, and when you run out of it, you just go and get more. When you look at a startup and a company is paying $6 a square foot, you have to wonder, 'What are these people thinking?' "

"In February [2000], we had an offsite meeting, and we were three weeks from going public," says Farros. "The market was going ga-ga, and so we said, 'What happens when we go public and our stock price goes in the tank? What are we going to do about it?' We literally had a blueprint as soon as the market started going down, and the whole idea of moving the printing integration group to Minnesota was because, if the market went down, we weren't going to be able to get a secondary. We were already doing our initial public offering and were literally at the end of the IPO process and into the roadshow process and had already laid the groundwork for secondary offerings.

"So when the market slumped, people who were going for second round didn't get it, and if you were going for a B and were looking for a C, you didn't get that," says Farros of the April 2000 crash. "The spigot turned off. It was fun because we already had the whole thing scripted—remember how Bill Walsh used to script the first twenty-five plays? That's what we did—we mapped out what we would do if the market slumped. I think that's why we got out of the gate early with all of our cost cutting. It shows you kind of a conservative nature—the people in this company did not grow up in the last two years. We were all managing companies back in the '80s when it was really hard to get money. With all of those great things going for it, it still took nearly a year to raise our first round of money. Today if somebody takes a year, you've basically died five times over."

PARTNER WITH AN INCUBATOR

The importance for some startups to partner with an incubator cannot be underestimated. In an incubator, you get discounted space or free space, use of furniture and phone lines (most of the time for equity). In many of the great incubators such as the Panasonic Incubator and the Women's Technology Cluster, you get solid advice from professionals who've been there, done that. There are lots of other doors that open to you, as well. Some incubators are for-profit, some nonprofit, and some will help you because you're one of the company's investments.

iPrint.com was lucky enough to have incubator space at NASA at a time when they needed to save money. Incubators aren't for everybody, especially if you have a team of primadonnas who want a fancy office and reserved parking spaces. iPrint's team was hardcore about the bottom line and building a company with a solid core. "[The NASA facility] looked like a 1950s classroom. It had a Linoleum floor. They were nice enough to paint it gray—gray walls, cast iron desks. We found options because we look at this like it's our money, and the truth of it is that a lot of it is our money. Everybody in the company, by virtue of getting options, has a vested interest in the company."

Even today the company takes the same approach in its thrifty ways. One day the company had investors come to its facility and comment on its sometimes-matching furniture. "All of our furniture is liquidator stuff—a dime on the dollar. They were so excited and said, 'We can tell you guys are cost-conscious, because none of your chairs match.' And they said, 'We do the same thing, even though we're a multi-billion dollar company.'"

SUMMARY

Be careful what you wish for. There are a lot of startups founded every day, but don't waste other people's time and resources by starting a company that doesn't make sense. Or *cents*, in this case. Found a company on solid revenue models and proven need. Just because you're starting up a dot-com doesn't mean that your business doesn't need to have a strong foundation. People need to have a reason to come to your site, and they need even more of a reason to buy your product or service. If you can't prove your company out that far, it's time to go back to the garage for a time out.

CHAPTER 6

MAKING INFORMATION TECHNOLOGY WORK
The Mechanics of Dot-Com

T his is the tough part, the part you need to get absolutely right—and if you don't, you'll be throwing good money after bad until you have to close your dot-com doors. Your *IT*—information technology—is the engine that makes your company run. In other words, *IT is everything*. And it's one of those things where you don't have time or the money to make mistakes. Not ever.

This chapter is filled with straight-up technology from some of the world's greatest technologists. While reading this chapter, I could take the time to explain all of the terminology involved, but I won't. If you're not familiar enough with the IT side of your business, I don't want to encourage you to do this on your own. This chapter is targeted at CTOs and if you don't get it, you don't get it. Hand this book over to your CTO when you're done with it.

"If you look at the most successful players on the Internet, they have teams that are dedicated to creating, maintaining, and enhancing their websites. So it's not something you're going to do once, it's going to be a big part of your business."
—STEVE KIRSCH, founder of Mouse Systems, Frame Technology, Infoseek, and Propel

Even when you're only in funding mode, your investors want to know what you're doing on your front-end, your back-end and everywhere in the middle. So what does this mean to you? It means you better have someone in your CTO position who knows how to build IT and take them with you into pitch sessions. Angels and VCs alike know all about IT now, what works with their portfolio companies, and what hasn't.

A lot is happening in the technology field, and you have to prepare your company to be ready for those changes as they occur. Often, when you're in a VC meeting begging for funding, you'll find that you have questions flying at you that you may not be prepared for. Does it have a PDA application? Is it Internet-appliance ready? This is the wave of the future, and there are some very good reasons why they're asking you these questions.

It's a very scary proposition when you think that your IT will most likely be the biggest expense on your plate. It will also probably be the biggest asset your company owns. That will also be the department within your company that will have the most difficulty retaining people. In other words, if you don't have a handle on it, IT could be a big pain in your dot-com ass.

ENVISIONING THE FUTURE

You not only have to be an entrepreneur to run a dot-com, you also have to be a visionary. And part of being a visionary is anticipating the market. Judy Estrin, former CTO of Cisco Systems and CEO of Packet Design, anticipates the market on a daily basis and is looking years into the future for her guidance on what to do now.

"Over the next ten years, as we see a realization in the bandwidth area in the appliance and in the mobility areas, you'll see continual evolution of how we're using it," says Estrin "Some people ask 'Is the Internet over-hyped?' In some ways, absolutely. But in other ways, it's under appreciated. It is as important as anything we've seen in our lifetimes or our parents' lifetimes. As with industrial revolutions or the telephone, [the Internet] is another one of those big shifts."

Technology also plays a key role in security and privacy, both issues we'll probably see government mandated in the future. As raiding information from your users becomes more detailed and valuable, and stealing that information becomes more lucrative, there will be issues along the way and decisions you have to make regarding them.

"The areas that need to evolve before the Internet sees its full potential are the laws and the policies; the laws can be government- or industry-imposed," says Estrin. "To me, security and protection of privacy are big issues we have ahead of us over the next couple of years. There's a real tension between personalization and ease-of-use and privacy, because the way you personalize or ease-of-use with a single click is that you maintain information. And the more information you maintain, the bigger issue with privacy and the bigger burden you take on as a company to protect that privacy."

GREAT TECHNOLOGY: A WINNING PROPOSITION

A big part of building your IT infrastructure is structuring it with proprietary technology: patented pieces of code that you can leverage into assets for your company. Investors always find a deal more attractive if it comes with filed patents—defendable patents—for your proprietary technology.

"The biggest thing in waterproofing a business plan—and what I don't see happening—is that people forget there has to be some kind of assets there," says angel investor Royal P. Farros, CEO and chairman of iPrint.com. "And what I look for is really great technology. Then it doesn't matter what kinds of ups and downs you go through, there's something there—there's something you can sell, license, or transact. It's not going to go away, and there's not going to be fifty-two competitors coming in overnight because there are barriers to entry.

"So much of it is technology, and that is so different from the dot-com world over the last two years," says Farros. "You had people scratching their heads and saying, 'What can we do? We have to get into this space right away.' The whole dot-com world was thinking, 'I've got to get my URL today and start raising money.' It just didn't make any sense. If you have technology, you will always have something strong to fall back on. Even if your business doesn't work, you have salvage value, which means that there are some mergers and acquisitions possibilities. That's a win in business. Going public is not the only win out there. Getting acquired is certainly a big win, merging is a big win."

ACQUIRING TECHNOLOGY

Acquiring other companies for their technology is sometimes a way of building your worth, and your own technology. It may even change the perception of how your partners and competition perceive you. Whether it be for stock or cash, it's more common to find this kind of acquisition among startups these days.

"Opportunity creates opportunity. You never know how one event is going to lead to another," says Joe Kraus, co-founder of Excite@Home. "We bought our first company, called McKinley. On its own, it looked like a strange deal. People thought, 'Why would we do that?' We did it because we wanted to show the market we were the consolidators, not the consolidated. On its surface, as an individual deal, it wasn't a very good deal. It didn't end up producing much in the way of assets for us. But that deal caught the eye of AOL, who then did a deal with us. The reason we got a deal with Intuit—which was a good deal at the time for us—was because we did the AOL deal. Now at the time, we did the McKinley deal, we couldn't see that. But remember that opportunity creates opportunity in ways you can't predict."

IF YOU DON'T UNDERSTAND IT, FIND SOMEONE WHO DOES

Building your infrastructure is going to be like hurdling a huge obstacle in your company's road to success. "If you're not technologically focused, and you're going to manage a technology business, the most important person you're going to hire is the person who is going to manage that," says John Spottiswood, former COO of Bigstep.com, and former president of Match.com. "Make sure whoever you bring on—the VP of engineering or your CTO—are really rock-solid individuals. In other areas like marketing, business development, or customer support, you may be able to step in and fix a problem or diagnose something early. But in the technology area, if you're not a technologist, you're not going to see the signs early enough.

"With a lot of people, the more they are entrepreneurs, the less they are technologists. I know just enough to make me dangerous. A lot of people are out there with good ideas, but if they're not technologists, they really don't understand everything required to put together the infrastructure in which to build an idea. The key is, it will take more money and time to put together your idea than you think it will. There are some key decisions you have to make that are setting the stage for what the platform of your company will be. It's an interesting process. I can tell you, I had no idea that Oracle databases cost so much, and I had no idea that we had to have them for every single server. It's interesting as you move forward and look at redundancy systems and all of these things. It's important that the entrepreneur understands [these issues], and that it needs to be reflected in their numbers."

—LISA HENDERSON, CEO of LevelEdge.com

"Don't just say, 'We'll build it and then we'll figure it out later,' especially if it's an Internet-based business, because it's very difficult to layer on the business model later. With Match.com, we were pretty much a subscription-based service," says Spottiswood of the online dating service he helped build for an acquisition exit. "One of the problems built into our service was that we had a free trial period. But, you needed to have a certain number of people subscribing for others to want to join. When people's trial memberships expired, many joined the service in cities where we had a large mass. In smaller areas, though, we only had three- to four-hundred members. In Salt Lake City, for instance, visitors would search in a certain segment, and only one person would come up in a search, and potential subscribers wouldn't join. We were building the base, but it just became a negative cycle. So if the company had thought more about that business cycle early on, it could have built it differently. In those communities where they did not yet have critical mass—where they had enough people where they could support it—instead of turning it all statewide, nationwide, worldwide, it would have stopped the trial at a point where it had reached critical mass in those areas.

"Bigstep was built as a free site-building service," says Spottiswood, "which was a great way to attract customers, but a lot of work. We worked for nine months on figuring out how to re-engineer and rebuild the site so that we could create a business. You don't want to slow yourself down, you want to get out there quickly. Spend a week with your management team and decide how you want to make money a year from now. Even if you don't build it all to start, at least you won't do anything to redesign and rebuild without having thought it through in advance, especially in today's environment where VCs are going to be asking you how you're going to make money. It makes sense to really think through the business model and the customer proposition before you start coding."

BUILT TO LAST

Many companies realize the importance of building an IT infrastructure that will survive nearly anything—Women.com is one of them.

"According to analysts, we're going to be profitable next year," says Marleen McDaniel, chairman and chief executive officer of

Women.com. "We could probably do it now, it's all a matter of what you want to invest in. I'm still building out my infrastructure—we just bought a whole Oracle financial structure, and I'm still investing in the people to build the company I want it to be. I can foresee a $500 million company from right here. The question is, do you stop putting in some of the systems you want to do because you want to be profitable? You don't want to do all that stuff and then have to figure out where you will get the cash and if the market will allow you to. In a market like this, you don't want to raise more money when your stock price is in the tank. So some people did it smart and some people didn't. When we went public, we raised $90 million. So I'm one of the lucky ones who has the wherewithal to withstand this. Reel.com wasn't."

BUILDING INFRASTRUCTURE IN EXCHANGE FOR EQUITY

As an entrepreneur without a CTO, you've probably been approached by small companies, or two guys and a gal in a garage shop, asking to build your site for equity. Unless they have a list of companies up and running (so you can check their references), you'll probably find that they only know how to build a site with a Web building program, and they don't know how to build a back-end for scale and reliability. They also may not be the right people to deal with your e-commerce or your servers. What you need is a knowledgeable CTO who will be able to manage IT with ease, and who will make sure that whatever consultancy you hire is the right one for the job.

Teri Spencer, chief executive officer and president of ephibian (www.ephibian.com), started out working as a civilian programmer for the U.S. Army. It didn't take long before she built a crackerjack team that was handling a billion-dollar government IT installation. Years later, the team was offered an opportunity for venture capital to form its own company. Now this group of people has grown to nearly 100 in an IT house based in Arizona. Ephibian's clients include American Honda, AT&T, Bell Atlantic, Decimal401k.com, and Get2Net.

The company began realizing the importance of the dot-com industry and started to make inroads to find great companies to build infrastructure in exchange for equity. Now you can usually find the ephibian team hanging out at Garage.com events near the food and beverages tables, sitting in the atrium waiting to get pitched by entrepreneurs.

"We're talking to people, finding out what kinds of Internet businesses they're starting up, and the kind of specific functions they're having problems with—things they're finding as challenges," says Spencer about the kinds of projects that interest them. "We look a lot at the same things a VC looks at—we look at the team, the experience they have within that functional area; we look at their entrepreneurship, and if they have the fire in their belly to make it go even when times are rough. We also look at the market opportunity, and what percent of the market they're after.

"We take a look at those different aspects. Who's in that space? Has it already been done? What are the barriers of entry? What's the competitive advantage that will keep them out in front?" asks Spencer of the questions a CEO and their team needs to ask. "We want them to look at our technology, our relationships, and our Rolodex that we can leverage for them. Is it all in alignment? Is their synergy between us? We look at it like we're putting in real money, too, because those resources that we use to make their technology are costing us cash."

Our pitch is we'll lower your cost of operations, and you'll sell more. So it'll actually save you money to switch over to our software. Clients don't have to write in the reliability and scalability code distributed database; they don't have to worry about creating their own distributed transaction manager; they don't have to write their own system-monitoring tools. They can have fewer people administering the site, so they can focus their coding on value added features rather than reinventing the wheel."

—STEVE KIRSCH, founder of Infoseek, Mouse Systems and Frame Technology, and Propel

One of the things that finding a company such as ephibian does for a startup is give them a leg up on the competition, especially if you're not first to market and looking for funding. "We mitigate the technical risk as far as the investors are concerned," says Spencer. If you're VC and a company is asking you for funding and they have an equity partner to build its technology, that's half the battle. Then the VC's money will go into the long-term marketing aspects of this particular site instead of building an infrastructure by trial-and-error. The investors look very favorably on that kind of deal. They also look at it like they're getting a team who has worked together for twelve years doing nothing but technology. They're not going to have to hire a team and get them used to working with each other."

THAT'S ENTERTAINMENT!

Some CTOs have a lot of pressure from outside influences when putting their IT in place, but what CTO ever thought it would be Katie Couric's producers of the "Today" show cracking the whip? This happens to be one such case. You do what you can to get press for your company, and Half.com went the extra mile to make sure to seal the deal.

When Half.com, a site where you can purchase just about anything cheaper than anywhere else, made a deal with the town of Half Way, Oregon, to rename itself Half.com for a year, the media picked up the story and ran with it. The CEO was scheduled to go live with Couric and the town of Half.com, and the site needed to be up and running when the story hit. The show had been scheduled before the site's launch date.

"We were scheduled to launch the site on January 23, and the 'Today' show called us and said they wanted to do a story," says Sunny Balijepalli, CTO of Half.com, about the beginnings of every CTO's nightmare. "Of course, we were all very excited. But because of some

CONTINUED   >

scheduling issues, the only day the 'Today' show could do it was January nineteenth. Number one, that pushed our launch date up by four days. So now we were writing code until the last minute in order to get it ready.

"The building management came in [the night before the show] and said they had to turn the power off in the building because of some breakdown in a generator," says Balijepalli of the incidents occurring during the countdown before the site would be announced to millions of viewers. "Of course, our code was not done and not yet deployed to our co-location facility. The building's management did not give us an estimate as to when the power would be turned back on. I had eight engineers here trying to figure out how we were going to do this. Josh, our CEO, was supposed to be on the 'Today' show the next morning, and he was frantic because he could not do the show with the site not up and running, because it would be such a missed opportunity.

"I ended up taking people with laptops over to my one-bedroom apartment. There were eight engineers on my coffee table finishing off the code at two in the morning. Then we deployed the code through my dial-up ISDN line to the co-location facility. At 6 AM the 'Today' show was on. We made it, barely. It was surrealistic to see the site on the show with Katie Couric—it was basically a split screen with the mayor of Half.com in Oregon, Josh in Philadelphia, and Katie in New York at 7 AM. Here we are, coming into the office and seeing all this happening! It was an incredible visual, something I will never forget."

WHAT DO THE ORACLES SAY?

It's obvious that everywhere you go in this space, you're going to get caught up in the big debate about expensive platforms and costly licensing of code. Every product has its strengths, but do they outweigh their weaknesses?

And there is the great debate on whether or not to use Oracle products. Once you get done picking yourself off the floor and put your teeth back in your mouth after receiving your Oracle quote, you may still want to buy your software from them. It's scalable, it's reliable, and it's a workhorse. Half.com, which uses an Oracle database back-end, takes a huge amount of hits every day on its site, and that database needs to be up and running at all times. But is it right for you? Only you and your CTO can decide that for sure.

"We were the first investment CMGI ventures made here, but they were happy to do it. There are a lot of companies out west, and the competition for employees out there is just fierce. You could have half your engineering department get up and decide to build a company all their own and give you three days' notice. In Philadelphia, you have a tremendous talent pool, but you don't have the competition."

—JOSHUA KOPELMAN, CEO of Half.com

"Oracle powers some of the highest traffic sites on the Internet," says Sunny Balijepalli, CTO of Half.com. "We've been extremely satisfied with the performance of our database. Right from the beginning, we architected the system not for 500 or 1,000 users, but for millions of visitors on the site on a daily basis. Although that increases the complexity of the system, we knew that we would get there. And we have. If you look at our Media Metrix numbers, we were the fastest growing e-commerce site in our first three months.

"We started going into Java right after launch. When we finished our 1.0 version, we always knew that ColdFusion would not be our version 2.0," says Balijepalli. "ColdFusion is great for getting the project together and putting together a bunch of features making iterations on the project. But in order to move to a highly scalable system, we needed to move to a three-tier architecture that separated the business logic. Basically, separating all the logic says what the business rules are on the site and separates it from the user logic. ColdFusion combines them. We needed something that separated them into tiers. When we went to a three-tier system where we have a front-end—the UI—and a middle tier, which contains all the business logic, and [the third tier] back-end data store, we started down the path of how we were going to build our middle tier.

"We picked Java pretty early on, but we waited until after the launch because we were under pressure to get the product out the door. Java has a higher development time frame; it's not fast to build. You have to hire a lot of highly qualified software engineers who are into Java. You also have to be able to spend a lot of time on software design before you can even get the version out and take a look at it. We started right after the launch after the pressure was eased and we started building some of the business logic inside Java.

"For all of our Linux servers, we're using a commodity processor Pentium-based server rack mount, a generic hardware solution. All of our Solaris servers are running Sun. We're using a combination of Sun and Intel-based servers. The brand for the Intel-based servers we're using is Silicon Racks. There in the Valley, we buy the machines really cheap. We did a lot of research online, but for me it was leveraging the contacts I had and deals I had worked at my previous job. For me, it was bringing in people I already knew. Relationships are important—those are the people who are going to come through for you. When we had our eBay announcement, we expected a huge spike in traffic. I contacted our vendors, like our Sun reseller and Silicon Racks and hardware, right away, and they came through. They shipped hardware overnight and got it in place for us. It's very important—even if you have to pay a little extra—to have good vendors that are also partners, not to just look for the best price on the Web," says Balijepalli. "You want to have someone you can call in the middle of the night on a cell phone—and the Sun reseller we have has an account executive who we can trust and call at any time."

How do you make sure you're putting all the right systems in place before you shoot your IT wad? It's very possible that a mistake could cost you a job. Mission critical decisions are not made without thought, deliberation, and extreme research.

"One piece of advice is to talk to as many people as possible and to get a lot of advice from people who are in the industry and who have done it before," says Balijepalli. "There are so many things you can learn from the mistakes other people have made. So if you're doing this for the first time, make sure you talk to people about the choices you have made, like the tools, the platform, the software, advice on co-location, recruiting. Just don't rely on the sales pitches you get. Join organizations, and be extremely careful about the talent you hire, because they will be the reason you either succeed or fail. If you are going to outsource, make sure it's with someone you trust. If you're going to build a team in-house, make sure you handpick each and every person."

A Run for the Sun

eBay is a huge traffic site with widely promoted auctions, so having a robust site that will handle user spikes is critical. eBay has built up a wall to the press, and you can't even find a phone number on the site where you can contact its PR people. I finally did get the number through other channels, and after several weeks of calling, I was told that no one from the company would be able to make comments. So, still curious about its IT, I pulled this information off the website. The eBay site is built around Sun Enterprise servers running the Solaris operating environment, as well as Sun StorEdge storage devices. eBay has been running its infrastructure on Sun technology since its beginnings in 1995. The company is one of the Internet's most heavily trafficked sites, with more than 1.8 million daily unique visitors and over $12 million in daily gross merchandise sales. In lieu of having a *real* Sally-gotten quote, here's a sterile Sally-retrieved one:

"After carefully weighing our options and determining our needs for eBay's future system architecture, we decided that Sun has clearly demonstrated a proven combination of technology performance and service," says Maynard Webb, president of eBay Technologies. "Sun has been with us from the very beginning and has helped make eBay the success it is today. We will continue to work very hard together to continually advance eBay's site reliability and scalability."

What Bob (Young) Says About Open Source

So, now you know the upside of expensive, proprietary technology. What about the purists out there who believe that code should be free to live as an ever-evolving, no-license-needed-to-change-it thing? Well, I have to say, my mindset used to be if you don't pay for it, how can you depend on it? But after having talked with Bob Young, chairman and founder of Red Hat, Inc., he rocked my proprietary-code world, and I've turned my thoughts around about Linux.

One Friday night, I was touring the aisles of Fry's, one of the retail stores in which you'll find hundreds of the Valley's geeks, during any time of the day, looking for the perfect techno-toy. I was looking for the perfect product to satiate my techno-needs. I was looking at a Linux display—the one with Tux the Penguin. I was admiring the stuffed penguin (trying to figure out who actually owned the rights to the Linux mascot) and contemplating buying it for my friend, Timothy, a very devout Linux programmer. Just then a guy came up and started chatting me up about the virtues of Linux. Granted, it was a Friday night, and I wear no wedding band. I was a bit taken aback, because he began following me all over the store as we chatted. Well, I mistook his loyalty for the product for fanaticism. I'm sure if he had been able to talk about the product as coherently as Bob Young did, I would have been sold lock, stock, and barrel. As it was, I couldn't get through to him that I preferred paying for software for mission-critical applications, and I was only stopping to look at the damn penguin.

That said, I have to share with you the conversation that Bob and I had about the virtues of not having someone hold to your head a gun filled with licensing bullets every time you want to change your applications.

"What has enabled our success is having a genuine customer focus," said Young. "We're doing things that are really counter-intuitive to everyone else in the industry. But to us they made perfect sense, not because we spent so much time with our customers, but because we knew what they were looking for and what they could not get anywhere else. And that's what this open-source phenomenon is all about. It's a revolution in the way you think about computer software generally, but certainly about operating systems and infrastructure software specifically.

"Our dedication is not ideological. We don't believe in the open-source model because it's the right thing to do in some moral sense; we believe in it because it enables us to do things for our customers that our much, much bigger competitors—Microsoft, Sun Microsystems, IBM—aren't willing to do for theirs."
—BOB YOUNG, CEO and chairman, Red Hat, Inc.

"Historically—and mind you, history does not go back very long—prior to 1965, IBM used to ship all the source code to their operating systems with their computers. Only relatively recently have vendors realized by not shipping source code and by prohibiting users from making changes, they could make users dependent on them which would enable them to maximize their gross-margins charge to their customers. This is the proprietary, binary-only model—the one where all you get are the ones and zeros that only your computer can understand, and you don't get the source code that programmers work in. Most people can't make changes, and even if they do figure out how to make changes, it comes with a license agreement. Basically, if you read it, it says if you make any changes to this software—if you add new features that your customers need or fix bugs that are causing your system to crash—you can get thrown in jail for improving the software you're using.

"When we talked to customers and got involved with Linux, which was early on at Red Hat, we saw that what was driving Linux users' enthusiasm was the fact that, for the first time, the customer had control over the technology they were using. We built our business on this, and we have what looks like by everyone else's standards looks an absurd dedication to this open-source model. It gives us this massive market opportunity. That's the unique approach we come from—we're not a bunch of engineers who have identified a new piece of technology for making websites run faster and have hired some marketing guys to go sell it. It's the other way around—we're a bunch of marketing guys who understood that the customers were very frustrated with the way they were being allowed to buy and deploy software. And by looking at the open-source model, we discovered a solution."

One of the great things about Linux is that it drastically reduces the cost of entry for companies that wouldn't have been able to afford licensing agreements—or the time it takes to push them through. Perhaps that's why we're seeing a rise in the dot-com users who are using Linux and the amount of startups we're seeing in general.

"With the proprietary binary-only model, if you decide you want to build a better e-commerce web server for delivering turnkey customer services in the area of snowboards, and you're going after all the snowboard distributors to sell them this all-singing, all-dancing website, you would have to put two or three years worth of engineering dollars into building the technology first before you served your very first customer," says Young. "What's happening with this open-source movement is that you're collapsing the barriers to entry of new service providers. Suddenly, you can just download the Apache Web server and *poof*, you have a third of your infrastructure available on day one. There's a whole variety of open-source applications available for the Apache Web server. You can download Red Hat Linux and *poof*, you've got an operating system that you can run this Web server on day one. Suddenly, you have two thirds of the technology you need to deliver to your customers on day one. All of it, without any development cost or royalty cost on your part.

"The alternative to that for a startup is to go ahead and license the various pieces, but the problem is that, whether it's Microsoft, IBM, or Netscape, it's a long and expensive process to get those licensing agreements in place. And once you sign one of these licensing agreements, you've locked yourself in. In the open-source model, we don't control you. In this sense, we can't force our customers to pay royalties, and we can't force them to remain loyal to our technologies. They are basing their applications on our technologies. There's a whole variety of training, services, and support that we can sell them that they'll find valuable. But for the startups, the barriers to entry are collapsing because of this rapidly accelerating inventory of open-source tools."

KEEPING IT SIMPLE AT CRAIGSLIST.ORG

One website that has grown substantially since its humble beginnings as a one-man show is craigslist.org, which helps people find apartments, jobs, mates, you name it. Jim Buckmaster, CTO of craigslist.org, has his work cut out for him.

"We're currently logging around 20-million pageviews—'pageviews' is a much better traffic metric than 'hits'—per month, although the actual number is higher. Lots of pageviews are on proxy caches and don't make it into our log files. For instance, Alexa Internet (`www.alexa.com`), which uses a methodology somewhat similar to the Nielsen ratings for television, estimates our traffic at 39-million pageviews per month," says Buckmaster of the site's growth and how they track it.

There are a lot of pains a CTO goes through when a company grows substantially. Some of them can be expensive, others are less painful if you throw more programmers onto the problem quickly. "I've learned that the KISS principle is key—keeping it simple, insisting on open-source software, and sticking with simple development tools that support rapid development. All of these tasks are easy to find experienced staff for."

Buckmaster's choices for craigslist.org applications are SuSE Linux for webserver, database, mail, and DNS; and open BSD for firewalls. Their Web server is Apache, their Web development is in Perl, and qmail is their e-mail tool.

Many companies are jumping on the NT bandwagon, but craigslist is definitely not one of them. "I think NT is okay as a desktop operating system, but it is not well-suited to mission-critical web-serving environments," says Buckmaster. There are also large numbers of startups putting large portions of their funding toward buying expensive Oracle databases. Craigslist uses an open-source Unix database.

"Unix databases like MySQL have lots of advantages over commercial databases like Oracle," says Buckmaster. "For instance, it's free—instead of up to $25 thousand per server; it's simple to administer—no highly-paid DBA required; and it offers higher performance than commercial databases for most applications, efficient and modest hardware require-ments, and stability. We've not had any serious data-integrity problems, there's excellent documentation available on the Internet, and excellent interoperation with open-source Web servers and scripting languages.

"My best advice? Find a good open-source developer who can get you up and running quickly with a working prototype that provides a minimal subset of what you want to do," says Buckmaster of his best advice for a startup. "Do not do a lot of visual design and/or branding work up front. Your users don't care about this. Stick with open-source software and simple development tools, and you won't have any scalability issues. Technical scalability is assured, as are money and manpower."

FEELING A LITTLE INSECURE?

Like a lot of dot-com companies that are finding themselves a possible target for the frequent rampant hacking that's been going on, Half.com is very security conscious.

"Of course, there is a lot I can't tell you," says Sunny Balijepalli, CTO of Half.com. "We've approached security and the measures we take to protect our information from a really aggressive standpoint. We accept credit cards, like a lot of e-commerce sites, and there have been a lot of stories about e-commerce sites having their user information getting compromised.

"We are concerned on two fronts: intrusion—making sure that nobody is able to get into our servers and get access to the personal credit card information—and a distributed denial of servers, such as the attacks against companies like eBay, Yahoo, and Amazon. We work with our ISP to make sure they have adequate security in place to prevent denial of service attacks and [to be able to] throttle the traffic on our site if there is such an attack, and we work to isolate the attacker and reject traffic from that site. We've distributed our servers on various layers instead of making our servers completely on one flat level with one level of access. We've made multiple tiers, and that allows us to apply different levels of access control to each tier. Finally, we use encryption across the board when private information is being transmitted between our servers or being stored on our servers. We are also a co-located site."

"Security is surprisingly fairly good right now. Most of the people who break into computers don't get anything. They occasionally embarrass themselves or someone else. I don't know of anyone who has made a million dollars by breaking into computers—or even thousands of dollars. But I do know lots of people who've made lots of money off of selling security systems to prevent it. The idea of breaking into a computer to make lots of money is fiction. Ninety-nine-point-nine percent of all of the information online is not worth reading, and very little of it has value."

—CLIFFORD STOLL, techno-sleuth and author of *Silicon Snake Oil*

How do you know when you have enough security in place? And how can you tell if you've taken enough security measures to make your site safe? What are the real risks involved? Security is an immediate need that you should address. After all, it takes only one security breech in which your customers' credit cards are accessed, and all of the network TV news stations have you as their top news story. How much more branding to regain users' trust do you think you'll have to do after that?

"Look for the industry leaders in security and get both a hardware and a software product," warns Balijepalli. "And get periodic upgrades to those security measures as new threats are exposed. I would also look for something that has low performance penalties, because a lot of the firewalls and routers are very good, but they may cause a penalty in performance. Look for compatibility with your software. A lot of applications do not work well with firewalls.

"After doing all of that, bring in at least two independent security firms to do a complete audit of what you've built in before you launch. They will definitely be another set of eyes for things you might have missed. I would not completely trust your own staff's judgment. We brought in some security firms, and it was very useful. They did a complete security audit and an intrusion test where they actually tried to break into the system. Then they tell you how they did it so you can patch that hole. I recommend using a couple of firms. SystemExperts.com is one of the companies we used."

HACKED!

They say those who can *do*, those who can't *teach*. But in hacking, those who can *do*, and boy, are they teaching others lessons. Expensive lessons. So what is it about these hackers that causes them to seek, hunt down, and access information they aren't entitled to have? There is definitely a school of thought on the subject about hackers.

"Typically, the people who are arrested and charged for these things are normally 25 years old or younger," says Clifford Stoll, author of *Silicon Snake Oil*. "Typically, they're interested in showing they can do something. Some feel that by breaking into things, they can steal money and get rich. Others think, 'Oh wow, this is a great way for me to show off.' In other words, they are techno-vandals…no different.

"It does not take a great deal of computer competence to break into a computer. Just like it does not take brilliance and intelligence to break into a house. Quite the opposite. The person who wants to break into a house has a fairly easy time of it. Probably one out of ten houses is easy to break into, so that means all you have to do is try ten houses and you'll get into one house. We're accustomed to that, to saying that any decent, honest person isn't going to do this. Only a thief is interested in stealing these things. We've yet to develop the same idea about online security. That only an amoral, asocial person is willing to break into someone else's information bank and steal information," says Stoll of the way that the media tends to glamorize hackers.

Stoll first came to prominence when he was working at Lawrence/Berkeley Labs, where he was a systems manager. Quite by happenstance, Stoll found a seventy-five cent discrepancy in the department's billing logs, which had been caused by a break-in. "I said, 'I'm going to find out who it is.' And I spent a year tracking them down and eventually catching them and prosecuting them." And that he did, in a very highly publicized break-up of an international hacking case.

"Before that time, I thought, 'Information? Who cares about it?' Afterward, I thought by joining a network you join into a community, and we all have responsibilities to the communities we belong to. I have a commitment here, and people who break into my system—they're doing me wrong. And I'll be damned if I'm going to let this happen.

"I was quite upset to find that there are—just as in real life— online thieves and burglars who have no ethics and no morals. Simply that you are able to manipulate a keyboard does not mean that you are more honest, more decent, or more intelligent than anyone else. To me, the idea of a brilliant, clever hacker is untrue. I've never met a hacker who is capable of creative computing. In fact, breaking into a computer requires about the same skills that it takes to break into a house—some amount of fraud, a great deal of patience, and a great deal of mechanistic try-and-try-again techniques. Very little creativity or ingenuity is involved; it's a rather mundane routine."

Stoll is primarily a stay-at-home dad these days, raising his children, although he has kept a close eye on the evolution of the Internet and has formed some opinions of what he is seeing in the industry.

"Thirteen years ago, I knew pretty much everything about Internet security, but now the field is so broad that I have to say that nobody knows about Internet security," says Stoll. "I think it's a little like making your house or your business safe. First of all, you realize you have to put locks on your doors at the same time you realize that a business that has its doors locked all the time doesn't get any business. You can put bars over the windows of your house, but if you're not careful to make sure the windows are locked when no one is home, you've got problems. A business can very, very effectively hire guards to watch people who come in and out of the store, but if there's too many people coming in and out of the store you can't do anything about it. Pretty soon, you're paying more to the guards than you are collecting from customers.

"If a business is mainly doing e-commerce—mainly selling things online—the main problem is fraud, pretending to be someone they're not, or using someone else's identity to purchase something. You have the same problem if someone walks into your business and buys something in person," advises Stoll. "Stolen ID, false identity, stolen credit card, a bounced check—pretty much the same techniques are used to combat it. Back up on the credential, make sure it's authorized. Make sure that the person who says who they are really is that person, that they respond to an e-mail, respond to a phone call. If it's a purchase of $5 or $10, it doesn't make much of a difference, but if you start spending $500 and $1,000, it does. What I'm getting at is that it's foolish to go to great lengths to protect things that do not have much value. If you're selling very low-cost things—balloons over the Internet—it's not worth spending a lot of money securing your site. You don't stand to lose much. If you are selling diamond rings over the Internet—hey, it's worth checking up on the people you're selling to.

"Spend money and secure things to the value of the information. Fully protect those things that have intrinsic value," warns Stoll. "Don't apply high protection to those things that do not. On websites, only protect those that have high value. There's a cost to using security. Mainly, it slows everything down. The people using your website will get frustrated because, hey, it's slow going because computers on both sides have to either encrypt or decrypt. The greater the security, the more likely that ordinary people will have more problems accessing your information. So if you make sure you have extremely high Internet security and its encrypted, it may be that the people whom you want to get your information, your advertisements, won't be able to. Stores that require you to ask them to get things off the shelves to show them to you will sell far fewer things than a self-service grocery store where you can take it off the shelf and examine it yourself. The first one is high security; the second is low security."

HACKERS AND CRACKERS

Hackers and crackers are a common threat, and an e-commerce site may receive several break-in alerts every day in its effort to thwart them off. Although hackers crack networks simply for the thrill of the challenge, the FBI has seen more cases of hacking for elicit financial gain or other malicious purposes. While remote cracking once required a fair amount of skill or computer knowledge, novices can download scripts from the Web to crack a site. And while hacking tools have become more complex, they have also become easier to use. The distributed denial-of-services (DDOS) that occurred earlier in 2000 are a good example of the e-commerce chaos that these tools can cause.

A new kind of terrorism called *hacktivism* is taking place as people see the amount of press they can get by taking down a site. These kinds of events are committed by groups and individuals who overload e-mail servers or deface websites to push through a political message. These types of attacks generally do not alter operating systems or networks, but they do disrupt services. There was a case in 1996 in which someone gained access to the Department of Justice Internet website. The cracker deleted more than 200 directories and installed their own pages. The replaced pages were critical of the Communications Decency Act (CDA) and included pictures of Adolf Hitler, swastikas, pictures of sexual bondage scenes, and a speech falsely attributed to President Clinton.

The FBI is doing a little cracking of its own, including cracking down on virus writers (high-profile viruses in the recent past include the Melissa Virus, the Explore.Zip Worm, and the Chernobyl Virus). The Melissa Virus (AKA, the 'I Love You Virus') spread far and wide as lonely engineers everywhere opened the file in hopes of finding love.

Often the first line of defense after an Internet break-in has occurred is to report it to local police. Then the case is passed on to the FBI. The FBI has only 193 agents in FBI field offices nationwide assigned to investigate cyber crimes. The organizations with which the FBI partners to catch cybercriminals are the Secret Service, the Internal Revenue Service, and Carnegie Mellon's Computer Emergency Response Team (CERT). The FBI's agents heading up the Computer Analysis Response Team (CART) conducted 1,260 forensic examinations in 1998 and 1,900 in 1999. The agency anticipates cyber cases to grow to 6,000 by 2001.

COMBATING INTERNET SECURITY PROBLEMS

There is no doubting the need for some kind of flawless, seamless Internet security. As a matter of fact, the issue has left the realm of being a Silicon Valley problem to being a matter of national security. In February 2000, U.S. President Bill Clinton and Louis J. Freeh, director Federal Bureau of Investigation (www.FBI.gov), made a plea to the Senate's Judiciary Subcommittee on Technology, Terrorism, and Government Information to raise the FBI's budget from $100 million to $135 million to meet the increasing need for Internet security.

"The statistics tell the story," says Freeh of cyber crime. "Ninety percent of respondents detected security breaches over the last twelve months. At least seventy-four percent of respondents reported security breaches including theft of proprietary information, financial fraud, system penetration by outsiders, data or network sabotage, or denial of service attacks. Information theft and financial fraud caused the most severe financial losses, at $68 million and $56 million, respectively. The losses from two-hundred seventy-three respondents totaled just over $265 million. Losses traced to denial of service attacks were only $77 thousand in 1998, and by 1999 had risen to $116,250. Further, the new survey reports on numbers taken before the high-profile February attacks against Yahoo!, Amazon, and eBay. Many companies are experiencing multiple attacks; 19 percent of respondents reported ten or more incidents.

"Over the past several years, we have seen computer crimes ranging from defacement of websites by juveniles to sophisticated intrusions that we suspect may be sponsored by foreign powers, and everything in between," says Freeh. "Some of these are obviously more significant than others. The theft of national security information from a government agency or the interruption of electrical power to a major metropolitan area have greater consequences for national security, public safety, and the economy than the defacement of a website."

The just-released 2000 survey by the Computer Security Institute and FBI states that 71 percent of companies taking part in the study detected unauthorized access to systems by insiders. So, in this world of cyber crime, loss, and prosecution, what is a CTO's best defense in protecting information worth protecting?

"You've learned that technology will save you, it's just a matter of waiting and finding the right thing," says, Bruce Schneier, Internet security specialist, founder, and CTO of Counterpane (www.counterpane.com), and author of *Secrets and Lies: Digital Security in a Networked World*. "I don't believe that security is that way. Security on networks has been around for forty years, and every year [security issues] have gotten worse. And I don't see any indication that that trend will reverse any time soon."

Schneier relates Internet security with the real world issues of security.

"What kind of security can you give shop owners that people won't shoplift in their stores?" poses Schneier. "It's only in computer security that a client says, 'Why can't you solve my problem?' We don't solve security problems, we manage risk. We put some procedural countermeasures in place, we buy insurance, and we accept some risk as the cost of doing business. It's how we solve security measures in the real world. I maintain that we need processes, because the products are never going to save you. If you live in the real world, you know this. If you go to a store in the real world, you don't say 'I would like to buy an anti-mugging device.'"

Schneier believes that the main trend is to keep believing in the snake oil and keep buying products to protect your information, but that this trend is bound to get you hacked. "The move I like is one toward process. We basically do a burglar alarm service [at Counterpane]. The preventive countermeasure is going to fail, so you really need protection response. I can't sell you an anti-mugging device, but you can walk the street safely because we detect crime—we have processes that make the street safe. That's what we're doing. We are an Internet burglar alarm service. What Counterpane has done—and it's the first time we've ever seen this—is that we did a deal with Lloyd's of London (www.lloydsoflondon.co.uk), so if you have Counterpane monitoring your site, you can get insurance. It's kind of like if you have Lojack guarding your warehouse, you can get a discount on your insurance rates. You can buy insurance [as a company to insure against hackers], but it requires them to do a big security audit and tell you what products to use and policy rule. If you have Counterpane, then you can get the insurance, period."

Schneier doesn't believe that there is such a thing as a security product that prevents break-ins, only countermeasures that will catch the intrusions in progress.

"The reason why Lloyd's did the insurance through us is because we're fundamentally different. We're not a preventative countermeasure. Recognize that we're a way to deal with the security problem. That's really cool. I'm really psyched about that. When you buy security products, they promise they produce alert. They all do. It's millions of lines of information every day. Embedded in all of those audit messages are the footprints of attack, and if you could read all those messages twenty-four hours a day, seven days a week in real time, you could catch those intrusions in progress. We take all of the messages and remote them to our secure operations centers where human beings read them. You can't build an automatic computer system to do this because computers aren't smart enough to do this. Human beings are the best pattern tracker ever invented. You need to build a human computer cyborg to get the best of both. Computers do the automatic data shifting that they are very fast at, and humans do the high-level pattern matching to catch intrusions. And ring the customer up just like ADT would and call the client. We don't go after them. We're not vigilantes; we're a burglar alarm company."

"The problem you have if you install a bunch of products is that you have to update them, and you have to monitor them. There are always new vulnerabilities, always new attacks—every week there's something new. You can't stop all of that. We can.

—BRUCE SCHNEIER, Internet security specialist, founder and CTO of Counterpane (www.counterpane.com), and author of *Secrets and Lies: Digital Security in a Networked World*

"We're getting really good response because of the way we stop the problem. It's the same way you do it when you get insurance in the business world," says Schneier. "You're told 'This is your risk, this is how much it will cost to insure it.' If you're the CEO, you don't really care if you have a firewall. What you want to know is 'What's my risk, what's my exposure, what does it cost to make myself profitable?' If a company said, 'For one-hundred-thousand dollars, I will indemnify you against losses,' you don't care what they do; all you care is that you're protected against losses. That's what they think. That's what the technologists don't get—the technology is irrelevant. It's about risk management."

And what does Schneier see for the future of Internet security? "I think it will become harder in the future because people will realize that human process is the answer. It's a pretty unsecure world out there, if someone wants to kill you, they will kill you. We don't have these assurances in the real world; don't expect them on the Internet, either. It's okay, we can do businesses anyway."

SUMMARY

Your IT decisions will affect every aspect of your business and its success. Choose your IT team, hardware, and software with deliberation and common sense. Talk to as many people as you can possibly find who have been there and done it. Have experts give you feedback about your decision. And when you finally build your IT, make sure you find a means to protect it. In the end, all you have is your reputation. One good hack job, and your company might be down for the count. And brace well— change is coming, so be ready for IT.

CHAPTER 7

BRAND THIS!
The Branding of Your Concept

Here we go…this is the fun part. This is where we get to see a company shine—no matter how strange of light they do it in. This is the event in your company's life when you get your people involved in coming up with some fabulous hook that will catch your market's eye and connect the message with your company name—a process otherwise known as *branding*. Branding is a powerful tool. And it can go horribly wrong. If it does, your branding message may just last as long as it takes for you to come up with a new campaign, and spend millions more to coerce potential users into changing their minds about you.

One of the best efforts I've seen in technology branding is Apple's "1984" campaign. The commercial, based on George Orwell's concept of a populace controlled by the government, had the tagline, *On January 24th, Apple Computer will introduce Macintosh. And you'll see why 1984 won't be like* 1984. In the commercial, a woman armed with a sledgehammer is running down the aisle of an assembly hall, worker-drones seated on either side of her watching a "Big Brother" video screen. She flings the sledgehammer through the screen, and George Orwell's future is put to rest via the freedom of the personal computer.

The production of the "1984" Apple commercial, directed by Ridley Scott (who also directed *Blade Runner*), played only twice, the first time on December 15, 1983, on a remote Idaho station (in order to qualify for that year's advertising awards), and the second time, during Super Bowl XVIII. The commercial won 35 awards, including the Grand Prix awarded at Cannes, for Apple's advertising firm, TBWA\Chiat\Day.

In a sense, that commercial epitomized the shift from the Cold War era to the free thinking in the late '50s and '60s, which led to the creation of the personal computer in the '70s, a tool of evolution—of revolution. That was a branding strategy that's studied in universities throughout the world.

Intel came close in popularity with its guys dressed in "bunny" clean room suits who break into dance to the Ohio Players' funk '70s hit *Love Rollercoaster*. The bunny-suit guy-dolls are among the most coveted giveaways at most conferences and are available at the Intel store and other places where geeks dwell in thick groupings.

In the hey-day of dot-com, we were barraged by a number of dot-com branding commercials. My favorite was the Pets.com hand puppet thingy who hitches a ride with the Pets.com driver to personally deliver pet supplies in a very aggressive manner. But, as we all know now, even a great branding strategy can't save your dot-com assets. I haven't seen any dot-com commercials rock my world like Intel or Apple did, but I bet the best is yet to come—perhaps even one your company develops!

WHAT'S IN A BRAND?

The important thing about brand is that you first know what branding is all about. Marty Brandt, CEO and founder of Pro-Brand (www.ProBrand.com) brings a great deal of experience to the table when it comes to branding. Before starting ProBrand in 1993, he was the senior marketing communications and advertising executive at Sun Microsystems, responsible for brand-building programs worldwide. Prior to that, he spent 13 years at advertising agencies TBWA\Chiat\Day, Ketchum, and Campbell Mithun, working for major packaged goods and direct marketing clients. Marty is the co-founder of both Brand Tech Forum and the IDG PowerBranding seminars.

"It's a challenge for dot-coms to get noticed and get recognition, because there are far too many companies out there for any of us to absorb. We can't even sort them out in our mind, much less visit all the sites that implore us to come visit them. My issue with that is that seventy-thirty ratio. The companies that are spending seventy percent of their time shouting about what a great experience they offer are going to disappoint people—that's what happened after the [2000] SuperBowl frenzy for many companies. They spent a ton of money to get somebody to come visit their site, and the site bore no resemblance to what they promised and wasn't even ready to handle the number of people who came there. So the economic benefit was totally lost."

—MARTY BRANDT, CEO and founder of ProBrand

Today Brandt's Silicon Valley firm has clients such as Acer Inc. (Worldwide), BigStep.com, Compaq Computer, Creative Labs, CyberSource, Day-Timer Technologies, Dell Computer, Deloitte Consulting, ELetter, E-Stamp, Excite, Hewlett-Packard (Various Divisions), Intel, and SAP. In other words, Brandt knows branding.

"I started working with a wide range of dot-coms and early-stage startup companies more recently when they become more brand conscious," says Brandt. "Now companies realize they need to build some of the brand consciousness and foundation strategies into their business. We often get called in when companies are about to launch a new ad campaign or make a major announcement—that's when they start getting advice from different people about what their positioning or messages should be. They get a bit conflicted because they're not sure who they should be listening to. We're strictly brand strategy consultants, and so we don't have any vested interest in how they execute strategic recommendations. Although our work informs all of those variants, we're totally agnostic about how it gets executed. Clients appreciate that objectivity, because the only interest we have is what's right for the brand."

Brandt has watched as companies have attempted to brand without using a holistic approach, and has seen what happens when you create brand the wrong way. The quick and dirty approach to branding is one that's used most often—throwing a lot of money at commercials to build awareness, and bringing a recognized celebrity on board. Brandt knows there is a whole lot more to branding than that.

"The next big wave of branding is going to be shifting from what I call outside-in branding to inside-out branding. And more branding will reflect what's true and authentic about the values that flow through the company."
—MARTY BRANDT, CEO and founder of ProBrand

"I just came back from giving a talk in San Diego. A couple of people came up to me after the talk and said, 'We really like this. We'd like you to do some branding work for us. We have eight weeks until our launch date, what do you think? Can you work with us?'" Brandt recalls, shaking his head at the ignorance about brand that still permeates the industry. "I said, 'No.' They were still thinking tactical and, 'Let's be driven by a deadline to do something as fundamentally important as defining the brand essence of our company.' We're only interested in working with companies that want to drill down to where they really see what's at the core of what they're bringing to people and what differentiates them is something meaningful. In most cases, it comes from the heart and soul of the company.

"First of all, you don't have a choice about branding. Branding is not an optional activity," warns Brandt. "There is no such thing as instant branding. You often hear dot-com companies say, 'We have to go out and brand ourselves quickly.' Well, that in and of itself is a contradiction of terms, because it takes time to build some awareness of your brand. But you don't have a brand until your customers tell you that you have a brand. Your brand is not your logo, your symbol. It's the sum of all of your experiences that people have with your people, your product, your website, your service, your delivery, your e-mail, your users, your twenty-four-seven ability.

"Everything is shaped by perceptions that people have about your company," advises Brandt. "So the brand is really the totality of the experiences they have with you. It leads to the second thing that dot-com companies need to know—that branding is a business issue. It's not a communications issue, it's not a marketing issue. More companies are realizing that branding does not equal advertising. Advertising plays a role in driving awareness of a brand higher and faster, but that's not branding, so companies need to understand branding should be treated as a business process—everyone in the company plays a role in shaping the perceptions of your brand. So you kind of have to harness the whole organization in support of your brand-building efforts which requires that it rise up to a very high level in your organization.

"I've had encounters with clients where we've been asked to propose our work, and they've kind of accepted it, and we walked away from it because we didn't feel like they really got what we were saying to them. We always propose research because we want customers/consumers involved in these decisions. Too many dot-com companies have indifference or even an arrogance about research. I don't care what you call it, but get the end user involved in this discussion about what their expectations are. How are you differentiated? How are you going to fit into my life? What problem are you going to solve that isn't being solved? That's one of the things we look for in these companies—a willingness to put their concept to a test of some kind before they launch it and find out, after spending multi-millions of dollars, there's no need, it's not differentiated enough, it doesn't solve a big problem."

MAKING A BRAND LAST

In real life, lust settles into love, and hopefully loyalty follows. That's also what happens when you get seduced by a great website. How do you get that user from, 'I can't live without this site,' to being comfortable with you, bookmarking you, and finally to just use, for instance, only your search engine when tempted by so many others? Once you find out who your users are and how to get them to your site, you should concentrate on the nuances that keep them there. Change things as your users let you know in subtle, and not so subtle, ways what they want. So many dot-coms don't care what their users want. They listen to everyone else involved in the process—everyone except the user. And guess what? You're not the only game in town.

"I would encourage dot-com companies to look at the acquisition side of the business—bringing customers in," recommends Marty Brandt, CEO and founder of ProBrand. "Then focusing on hits and click-through and conversion, which gets a little further to economic value. They should really concentrate on retention—brand really pays off through loyalty. If you can harness the experiences that shape the brand in a way that creates loyalty, that's where the economic payoff is. Jeff Bezos, founder and CEO of Amazon.com, has a great saying that in the old way of thinking, seventy percent of your effort was put around shouting about your customer experience and thirty percent was about building a great customer service. Now, you have to invert that and put seventy percent on creating a great customer experience and thirty percent on shouting about it."

But, as the cards fall in this part of the dot-com era, even Bezos has proven that even with a flawless branding strategy, everything else—including your revenue model—must fall into place.

"Loyalty results from some authentic reason for engaging in the relationship. That doesn't mean there won't be room for Priceline that has a different kind of emotional dimension, which is 'I want the cheapest damn flight possible, and I don't care about the hassle I have to go through.' There will be a segment that will be driven to use it. Increasingly, there's a bigger segment looking for more emotional gratification from their relationships with websites—relationships that will save them time and reduce stress. We're in this just-in-time living mode, and the fundamental economic justification for brand is to make someone's life simpler. You don't have to go through a difficult decision about who to go through anymore—if you're a loyal Amazon buyer, you don't think about it anymore. Where do you go to buy a book? You know that Amazon is going to be nearly the best price, and even if it's not, it's not worth going somewhere else."

—MARTY BRANDT, CEO and founder of ProBrand

"Brand is linked inextricably to the culture of a company. People engage with brands with the expectations that they're going to solve some problem, to accomplish some task, or inform themselves in some way—and they want to accomplish that very task and are goal-oriented in many ways when they engage with a brand in the Internet world. So they want that experience to be productive, satisfying, and engaging. The delivery is very much influenced by the culture and values of your company. Schwab is a beautiful example of the values of a culture-driven organization that engages their people and their website experience to reflect those values and around trustworthiness, being responsive, and empathy with their customers. That shows up in these experiences that shape the brand perceptions. These things are linked. Bezos and Schwab have concluded that in the Internet world, the real source of enduring differentiation in competitive advantage, is going to come from the culture of your company. The culture is linked to the brand, the brand is linked to loyalty. Loyalty is linked to economic return, and all of these things are linked together. The companies that focus on being real clear about brand values are at the core of what they are— like Bezos with customer obsession, that's not just a slogan, they live by that value. That's the next area of brand development to focus on—how do we create and harness the culture of the company in a way that creates a great brand experience?

"AOL has built a *churn assumption* into their model, and as long as they can bring enough people in on the front-end, capture the revenue through their partnerships, and keep their total number up, they can get away with letting people down on the back-end and not having loyalty. And in fact, their loyalty isn't very high. We looked at some really interesting numbers on loyalty that came through from a company back east called Digital Idea. They just came out with a dial-score measurement, which is the first industry measurement that I've seen on loyalty in the dot-com world. And it shows some pretty surprising numbers. The highest they've identified in this first wave is a site called BabyCenter, and it comes in at thirty-five percent. It's based on the strong bond and relationship they have with expecting mothers and its ability to personalize the site."

FOCUSING ON USERS

Finding out what your users want is half the battle. More and more dot-coms are turning toward the use of focus groups and harnessing their own user data to find how they can benefit the user's experience. Two of the online services concentrating on user experience data are Greenfieldonline.com (where people register online and get an account and earn Web currency for participating in online user surveys) and DigitalIdea.com.

"The rap against focus groups is very unfounded," says Marty Brandt, CEO and founder of ProBrand, of the value of the human opinion. "We've had clients that have actually changed the definition of their business as a result of our consulting with them. We've been doing some pretty interesting work for ELetter to redefine what business they're in. They thought 'We're kind of in the mailing business.' Then they thought, 'Are we in the direct-mail business, or the mailing-production business, or the printing and mailing business? Perhaps we should be in the customer-communications business, because what we're really helping customers do is communicate. We may want to do some e-mail mailings and that kind of thing.' We worked with ELetter customers to uncover what it was that ELetter was doing for them, and we found out what they were doing was something totally different, something much bigger.

"They were automating tedious processes for their clients," says Brandt of how ELetter's focus changed after some investigation. "The idea of doing short-run mailings of a hundred or a couple thousand is incredibly tedious and a chore that small businesses hate to do, it's very time consuming. What they love about ELetter is that it takes the chore away from them and automates it and spits it out, and they don't have to worry about it anymore. So the benefit is clearly less stress and saves time. We defined that what they're doing for a client is not just printing and mailing, but automating tedious tasks they wish someone would come along and take away from them. So, ELetter is in the business of automation services which allows them to automate lots of different things like billing and invoicing and management of databases and list procurement, and all those things that are tedious, mundane, and time-consuming tasks.

"Their space is so much bigger than the printing and mailing business," says Brandt of how focusing on what the client wants can be much more than what you're giving them. This happens only when you go out and talk to people who are engaged and need your services. We really try to find out where the emotional stuff—connection, opportunities—are. That's where research becomes very powerful."

MARRIED TO THE BRAND

Reputation is something a company must hold near and dear, and fight to the death to protect. A reputable name will help you attract reputable partners that will help you build your brand by association.

"One thing we decided early on was to focus on being a matchmaking service," says John Spottiswood, former president of Match.com. "There was an opportunity at that time to go in a lot of different directions—to broaden the brand Match.com into things other than people, providing matching services with services. We decided to stick with only matchmaking so we didn't diminish the brand."

Match.com decided to rely heavily on focus groups, experts, and partnerships to form its site. "After I got into the company, I started talking with the people who were using the service," says Spottiswood of his interest in his users' opinions. "I found out they tended to be professionals working a lot of hours, and the men tended to be engineers. It was a mix of people who were casual daters, and those looking for people who were looking for life partners. It was really serving a valuable need for a broad section of Americans. And yet it was only reaching out to a very small section of its potential. So I saw a very critical service that could do a lot of good for a lot of people.

"We relied very heavily on partnerships with sites and with media outlets that would reach out to women," says Spottiswood of the early work on the site. "We had a dating expert who was also a relationship counselor, and we focused on building her up as the face of Match.com because we really wanted to have the site appeal to women. Men feel very comfortable in reaching out in what can be a somewhat impersonal manner through dating services; women don't. So by building out the site to be a very clean, friendly, well-lit site, and partnering with sites that appeal to women, we went to slightly over fifty percent female by the time we sold to Ticket Master/CitySearch in 1999.

"In all of our branding, we stuck by our red-heart logo and our tag lines. And the other thing we did that was successful was really focus on our member success. From day one, we tracked all of the success stories—people who got engaged and married through our service—and we kept tabs on over a thousand marriages. And if they gave us their permission, we'd refer the press to them. We had marriages in just about every state, and whenever we got a media call we immediately looked through our database and referred them to those individuals who agreed to help us promote our service by telling their personal story. That has been the biggest success in building our brand nationwide.

"Because we were part of a corporation, we had a focus on profit, which was far different from other Internet companies at the time who were pretty much free-spending," says Spottiswood of the dot-com that had been part of a corporation and then sold as an individual property. "We'd go out and do partnerships with every major Web property, from Yahoo to Excite to AOL, Women.com, and iVillage.com. We had to do those partnerships in a very cost-efficient manner. We had to look at the value we gained from a subscriber and how much we could afford to pay per subscriber, and then we would negotiate deals. We would pay a certain amount of money for a guarantee of a certain amount of subscribers joining through that partner. The money was there if we could find cost-effective ways to utilize it. The money we spent generated profit for Match.com."

"We're seeing less companies receiving funding that are trying to sell to consumers because most of those markets have been cornered. And you have companies like Amazon and eBay that are eight-hundred-pound gorillas, and it's difficult for a new company to come in and compete. You have a company like Amazon, a clear leader in their space. They've spent millions and millions of dollars on marketing, and they're still not profitable. It's even questionable whether Amazon will still be around on its own for the next couple years. So how does an up-and-coming startup intend to compete with a company like that? The companies that we're now seeing emerge are companies figuring out technologies that can enable certain processes to be more efficient using the Internet."

—JASON THOCKMORTON, co-founder of LaunchSquad

Spottiswood credits partnerships with respected brands to the success the company did achieve. "Partnerships did a few things that legitimized us as a high-class, high-quality site for online dating. For instance, for iVillage, we built a dating guide and relationship section provided by Match.com, with links throughout it to Match.com. It was really meant to help people find their right match as opposed to seeing a tacky banner on the side of a page.

"If you were single and on the Internet and saw Match.com one time, you might just think, 'Oh, that's interesting.' If you start seeing it over and over again in multiple places, you're going to take a serious look at dating online," says Spottiswood of how to bring users to your site.

"Signing the partnerships was challenging, and we were in a fortunate position of having the best service *and* a service that matters to the partner sites. For example, Women.com would have felt comfortable linking their users to Amazon, but they would have felt just as comfortable linking them to Barnes & Noble. But in dating business, we had the argument that we were the only credible dating site out there."

This reputation helped Match.com gain a foothold early on, because they knew that sites such as Women.com and iVillage would only link to them if they had a high quality service. As a responsible dot-com company, you should really be concerned about where the links on your site go—your users will hold you responsible for any bad experiences they have that are associated with your site.

BRANDING WITH A STORY

One thing I always hear from both investors and the media is that it really helps to have a personal experience to link a company's mission. You may have to get a media coach to help you find your story, but the reward is fulfilling part of your identity. You need a story people can repeat:

"Did you know that dot-com was started because…
Isn't that amazing?"

That could be you they're proliferating with a viral story that will be repeated again and again.

One company with a great story the media loves playing on is LevelEdge.com. CEO Lisa Henderson has a built-for-press company. Henderson was raised in a small rural town in a family that believed more in work ethic than education. From the age of nine, she pumped gas at the family gas station after school and during her summer vacations. Now, Henderson—a tall, savvy woman with a shock of red and blonde hair who is one of the hippest dressers you will see in dot-com—is the belle of the media ball. She is dot-com personified.

"We've had a business and a unique position. Every one of our student athletes, who are sending their MyEdge Profile, is sending about six other people to us. Every parent is talking with two or three other parents, and every coach is talking to four or five other coaches. We've been able to build our customer base on a very grassroots basis. We've very lucky that we're not a company that requires $20 million a quarter in advertising."

—LISA HENDERSON, CEO, LevelEdge.com

"We didn't have much money, and there wasn't much of an emphasis on education," says Henderson of her childhood. "My father only had a seventh grade education, my mother finished high school. My family's values were in working hard. So when I said I wanted to go to college, my whole family was thinking 'Why would you do that?' I was saving money for school when some friends of mine invited me over to watch a pre-school tournament at a small private university they had received scholarships from. They were soccer players, and I played soccer with them in a division not related to the school. It was the third game of the day and it was very hot and the team was starting to look kind of weak. The coach looked at me on the sidelines and asked me if I knew how to play. He put me in and I scored two goals. He asked me what I was doing the next day, and I played three games and scored four goals. I left that day with an offer of a $2,000 scholarship."

The coach introduced her to the softball and basketball coaches, and Henderson received scholarships from them all.

"Our charter with our clients is to help them gain visibility through the media. We understand technology and the way the press works, and we think long and hard about every client that we take, how this story will be told to the press, and, in return, how the press will receive it. That is our strength, and we think it's quite a simple process—one that is neglected pretty seriously in the world of PR and marketing, in general. There are a lot of practices right now [in the marketing and PR industry] that are alienating our community with the press, because people seem to think that press releases are equal to awareness. But the reality is, they aren't. The way to go about raising awareness is coverage and stories. The way to go about that is not a press release, it's by knowing a way to tell a story and working with the reporters in such a way that they are going to be able to tell the story."

—JASON THOCKMORTON, co-founder of LaunchSquad

"That was it, the beginning for me," says Henderson about the seed that was planted many years ago that inspired LevelEdge.com. "I often think about how I got lucky that these friends just invited me with them to the game and how things unfolded. I believe I would have gotten to college somehow, but the *way* I got there was something I often reflected on. I found myself in the middle of this thing called the Internet, which was amazing, and I thought, 'I wonder if there's something I can do on the Internet to get people scholarships?'"

After 10 years as a senior research analyst and product manager at Ralston Purina, Henderson took a job with Autodesk after a friend put her resume in front of Carol Bartz. Henderson was hired to head up product development from a consumer perspective. The product allowed people to design interiors with software and included a website where more than 60 major manufacturers allowed them to publish their content on the site.

"The media is interested in technology stories instead of business model stories. Two or three years ago, new companies came online trying to introduce new ways to do things on the Internet. I think the value of that has diminished pretty significantly. Reporters are looking for the next Cisco or the next Intel, or what technologies are going to emerge to make things better. We really look for the technology stories, and our motto is looking for stories that haven't been told. So we look for a fresh story, and one that the entrepreneur has done a good enough job convincing their potential customers and partners. Then when they launch, we can come to market with a lot of validators. We use the example of blowing up a balloon—one of the things we recommend is that we want our companies to be as quiet as possible for as long as it takes for them to build up their story to achieve critical mass and validation."

—JASON THOCKMORTON, co-founder of LaunchSquad

"We had a crazy vision that people would buy furniture, refrigerators, and wallpaper online," jokes Henderson about how out there that idea seemed at the time. "This was back in the days when Prodigy really had a foothold. So we used to call Steve Case and ask how commerce was going to happen online. Prior to it really evolving to that stage for Autodesk, we divided the business, and one part became GoodHome.com, which raised $50 million in venture capital a year ago. That was my first taste of the Internet, and I remember we used to just sit in a room sometimes with Carol and other executives and just talk about the limitless potential of the Internet."

"I've [marketed and developed] over a hundred new products in my career—a hundred ideas I've come up with for other companies. I knew the moment I found one that had a business value and a social value as well, I'd quit everything I was doing and do that one myself. That's exactly what happened, and here I am."

—LISA HENDERSON, CEO, LevelEdge.com

Since that time, Henderson began work as a consultant and helped launch Lucy.com when it was just two people in a kitchen. It is now the leader in women's sports apparel. She then went back to Autodesk as a consultant to spin-off BuzzSaw, which recently raised $90 million. Henderson then worked with serial entrepreneur Steve Hoffmeyer, who had sold Reel.com (now a dead dot-com) for $100 million. The two worked together on a website called HungryMinds.com.

A NOVEL APPROACH

Another well-told story of a successful company is that of Half.com, a company recently acquired by eBay. The company has a great story from the very beginning.

"If I'm in a room full of people and I say, 'Put your hand up if you've read Grisham,' every hand goes up," says Joshua Kopelman, CEO of Half.com, about the company's concept. This was part of the company's original funding pitch. "And if I ask, 'How many of you have read a Grishham book twice?', not many hands will go up. Then you pull out one of those Grisham books off the shelf and it says $28. Imagine how many of these books are on people's shelves, and they'll never be read again. What if you could take every book you've finished and every CD you're tired of and get half your money back, and if every time you wanted a Grisham book, you could get it at half price?"

Sounds like a great concept, right? What about the kernel from which this concept sprang? The press loves this stuff.

"It was more of an evolution [than an idea for a dot-com]. It was that John Grisham thing that caused it. My wife hadn't read a Grisham book, and I was on eBay because I collect stamps. And my wife said, 'Could you get me this Grisham book?' Well, immediately I went to Amazon.com and I thought, 'Wait a second. There has to be copies of this book on eBay. I saw two dozen copies of the hardcover book, and the only thing they all had in common was that there were no bids, not even a dollar. On Amazon, it was one of the top four thousand. And yet they have it on eBay, and they can't even sell it for a buck. I thought, 'Isn't there a way to fix that supply-and-demand inefficiency?'

And this is how Half.com came about. A human need tied into a human story."

WHAT'S IN A GOOD NAME?

And I don't mean a *good* name, I mean a site with a good reputation that gives you a warm-fuzzy when you hear the site's name. A good feeling connotes a good experience. Good experiences build loyalty. Loyalty is everything in this business. These days, an excruciatingly painful amount of your dot-com's budget goes toward marketing and branding to build user loyalty. Before April, 2000, it was not uncommon for a company to spend upwards of a $100 million on building a brand. Today, in this climate, companies spend what they can afford. Branding is expensive and rarely happens by fluke.

One case of completely accidental branding comes from the heart of dot-com, San Francisco, where you find a company that started out with one guy and a computer. Craig Newmark, programmer extraordinaire and CEO of craigslist.org, began the company as a way to help out his friends by posting apartments and events on his site.

Newmark had observed people on the Net, on the Well, and in Usenet (an early form of dot-com, for you newbies), helping one another out. In early 1995, he decided to jump in and start posting cool events around San Francisco, like the Anon Salon and Joe's Digital Diner. It spread through word of mouth and became large enough to demand the use of a list server, major-domo, which required a name. Newmark wanted to call it "SF-events," but his friends suggested calling it "craigslist" to reinforce its personal and down-to-earth nature.

"Paying $50 thousand to come up with a company name is pretty pathetic. For one thing, it's a very bad use of capital—almost as bad as throwing a launch party at a tradeshow to feed your competitors. It also shows that the founders aren't very clever people. I would be embarrassed to have used a naming company. Instead, entrepreneurs should marry smart women It's a true story that my wife came up with the name of Garage.com. I don't want people to think I'm sexist—i.e., that only men are entrepreneurs. However, if the CEO is a woman, she should not ask her husband to help name the company, because most men are clueless."

—GUY KAWASAKI, CEO and founder of Garage.com

Over time, people started posting items on the list in different areas—jobs, stuff for sale, and housing. Now, not only has the site become known as one of the hottest job sites (giving Monster.com a run for its money), craigslist now has local sites for several other states and is running in the black. Craigslist was started with no venture capital and has grown with profit. (Hey, can you believe that in this day and age?!)

Unlike others of his ilk who have gotten a bit too digerati for their own good, Newmark is a nice guy. When the agents of Cindy Crawford (eStyle) and Whoopi Goldberg (Flooz) turned me down for interviews (forgive me if I thought it was a spokesperson's job to speak) about celebrity dot-com endorsers (even for my *Newsweek* article on dot-coms!), I knew I could count on Newmark to give me the inside scoop. Not only is Newmark a great success, he's also humble. "Having a site with my name, I find I get more attention than I want," says Newmark in regard to his naturally shy programmer personality. "We all want a little extra attention, but we all have a threshold. I'm operating around the margin of that now."

Word traveled fast about craigslist.org when Craig ended up on the "Today" show, interviewed by Katie Couric as one of the 10 top bachelors in Silicon Valley. The entire story of craigslist.org is like a fairy tale, where a Java programmer finds himself at the head of a very successful job (housing, personals, etc.) listing site that is pulling away business from large corporate sites. Now craigslist has more than 20 employees, and the company works on a bootstrap budget with nearly no funds appointed to marketing and branding.

"Basically, loyalty occurred by doing our version of the right thing," says Newmark of the branding the site has received without even working at it. "Our site is about giving each other a break, speaking in a human voice, not business speak. We've had a genuine commitment to giving the community a voice for well over five years, and we've created a culture that way. We've created a genuine commitment to using the technology for community outreach and nonprofits, in particular.

"It's not so much branding, but a culture. The culture in itself is the value of our site. In terms of getting the bills paid, people like our site for posting jobs because of the culture built up around the site. There's no marketing in any conventional sense. It's an insignificant part of what we do."

Craigslist works closely with the Bay Area community by providing a platform for nonprofits via its site. Craigslist also sponsors parties where it helps raise community awareness for nonprofits, and these parties are always packed wall to wall. Part of craigslist's success is the company's belief that it should bring awareness to worthwhile causes. Recently, craigslist.org worked with Amnesty International to get the word out through its community when political prisoners are identified. Several prisoners have been freed without having been tortured thanks in part to the flood of letters that came from the craigslist community via its links to the organization and the craigslist community's action to take a stand by writing letters demanding prisoners be set free.

"We all have problems getting through the day, but if you just got picked up by the secret police and you're lying in a cell hearing a lot of other prisoners screaming, you're in Titanic-ly deep shit," says Newmark of one of the reasons the company became involved in Amnesty's plight.

I think the thing about craigslist that makes it so successful is it has a real Craig—kind of like the Jeeves character from AskJeeves.com, but much more successful at making a profit—someone who makes you think they care. And when you go to parties you get to meet and talk with him. He's one of our dot-com royalty, so you'll hear about Craig sightings in the city like you would the mayor. He's the geek who made it, and people like and support the underdog.

It helps to have a spokesperson everyone can relate to, as well as a company mission. We all know about the bad boys of dot-com heading their companies for purely financial gain—would you go there because you wanted to, or because they just have a product you need? In these times, loyalty is the soul of branding.

THE FACE OF THE BRAND

One of the fastest ways to gain recognition in branding is to latch on to a celebrity who already has brand. This is a double-edged sword. If you pick the wrong celebrity, one scandal on their part can plummet your stock. It's the same thing if you partner with a company that tanks, and you have to find a way to gracefully bow out and scramble for damage control. One of the things you have to do is think long and hard about what you want your brand to convey.

One of the reasons why Priceline.com did a deal with William Shatner to be its spokesperson is because his voice was recognizable on radio, a very important quality for a company who didn't have the money to invest in TV spots. As the company received more funding, the company was able to purchase TV spots. Whoopi Goldberg seems to be doing well for Flooz; and Cindy Crawford is not only the spokesperson for eStyle.com, she's taken an active role on the board of directors. One of the many hurdles of attracting a celebrity to your table for discussions is, well, how the hell do you find one? One way is to call the Actor's Guild (323.954.1600) or one of the legendary talent agencies, such as the William Morris Agency or BMG.

Robert Levitan, co-founder and CEO of Flooz.com, said that they realized they had no brand equity, so they had to cre-ate some attributes and attach them to their products and serv-ices in a hurry. In effect, they got Whoopi on board to be their brand. It perpetuates the brand-equals-buzz myth, and if Whoopi becomes the representation of the brand, you'd better hope that her attributes are the same as the Flooz brand attributes. If that's fine, then it can probably work, but too many companies say, 'Hey, so and so is available. Let's get them,' before they define their values.

BUILDING THE CEO BRAND

There are a lot of different reasons why CEOs are sometimes built into the brand. If someone has a reputation for building strong technologies and companies, then the CEO's name will probably become synonymous with the brand. And if you have a bad-boy CEO, someone who gets popped e-mailing teenage girls on the Internet, yeah, that'll have some repercussions, as well. Especially if you have a brand such as Disney backing you. Depending on the company, the CEO may become the brand's champion. For those companies that have succeeded in branding—AOL, Amazon, Yahoo—we automatically think of the CEO when we hear the names of the companies. If your CEO isn't ready for prime time, you should seriously consider professional training. One slur, a joke in bad taste, or a stupid move will tear down whatever good branding you've managed to place and set you back to ground zero.

HOT AND BOTHERED—IS IT IMPORTANT?

Many companies are using the hard-slam, 2 AM drunk, 'Hey baby, I can make you feel good' approach rather than easing into a long-term relationship with their users. Companies are dumping hundreds of millions into giveaways. But how long can that rev model last?

Remember when iWon.com was giving away $10 thousand a day when you signed up for its search service? Well, they still are, but they've cut way back on their TV commercials. But how long can they keep giving away $10 thousand a day before it becomes a problem? And how much stickiness does $10 thousand a day get you? I remember when I first went to the site, I was appalled at the number of cookies they were trying to download (you can check this by turning on permissions for cookies in your browser preferences). On top of that, I wasn't all that impressed with its UI, and I had a lot of difficulty trying to register. I tried nearly a dozen times, and their site kept crashing my computer. It was frustrating, and I ended up writing a note saying so to the webmaster (who seemed empathetic to my cause). It only takes one bad experience to turn all those advertising dollars into confetti when you're looking at cost per user. It costs a lot to get those users back. I did try and get iWon's perspective of their branding strategy for this chapter, but they turned down the invite for an interview on several occasions. Lots of dot-com companies tried the grand giveaways (most of them before April, 2000), and many of them are dot-com no-longers. This is the kind of marketing plan that venture capitalists will roll their eyes at if you pop up a PowerPoint slide that calls for branding in the millions.

Excited About a URL

URLs are a big part of branding. Sometimes your domain name can make or break you. Some URLs were just meant to be, even if they come about at the eleventh hour. Excite.com is one of those companies.

"Excite came about because the original name of the service was going to be Bullseye.com," says Joe Kraus co-founder of Excite@Home.

"We had a guy named Roger Black, a pretty well-known designer, put together a whole concept around BullsEye.com. Being eternal optimists, we were supposed to launch sometime in October, and here it was September and I still can't get the guy who owns Bullseye.com to sell the URL to me. It was, at one point, pretty clear that this was an emotional issue for him, and we weren't going to get it, so we had to come up with another name. We met with our ad agency—at the time it was CKS—and we had a huge brainstorming session and put hundreds of names on a wall and narrowed it down to five. One was Excite, one was Ferret, another Swoop. I don't remember what the others were. The criteria were that it couldn't be a technical name, it had to be consumer-oriented, it had to have energy, it had to be broad, and it couldn't immediately imply something like 'search' because we knew over time our business would be more than that. So it had to have meaning packed into it, and clearly the URL had to be available.

"*Excite* met all those criteria. Literally, we were going on press tour to pre-pitch monthlies for the launch of Excite with our name on the press release blank for a name. We finally decided on Sunday, changed the name to Excite, printed them out, and left on Monday."

The Excite.com site (now Excite@Home.com) has been an incredible success and recognizable as one of the great branding successes of the dot-com decade.

Summary

Branding is not a marketing, advertising, or PR issue. It is the fine art of weaving all of the important elements of your company together to present your dot-com as a believable, reliable experience. It's your responsibility to make sure your company has a brand that will pull it through the tough times ahead, because when the market is tearing down your valuation, you'd better make sure the analysts, the press, and your users are on your side, or you will be dot-com dead.

CHAPTER 8

BUILDING A COMPANY
The Key Elements of a Winning Environment

L et's say that you now have a brilliant executive team in place, and you're looking to fill all the positions in engineering, marketing, PR, bizdev, and everything else down to interns (and never underestimate the brainpower of an intern). Hopefully you'll also have an HR exec who has killer contacts, especially with recruiting firms. If not, I'd say that would be your first order of business about now.

Currently, none of the dot-com companies I know of that use traditional advertising (newspapers, trade pubs) are having as much luck as those using headhunters or the Web to pursue new hires. The companies not using headhunters or recruiters are saving a few bucks—or many bucks, in most cases—but in keeping positions open until they find the qualified candidate, they are shortchanging their company's time to market. So how do you go about recruiting in these days of such high competition? It's the time-to-market challenge that will be chewing your ass until you do get qualified people to fill your open positions. It may be an HR issue at the beginning, but it soon becomes everyone else's problem.

"Recruiting is almost like the process of setting up a blind date. You're setting up two people together, and you hope they're going to love each other, but the chance of that happening is really low. You're basically trying to prep each of them with as much information about the other so the surprises are few and the likes are great."
—**SID VALLURI, vice president and general manager of Korn/Ferry's FutureStep.com.**

I've seen the lack of engineers bring down an entire company because it didn't have the people to build the website's infrastructure. Without the full-blown product in place, it's difficult to get your sales team jazzed (because they can't sell a working product) or get PR or marketing involved (because they have nothing to tout, you can only take a demo so far). The company, after they nickel and dimed about hire-on salaries and balked at the cost of headhunters, finally brought a recruiter on board (the recruiting up to this time had been done by the CEO). The recruiter was so beaten up by the CEO for not being able to bring someone on board, (via their guidelines and budget) that he quit.

Soon the company was so hard up that it hired Oracle employees to come in at night after work (after their day jobs) to manage the project. You can't build a company on off-hours—especially with people who've already spent their brain-power for the day elsewhere. It rarely works. The people who were part of the company—an intricate part of the company—got tired of being worked to the bone because others weren't being brought in. They hung around for five months and, with no end in site, left the company. And with them, so went the documentation. After nearly a year-and-a-half, the company has gone through a complete turnover from everyone in the executive team. Even the founder has left. This company still has plenty of capital, but it doesn't have the personality or resources to keep and maintain good people. The company lost its time-to-market advantage and is floundering to find another product to enter the market with. The red flags were there all along, and the experienced CEO should have seen them. The company bought the Vaseline and dot-com screwed itself.

USING A HEADHUNTER

Now that you have the capital, it's time to bring in the big guns and use a headhunter or a recruiter. Large corporations have actually brought headhunters from the big firms to set up offices at their own headquarters just to get a jump on the competition. What this tells me is that you're up against some pretty scary competition.

I advise you, if you have the cash, to encourage your HR people to use headhunters. You have a product to put out, and time is against you; you shouldn't need any more encouragement than that bit of knowledge. You may save some money doing it yourself, but you may also lose your company if you're a spendthrift. This is not the place to be tight in your budget.

Sid Valluri, vice president and general manager of FutureStep.com, Korn/Ferry's online recruiting service, says that FutureStep's database of middle and executive management and technology specialists has grown to 800,000 people, most of whom are looking to move into other jobs. Seventy-five percent of those people are open to relocation. The majority of these applicants are in the $75-150k wage range, with others on the very top notch of the glamorous digerati pay scale. What does this mean to you? It means if you are located in Silicon Valley or another blossoming technology area where housing prices have gone through the ceiling, you will probably find your people by using a national (and worldwide) database, but you will pay through the nose in cost-of-living increases, relocation fees, and bonuses. You knew this from the beginning, right? It's expensive to hire and maintain good people. David Packard set a high standard a long time ago that was felt by employers all over the world. We all have a lot to live up to now, so get used to it.

Finding an IT genius in the Appalachian Mountains means that you'll have to pay her moving costs, probably a hiring bonus, and a competitive wage that will tempt her to leave the deep blue mountains of home and her mansionesque five-bedroom home she paid $200k for five years ago.

Thinking about hiring someone just out of school? Not as easy as it used to be. Recruiters are making a living by hanging out at universities and handing out cards with their cell phone numbers so they can be reached one minute before the next recruiter the grad has on their list. As soon as these kids graduate, and in some cases before, recruiters have them in jobs a week later at starting wages of $75k–plus. Many did internships at major companies and were groomed for hiring upon graduation, or even before. Believe me, the smart, ambitious ones have been identified, bagged, and tagged.

The advantage of using a recruiter is that they are already tied into those who are eager (and for the most part, single and willing to move) to be a part of the industry—the risk takers. You find a lot more risk takers at this recent grad level than you do with someone in a comfortable job at an established company at which they have a routine and can do it without much effort. And many of these grads, although they've been warned, haven't been jaded by the recent Internet fallout and consolidation trend. They still think they can be millionaires, and bringing that kind of enthusiasm to a company can be the shot in the arm that your dot-com morale may need right about now.

What is the biggest advantage in going to a headhunter? That would probably be the recruiter's vast number of applicants to choose from. That's the first sign of a good recruiter. The first question to ask them: "How many people in your database have the experience you're looking for? And how much time do you think it will take to fill the position?" Having a large number of people to choose from is important not only because you want an employee with the right skills set, but also because you want someone who will fit in with your culture. You may have to go through a lot of princes to find the right prince—remember, you are paying for these recruiters to bring you princes, not frogs. But you might want to constantly review your standards vs. market standards to make sure you're in the ballpark for a prince.

RECRUITING IN THE POST-APRIL FALLOUT

"The hard part is not finding qualified people. The hard part is getting them to leave their jobs," says Daphne Albert, founder of ABA Associates (www.abaassociates.com), a San Francisco Bay Area recruiting firm specializing in executive-level management. "I don't think that the concept of Internet-time can be overstated, it's not a cliche—it's a *real* thing. Six months ago, it was really easy to get people to move into another job. All I'd have to do is mention *startup, pre-IPO, early stage* in my messages, and people would call me back nonstop. It was a different environment. Now what's happening with the market becoming more efficient is that a lot of bad companies that never should have existed are going by the wayside. People are getting skittish. The media is sensationalizing it, and even people in the industry are buying into whatever the buzzwords of the day are," says Albert of the mid-2000 spring/summer of fallout and consolidation.

"It's a more difficult environment to recruit from," Albert says of people who want a sense of security because they're reading about all of the failure stories. "People's tolerance for risk has gone down now as they realize what the reality is surrounding the risk. Risk was almost a glamorous word six months ago. Now people are risk-adverse. I'm calling the right people to fill the positions, but getting them to leave a comfortable situation is much more difficult."

BUILDING A LIST AND CHECKING IT TWICE

My friend Kim set goals when she began husband hunting. She sat down with a list of the things she wanted from life and from a spouse, and when the appropriate time came in the dating sequence, she would sit down with her men and ask them what they thought of her goals. Well, Kim had a baby this year—her first. She married her husband David nearly six years ago.

David was one of the guys she subjected to "the list." She had to kiss a few frogs before setting her sites on David. He passed Kim's test, but there was some give and take on both sides, compromises that, in the end, worked out just fine.

This targeting story should be passed on to every startup. Many companies begin their search for employees with no sense of goal setting, no honed list of skill sets the employee must have or specific experiences they wish the candidate to have lived through. They just don't think through what they really want. In using a recruiter to shop for a candidate in this way, they lose a lot of time and money in the process.

"You can't just say 'We've got a deficit in marketing. Send us a marketing guy,'" says Sid Valluri, vice president and general manager of FutureStep.com. "That's not a heck of a lot to go on. You're just saying, 'We have a weakness, and I want somebody who will be a strength for me.' If you specify what the weakness is, why it's a weakness, where you are trying to take your company, and what sort of strengths and experiences are you looking for in a person—that is the information that will help rectify your situation. Then a recruiter can help. "After you've given the recruiter everything, you also have to realize that this is an extremely competitive job market, and you're not going to get everything you want," Valluri says, advising dot-coms to keep perspective. "All you're doing is setting the guidelines for the recruiter. Then you have to step back as an employer and realize that you're paying market competitive wages, that your stock has a fair hope of doing well, and that you're out there competing with every other dot-com and every other established company for this individual."

Let's say your recruiter is rounding up 10 people to present to you. What do you have to know about the job package you are offering and how it might affect the pool of candidates you can attract?

"I have to give them a compelling reason to move," says Valluri, a seasoned veteran of playing the mediator who has reason to make both the client and the individual happy. "If your reasons are only marginally more compelling than someone else is able to offer, you have to be realistic about the compromises you have to make and the kinds of people you're going to find."

For instance, what about money? How much more do you offer than the company competing for this person?

"If the job typically offers $100 thousand a year, and you're offering $150 thousand plus a king-sized stock package and six weeks vacation, you'll get a lot of talent applying for your job," says Valluri, who knows that some companies will even surpass that amount and package if they need someone in the position ASAP. "But if the job typically offers $100 thousand, and you're only paying $105 thousand plus a little more stock and a little more vacation, people aren't going to start banging down your door. So when your recruiter finds you ten people who are interested in the job, a lot of companies say, 'These people aren't good enough—find me ten more.' All they're doing is having an unfilled position propagate month after month until they finally realize that, for what they're offering in this job market, they can't find a heck of a lot better. If they could, they wouldn't be coming to us in the first place. Some companies think that just because you pay an executive recruiter to find people that the recruiter can do magic for you. They can't do magic; they can just find the best people in that price range."

BUILDING MASLOW'S DOT-COM PYRAMID

So how do you know you've satisfied Maslow's hierarchy of needs for your candidate? First, what are the needs that must be met?

- Attractive market salary

- Enticing stock package

- Great vacation time

So that about does it, right?

Not so fast. You're up against *stiff* competition to tempt talent to your company. Many companies are offering BMWs, vacation packages, and gourmet chefs to make the pot a little sweeter.

Two dot-com companies in the Bay Area offer weekly visits from "massage therapists" in the privacy of their own homes, hotel rooms, wherever. This benefit is kept extremely confidential (I suppose, if you don't include me, a member of the press, knowing). I was doing some research for a men's magazine about how Silicon Valley men blow off steam when I came across this tidbit of information.

In attending startup party after startup party, I kept running into the same stunning women. These women—leggy, smart, and statuesque—all seemed to be of an ilk not usually found at startup companies. In talking with several of them, I found they were working for an escort service. The name of a particular agency kept coming up. I made an appointment to see the mistress of this company, and she promised to give me the scoop if I promised not to mention her company clients by name. She made me sign the Mother of All NDAs. Only in Silicon Valley...

How do you approach something like that comfortably in an interview, anyway? 'By the way, we realize you have needs, and seeing as how you're an engineer without a whole lot of social skills, we're going to make sure you have those needs met so you're more productive.'

The mistress summed it up nicely when she said, "If it keeps the guys at their job, and it keeps my girls working in a safe environment—we've never had a problem with these guys; they're pretty harmless—then what's the issue? Everyone wins."

And so it goes. In making routine calls to the two companies in question, I found that their retention rate for senior engineers was flawless. Just to clarify a point, neither company has women on their senior engineering teams.

So let's get back to the needs we can actually address at the workplace without fear of being slapped with a lawsuit.

WHAT'S STOCK WORTH THESE DAYS?

"In the early days, because stock was a novelty, you could short-change people on cash and give them stock," says Sid Valluri vice president and general manager of FutureStep.com, about how the market has shifted. "Now that people are becoming more aware of the risk in stock, people are saying, 'If you want me to stay for a long time, give me stock. But if you want me to work right now, you have to pay me a fair market wage.' We see that people are less willing to leave a secure job for a startup just because there's a stock package there.

"People have also come to expect some kind of flex in their holiday schedule as an important part of their job satisfaction," Valluri says of the added incentive of having a flexible schedule. "It's surprising how much of an impact it can have on your life. Some companies will have a half day all the time on Friday, and that incentive becomes more attractive now that wealth is becoming more prevalent. People are focusing on quality of life. Getting a half day off, working one day a week from home, or just having flexible hours during the day are the things that are actually attracting people."

So what are the incentives that keep you on after the call girl and stock thing gets old. Perhaps your BMW doesn't shine quite the way it did when you first laid eyes on it. And that gourmet chef? All he knows are recipes that can be found in Jacques Pepin's dated cookbook. Eventually everything becomes passe. So what are the emotional ties that bind?

"It's the personal satisfaction derived from a job that means more," says Valluri. "Let's say your company is paying the lease on your BMW for so many years, but in reality, the cost of that BMW is $300 a month. But, if you have the option of getting $300 more, you might decide to do something else with it. It gets someone's attention at first, but it's not necessarily what's going to sustain a flow of good talent into the company. If it did, every company would do it. Looking at Maslow's hierarchy of needs here is so appropriate when talking about incentives to take and stay at a job. Once basic needs are met—job security, financial security, and rewards from having done a good job—then quality of life becomes so important. Those companies that are more willing to improve their employees' quality of life are the most successful in attracting and retaining people."

RISING THROUGH THE RANKS

Another big incentive in going to a dot-com is how quickly people rise in the ranks, something they wouldn't ordinarily do at an established company. How long do you think it would take an admin to rise to director of content at, say, an established magazine? I've never seen that happen, but I've seen two people—one with a degree in art history and the other in psychology—rise to the top at dot-coms.

"Money is a great reward, but one of the biggest rewards of working is the satisfaction of having accomplished something," says Sid Valluri. "You can get that faster at a startup than you can at a big company because a startup needs someone to do everything. If someone can't do something and you step up and do it, so much the better for you. And that's the kind of person who succeeds at a dot-com, not someone who needs a very structured job description."

AN ENVIRONMENT YOU CAN LIVE IN

There are a lot of reasons why people choose to work in the places they do, and many of those reasons are purely emotional. They want to work with people whom they know (and who have now received bonuses for referring them—this is a win-win situation if it works out). Perhaps they saw the company listed in the top 100 places for women to work. Whatever the reason, if the company has a culture, chances are those pieces of it were placed there carefully and ever so intentionally.

"The first thing you need to see when you bring someone in is that they're excited about what you're doing. They need to buy into your company's vision, your mission and your company's values. The shared vision is important because people need to rally around it—all the departments need to share the vision, it's what pulls a company together. I don't think the importance of a cultural fit can be overstated enough."

—DAPHNE ALBERT, founder of ABA Associates

Let's take, for instance, the company's values and ethics. Steve Kirsch is worth in the proximity of $200 million or so. He's a low-key guy who happens to have founded Infoseek, and before that Mouse Systems and Frame Technology. Kirsch, 43, and his wife Michele, founded a $75 million foundation and are believed to be in the top 10 of America's philanthropists. Still, Kirsch packs his briefcase in the morning, eats an orange at his desk for breakfast, and carries on the business of the day. And what is that business? The website gives this description of the goal the company aims to achieve: *To become the standard platform for developing and deploying e-commerce applications.* For our purposes, the company could be selling widgets; what I want to tell you about is that the company hired an ethicist by the name of Tom Shanks, a former Jesuit priest, to help visualize the company's behavioral guidelines.

"When we first started the company, we said, 'What are the things that are important to us about the culture we want to build in this company?" says Kirsch about Propel's philosophical guidelines. "And so we talked about things we thought were important, then we wrote them down and narrowed them to a list of a dozen. Then we got feedback from the company and we added one more—live a healthy, balanced lifestyle." In other words, play well with others and prosper. The company has found a way to live within these guidelines and is growing in large strides.

Shanks, taking the company's goals to heart and the culture Kirsch and others at the company wanted to create, formulated Propel's 13 commandments that are posted in the company's lobby. Propel has established this set of philosophical guidelines and core values to shape its company culture. The following are the commandments listed:

Think and act like an owner.

Have fun.

Recognize accomplishment.

Keep a balance in your life.

Teach and learn from each other.

Communicate without fear of retribution.

Require quality beyond customer expectations.

Improve continuously.

Go the extra mile to take care of the customer.

Play to win-win.

Act with a sense of urgency.

Make and meet commitments.

Give back to the community.

Other companies have similar mantras and goals they try to achieve. One company that has made news everywhere about how it motivates its employees is Excite@Home. Founded by Stanford alum, the Excite@Home campus may catch you a bit off guard. Its giant tube slide that dips from the second to the first floor is the first sign that you're not in Kansas anymore, Toto. Mountain bikes line the walls, big beanbag chairs huddle in circles, and the space is peppered with a few of those big rubber balls with handles you sit on and bounce around on. There's a get-it-yourself juice bar, an indoor basketball court, pool tables, and huge rubber balls that people lay on face to the ceiling to get the kinks out of their code-ridden shoulders. There are beer bottles in the trashcans (probably from the night before). And I can't even begin to describe the anarchy of Excite's cubical landscape. One thing is certain, all of these people look pretty damn happy. And this is my third trip to the company; they can't always be putting on such a good show.

In a series of interviews with employees I found that many of Excite's employees live together in groups in nearby apartments and houses. They really enjoy being together. This is a culture that has fun written all over it.

When recruiting, the first thing you need to be aware of is that people need to buy into your culture. Remember that first wife you married—for better or worse? It was never going to get to the *worse* part because you would change her before that happened. Yeah, right. If you've learned nothing else from living in the real world of relationships (and I'm assuming you're not one of those 40-year-old techno virgins I run into from time to time), heed rule number one in recruiting people to fit the company culture: *People do not change.* Bringing a hardcore IBM micromanager to fit into an Excite situation—I'm betting—wouldn't work too well.

Recruiters know what a company's culture is before they even pick up the phone to invite someone to come in and talk about a job.

"Every hire is a crapshoot. You learn as much as you can through interviews, references, and background checks, but it's still a crapshoot. All you can do is try and reduce those risks in every way you can."
—TRACIE DECKER, human resources director at ELetter

"We try to make sure the person is the right person for the company's culture," says Valluri. "That's the number one reason why people don't stay in their job. We test people to see what kinds of cultures they'd be best working in. For instance, at HP there has always been a great deal of consensus and people don't make a decision without holding hands and singing *Kum Ba Yah*. At Apple, people disappear behind closed doors and, every once in a while, come out with a great product. There's a big difference between company cultures."

IS YOUR MIS GUY A SERIAL KILLER?

Let's say you've found someone you want to hire. If you've used a headhunting firm, what due diligence, in detail, did they perform? If they didn't do enough to satisfy you, you may want to do more before bringing that person on board.

I don't think it would surprise you to learn that many employees are getting their jobs by embellishing, or outright lying, on their resumes. Perhaps you're guilty of it yourself? So why are people lying on their resumes? And what are they lying about? One company working to detect resume fraud is HireRight (`www.HireRight.com`), an Internet-based company that checked out the resumes of more than 200,000 applicants in 1998.

"Our offer letter states that the offer is contingent upon the successful completion of a background investigation. There's nothing more I can do to be more upfront with you other than jumping up on the desk and shouting, 'It's now, I'm going to do it! Anything else you want to say?'"
—TRACIE DECKER, human resources director at ELetter

HireRight recently released some interesting statistics that show how rampant resume fraud is in the United States. The company's numbers show that

- 80 percent of all resumes are misleading.

- 30 percent show altered employment dates.

- 20 percent state fraudulent degrees.

- 40 percent have inflated salary claims.

- 30 percent have inaccurate job descriptions.

- 25 percent have companies listed that no longer exist.

- 27 percent listed falsified references.

The due diligence process is quite simple. When using a typical application form, you put your John or Jane Hancock on the bottom of the page stating that all the information you just filled out was factual, and you give permission to your potential employer to try to prove otherwise.

Some personnel directors believe that applicants have earned degrees in fiction writing rather than engineering or computer science. Keeping applicants honest has become a fulltime job for many people. Startups and mega corporations alike are going beyond calling references...*way* beyond.

When you hire a company to check out the facts on a resume, they do this in a number of ways. These checks and balances may include a thorough check into the applicant's Social Security history record. Social Security records give the exact dates of when employee contributions began and ended at every company they've ever worked for. A police background check is done, a complete rundown of credit records is obtained (including monthly credit payments), and education records are tracked down. There's also a thorough check into references to make sure the person they use as a reference actually has, or had, the job title they claim. This part of a background check—the checking of the references—always reminds me of the "Seinfeld" episode where George, to stay on unemployment, uses Jerry's telephone number for his reference at Vandelay Industries, a fictitious plastics company where he'd recently applied for a job (later George became Art Vandelay, the architect, to impress the chicks). This is why building a check into an applicant's references as part of due diligence is a great idea. So why should you be so paranoid when hiring?

"A lot of hiring managers are in such a hurry to get people in the company that the hiring manager interviews someone, thinks they look good, and brings them in. You can't do that here, and you shouldn't do it anywhere, because whoever you bring in touches so many others that we throw them in front of a lot of other ELetter people. If someone says, 'I don't have a good feeling about this,' then we hit the brakes and find out why."

—TRACIE DECKER, human resources director at ELetter

"Many employers won't hire someone with a lot of credit liability," says Ralph D. Thomas, private investigator-turned-author (*Pre-Employment Investigation for Private Investigators: How to Start and Conduct Pre-Employment Screening Services*, `www.pimall .com/nais`) about potential liability. Why is credit liability, or even pending lawsuits, so important to a hiring manager? Human nature. Desperate times call for desperate actions. Why hire someone who may be living beyond all their means and put them in charge of a budget, expensive equipment, or company secrets? Why, indeed?

"At a previous company, we ran a background check on someone who was a convicted murderer," says Tracie Decker, human resources director at ELetter. "But on the application, he had written that he had been convicted of a felony. The biggest part of the background check is finding out if someone lied, were they upfront? He'd been in a bar fight when he was 19 and hit the guy in the head with a beer bottle and the guy died. The company did hire him—he'd been upfront, he'd gone to jail and served his time. Had he been a rapist or a repeat offender of violent crimes, would we have done something different? Yeah, we would have."

TESTING THE EXPERTS

What if the background checks out just fine? Have you then overcome all of the hiring hurdles? Don't pack that lunch so quickly, Code Boy. What if you have a technology you're hiring for that even your own CTO doesn't know enough about to qualify the applicant?

With technologies being developed every other day, even a CTO can't be expected to know everything. One company exploiting the fact that you can't know everything is ReviewNet (`www.reviewnet.com`), a service that tests applicants virtually (via Internet) to detect if an applicant's skills are real or only virtual. The service tests applicants via an Internet-based quiz using their computer at home, or at the potential employer's site. The test is timed, and an evaluation lets the person giving the test know how much time it took the applicant to complete the multiple answer quiz. Then, ReviewNet gives the applicant's company the test score, including the correct answers *and* near answers. Even a non-technical HR director has the ability to hire qualified applicants, or disqualify the ones who don't make the grade. ReviewNet also has another service where a specialist in a particular field will telephone and give an oral test.

OPEN YOUR KIMONO?

Now that you know everything about that person sitting in front of you, how much should you tell them about you? In my view, if someone is going to leave a good job to come to work for you, you should definitely open the kimono. If you're using a recruiter to staff your company, then you probably don't have to worry too much about this coming up. The recruiter will fill them in about your company, but there will probably be some missing pieces that need to be placed when you come to the table.

But if no one knows anything about you, they'll ask around—and on my user lists (such as SFWOW.org), I see tons of e-mails that read, *I need info on such and such company, they offered me a job, anyone know anything about them?* These inquiries are answered off the list so people don't get into libel lawsuits, but I've been told of some real shockers. How can an applicant know what to believe?

The best thing is to sit them down and be straight-up with them. You may be hesitating because chances are your recruiter has pulled them from a company that will probably be a competitor of yours. So how do you avoid having your information spread? You try to alleviate doubt. Try to quell their objections with support and confidence rather than the hard facts that you may not want out there yet. I would begin by setting up a series of interviews with people in your company for this person to talk with—people who will tell the company story, talk about what a good experience it is to work there. Then, if they pass the litmus test with your people and want to know more, tell them. Show them your business plan. Show them your Power-Point presentation. Tell them who your investors are. After all, this is their future that's weighing in the balance. But what about the confidentiality of your company information?

"You can certainly feel free to have anyone you come in contact with sign a nondisclosure agreement if you're going to be discussing proprietary technology, and you absolutely should," says Mark Radcliffe, partner at Gray Cary Ware & Freidenrich (www.GrayCary.com) and co-author of *Internet Law and Business Handbook* (www.LaderaPress.com).

TO COMPETE OR NOT TO COMPETE

When you're hiring someone from the enemy, or leaving your old company to form a new and improved company with the same basic product, what rights do you have that will save you from being tied up in court for years?

"When you hire somebody from a competing company, you have to make sure they're not bringing over any technology that will taint your own," says Mark Radcliffe, partner at Gray Cary Ware & Freidenrich (www.GrayCary.com) and co-author of *Internet Law and Business Handbook* (www.LaderaPress.com) about some of the basic guidelines. "You also need to make sure that if you're hiring people in squads from your competitor that you don't do it in such an offensive way that they don't sue you for some kind of unfair interference of business. There have been suits like that.

"There was a recent suit claiming trade-secret misappropriation because someone was hiring away from a company and the judge basically said the first guy hired away gave away confidential information about the other people's salary. So, in this case, there was a misappropriation of trade secrets in that way, though the judge did rule that there was no exposure of confidential technical information. You have to be careful of this. You have to sit down with your lawyer and get a framework so you don't make mistakes."

There are other kinds of issues you need to beware of when hiring your competition's employees. "I think you should have an attorney explain what the issues are to you. Most of my clients don't ask us to vet every employee. They ask for a set of guidelines—a framework within which to make decisions—and then a lot of them are gray areas. You don't want to be in a situation where you don't understand the risk that you're taking," warns Radcliffe about the pitfalls of not having an attorney who understands the issues.

"For instance, most of the states will enforce non-compete agreements, and so people in California don't really think about that. There are people who are under non-compete agreements and they may be enforceable if you're not bringing them into California. Non-competes are basically unenforceable in California, with certain rare exceptions. For example, if you sell your company and you have a non-compete, it's enforceable if you own a substantial piece of the company. But in other states, any non-compete is enforceable. So if you're hiring someone to staff your New York office, and they have a non-compete agreement with their last employer, that may be enforceable. It's a good idea to prevent this problem before it exists. Many entrepreneurs say, 'I don't have the time or the money to see an attorney.' All I have to say about that is that it will be a lot more expensive later. And there have been cases where the rights were so screwed up that people won't invest, and it killed the company. It's important to remember that most venture groups get ten-thousand plans and they fund twenty—they're pretty much looking for reasons to turn you down. Having a rights situation is an easy one."

GOLDEN, MINK-LINED HANDCUFFS: TIES THAT BIND

So what happens once you've found someone who might be right for you? If it's a thumbs up and their personal due diligence has panned out, your recruiter helps hammer out the package and makes an offer. "There are always trade-offs," says Sid Valluri, vice president and general manager of FutureStep.com, "especially if you decide to move to Silicon Valley. You may decide you need flexible hours so you can avoid a heavy commute. All of this is negotiated."

Of course, you're going to offer your employees stock, and of course, they're going to expect it. But stock at most startups these days is looked at like funny money. If it makes something of itself, it makes something of itself; but generally people's enthusiasm has tanked because of the stock dips and the companies that have gone under. I liken it to the first time you date a guy who wears a hairpiece. You probably don't know it (if there is a god), it looks completely natural. But then one morning you notice something strange. You realize it's a hairpiece! You never look at men's hair the same way again; even in casual relationships, you're always eyeing it, looking for the weave or evidence of plugs. That one hairpiece has freaked you for life. You know what I say to that? If hair is so important, date college boys. Nothing is as it seems; if you want to make money don't count on your stock.

"It's not like it was twenty years ago—you don't work for IBM for twenty-five years, retire, and get a gold watch. Now if you stay in a job for more than five years, you get people wondering what's wrong with you."
—SID VALLURI, vice president and general manager of Korn/Ferry's FutureStep.com.

In a matter of speaking, the same is true for startups. If the people you're interviewing don't care about owning stock in the company and aren't excited about the opportunity to build a company, take a pass. Risk-taking dreamers are the stuff of startups. If you ever get someone who says, "I really don't care about the stock," dump 'em. They have no vision to bring to your company, and they will probably be the first to leave. Find someone who is passionate about your product or service, someone who has done some research about your company and is in your office for one reason—they *get it*, they share your vision.

BUILDING A COMFORTABLE NEST

Making a workplace a comfortable place for your employees to nest is important, and a critical thing to do if you want to make it easy for them to hang up that phone the next time a recruiter calls them with a job offer.

"I do have a challenge, and it's that the job market is so tight," says Tracie Decker, human resources director at ELetter. "We have very little turnover right now, and I think that's in part because we're so young. There's a definite culture here that big companies don't have anymore, if they ever had it. If you can be competitive in your salaries and benefits, that's the first step. But people have to want to come to work every day. At places like Oracle, that's a tough thing to come up with, but ELetter can offer an exciting startup atmosphere."

ELetter has lunches for its employees every other week, and you can, on some hot days, find the company going out for ice cream at Ben & Jerry's or off at an IMAX movie at the Tech Museum. On other days, they're out having a BBQ and letting loose with high-powered water guns. Sometimes it's the simple pleasures in life that make your house a home.

USING YOUR OWN RESOURCES

If people love where they work, they tend to bring with them people who share similar values. Sometimes it can take some finagling for them to convince a friend to leave another job, but it can be done.

"We've done a lot to make finding people easier," says Kim Fischer, CEO of AudioBasket, a company that designs personally tailored audio news for PDAs and other means of media transfer. "We have internal bonuses, and if somebody refers a candidate who gets hired, they can get $5,000. We have a lottery in which, each time you refer someone for a position, your name goes into that lottery and people can win a trip to Mexico. We do everything to foster an environment where everyone is involved in the recruiting process."

"I think you start running into problems when you start throwing in as many perks as you can," warns Decker. "Anyone is hard pressed to beat the perks a company like Oracle can offer—how nice the buildings are, how good the food is, the health club, you can get your dry cleaning done, your pictures developed. I think the message you're sending when you offer all of these perks is that you don't want people to have a personal life outside of the workplace. Do we offer good perks? Yeah, I think we do well for a small company of one hundred. But, I'm not so sure that's what keeps people here. You can get those things anywhere—what you can't get anywhere is this sense of excitement and availability to your senior people and co-founders. Even in most small companies, those people live in a rarified atmosphere and don't get off the mount to meet with *the people*. Our co-founders and senior people hang with them, have dinner with them, they understand the technology and know what's going on. You want to see an engineer happy? Give them an opportunity to sit in the CEOs cubicle and talk about what they're doing and what the next functionality on the website might be."

TALES OF GREED FROM THE UNDERGROUND

Recently, I heard a very sad story from an investor. They funded a startup with a huge chunk of money and tried to give the CEO mentoring. The angel caught wind that the company was using programmers from another country who they were enslaving with its power over their visas. These guys were working like slaves, being paid a very small fraction of what U.S. Java programmers were making, and they weren't getting any stock. It was a sweatshop—Silicon Valley's version of Kathie Lee's clothing factories. It still happens, even in these modern times in modern places. The investor was furious and demanded that the CEO start treating his people fairly. The CEO told the investor to butt out. As a matter of fact, the CEO had kept 80 percent of the stock in his company (this is an unheard amount in the Valley). Although it was too late to do anything about the money, the investor swore to not invest in any further rounds and to tell others not to, as well. This will probably kill the company, but some people do have ethics.

"When it comes to raising money or giving options away to employees, wouldn't you rather own one percent of a billion-dollar company than ten percent of a failure?"
—KIM FISCHER, CEO, AudioBasket

After I told this story to Kim Fischer, CEO at AudioBasket, she had some pretty strong comments. "I think the company is the team," says Fischer about sharing stock. "It's a tough market, and maybe these guys are locked up because of their visas, but tell me who they are and I'll go get them visas and bring them over to AudioBasket. I think that's nuts if you don't give away parts of the company. It's not about generosity, it's actually about selfishness—if you don't treat your employees well, they're not going to stay, and you're not going to have anything. It's the employees and investors and a lot of other people who are going to make the company a success. And at AudioBasket, our most valuable asset is the team. We want to make sure that everybody is incredibly happy. And like you said, the investor isn't going to invest anymore in the startup. I think that story in itself is enough to tell people how they should treat people."

Unfortunately, it's not the only story I've heard lately. One of the webmasters I work with has been mentoring a Vietnamese gentleman working via a green card. The webmaster has been teaching his friend Flash and Director and getting him going on little projects to build his skills. To make ends meet, the guy was working at a manufacturing plant (semiconductor-related) on a graveyard shift where he was forced to breathe air that was not safe. He would take aspirin all day long at the webmaster's house to relieve the headaches from the fumes he'd inhaled on the nightshift. Everyone who complained had been fired, and those were few and far between because people need those jobs (usually their second or third job they are holding simultaneously) to make ends meet in this fantastically expensive environment of Silicon Valley. Finally, the guy quit because his health was going down the tubes. Now he has a dilemma: Should he or should he not report the company to OSHA? He ended up not reporting them because he didn't want his friends to lose their jobs if OSHA decided to shut down the factory. These are the evils we live with in this Valley.

A TALE OF MICROMANAGEMENT

Just in case you haven't noticed, the whole thing about being part of a startup is that you will be released from a corporate atmosphere. You get to rip off those nylons and toss them from your sunroof going 85 miles an hour down Highway 280. You get to say goodbye to ties and dress shoes and heels—man, they're *so* gone. You get to buy a whole new wardrobe that includes shocking colors, funky designs, and torn jeans. You finally get to have your nose pierced. These are all cool things, but what did you give up for these freedoms? Well, let's start with that cushy job you used to have at Sony, Panasonic, Apple, Oracle, Cisco, 3Com—wherever you migrated from. Big deal, right? You have signed on with a company you feel is worthy of your coolness. Although you have as much chance of striking it rich as you do winning the lottery, you've given up your stable job, and, in most cases, your excellent pay and your steady-growth stock options.

So why would someone want to toss stability to the wind at such a thin chance at being rich? The ups, the downs, the long hours, the sleeping under your desk and consuming more Jolt Cola than anyone would consider safe—*it's all yours, baby*! Could you want for anything more? Hey, even if you're an admin entering the job market, you just bought an e-ticket to ride The WWW Beast.

One of the biggest issues a company will ever face is bringing in somebody who doesn't fit with the culture their employees signed up for. That means you don't bring a neo-Nazi to manage a startup. People have left corporate life because they want to bring their creativity to *your* table. They have left the timecards and 8-to-5 job behind to gift you with their brain-power. They *get it*—they understand your dream and want to help you achieve success. They don't need a storm trooper finger-flicking them on the back of the head to help them produce.

This is the biggest problem I see with established startups. These are the ones who already have funding and are on their way to building a product—the absolute deadliest time to have your engineers leave a company because of the lack of documentation that takes place at this stage.

It happens when the executive team feels they could be driving their engineering department a little harder to reach time to market goals faster. They're running scared because of an announcement they just heard about a possible competitor in their space. All of a sudden, the exec team gets a bug up its ass and brings in a guy known for cracking the whip. Well, e-boys and girls, let me tell you a little story about micromanagement, probably the best example of micromanagement this Valley has to tell.

In 1947, a disruptive technology development occurred when three engineers, Walter Brattain, John Bardeen, and William Shockley, from AT&T Bell Telephone Laboratory, demonstrated the principle of amplifying an electrical current using a solid, semi-conducting material. These creators found a kick-ass alternative for the vacuum tube. Shockley would win the Nobel Prize (that came with $38,633 for each member of the trio) for his participation in the technology.

Shockley, who emphasized that he was from a long line of bluebloods traceable to the Mayflower, left Bell Labs to build a company of his own. He would set up a semiconductor lab at Beckman Instruments for a short time and then his own company Shockley Transistor Co., where he would use his reputation as a brilliant engineer to hire smarter people to surround himself with (at least he got that part right). His last claim to fame would be bringing those brilliant engineers together who would then change the world.

His team? Gordon Moore, C. Sheldon Roberts, Eugene Kleiner, Victor Grinich, Julius Blank, Jean Hoerni, Jay Last, and Bob Noyce. Any of these names sounding familiar? The guys would endure three days of intense psychological testing. They ignored the red flag of a control freak and took the opportunity to work in an exciting, burgeoning technology field in sunny California.

Soon after Shockley formed his startup, his eight engineers, who would birth the semiconductor industry and become our icons, walked out en masse. Shockley's people skills, or lack thereof, had killed the team's creativity. It was 1957 when Shockley's team that he would publicly brand "the Traitorous Eight," created Fairchild, the company that would spin off hundreds of Silicon Valley companies.

"His management style, to say it kindly, was *original*," says Eugene Kleiner, who would later build a legendary reputation in venture capital. "He tried to micromanage some very creative people. I've worked with different kinds of managers before—some were good, some were not good. He was unusual about the way he handled things. He tried to punish people, and it was very *unusual*. He almost treated us like children. It just didn't work."

Later, Shockley taught at Stanford but veered from technology and began spouting his very controversial views about IQ and race. He was burned in effigy on the campus. The moral of this story? The more things change, the more they stay the same. I don't have any explanation for Shockley's behavior with the exception that he was homeschooled during his formative years and never learned to play well with others. Had he learned to be a great manager who nurtured his creative staff, he might have died one of the Valley's giants instead of a despicable footnote.

COMPANY DIALOG THAT WORKS

Kim Polese, one of *Time Magazine*'s 25 Most Influential People in America, is at the helm of Marimba, Inc. (www.Marimba.com). Polese leads a successful Internet-based software solution company. So how does she run a company in which revenues are up and employees feel they're an intricate part of the company's successful bottom line?

Polese credits Marimba's high retention rate and spirit of teamwork among employees to listening. Marimba is the kind of company about which people say, 'I wish my CEO were like that.' If you have something to say to this CEO, come on in and have a seat. Is this an effective way to run a startup? Growth at Marimba has been steady, as are revenues—up $6.9 million— up 87 percent from 1998.

"One of the things that is critical about creating a solid company is the bond that people form in the workplace. It's about feeling like you're an important member of a whole team—the company itself. We don't want people to feel that they're here to do their one little job. Being connected to the company, to the executives, and to the other people who work at the company, is very important to employees. If you feel that you can ask questions or make comments to the people running the company, it makes a big difference."

—KIM POLESE, CEO, Marimba

So how did Polese arrive at her policies that seem to work so well? Polese was once an employee for a company that was at the same stage Marimba is currently. It was there where she first gleaned how helpful it would be to know what was going on in the rest of the company.

"I had a sense about how the company worked, but not completely," says Polese, who feels that being informed is important. "Back then, I felt pretty uninformed about how a company achieved market growth, about what kind of decisions a company makes when it decides what the next product will be, about how you actually go out in the marketplace and sell to the customer, and about the mechanics of winning a sale. I feel it's important to learn about these things because this is what career growth is all about. I want people at Marimba to know that they're not only here to perform a function, they're here to learn and grow."

Polese has implemented several programs to make sure employees are heard at Marimba. One of the programs is "Lunch with Kim," a monthly meeting for six to eight employees who join her for lunch at a local restaurant. If you work at Marimba, having lunch with your CEO is as simple as putting your name on a list.

The 188 Marimba employees clearly have an opportunity to sound off about what they feel is important about their jobs and environment. Polese feels that input from people who have a vested interest in what happens to a company is essential. "Basically, we're all moving so fast—every company out there is—that the six members of an executive team can't possibly have it all figured out. We don't know every nth degree of everything going on out there. We often aren't close enough to every issue or technology to be able to provide that kind of input.

"As a manager, when you lose touch with the people who work in your company," warns Polese, "you've really lost everything, because everything flows from communication. The successes you have in winning a deal, or in getting a product out the door come from people working together within the company to make those things happen. We're not just little islands unto ourselves, we're a team."

HERDING CATS

I've heard it said, and I wish I could remember by whom, that managing a startup team is like herding cats. With the small bit of managing of creative teams I do, I can see the issues that would arise daily—if not hourly—at a large startup. Creativity is such a tremendous force once it gets rolling. And roll it does. If you do anything to manage it, you may screw up momentum and be looked at as a micromanager. And as we've learned about the infamous micromanager, William Shockley, people will leave if you pull the reins in too tightly. So how do you keep the look and feel of a startup environment without stopping the creative juices from flowing?

"Group creativity begins with an idea—the vision of a singular person. Usually, a creation is built around a mental template, structured from experience or training—pure creation rarely occurs, if it exists at all. The best individual creations aren't spontaneous eruptions of ideas. They result from often frustrating trials. In other words, creativity is hard work."

—DONNA SHIRLEY, former manager of the Mars Exploration Project

Events such as the Mars landing don't happen on their own. It was Donna Shirley's personal vision that helped generate and harness the innovative creativity of the Mars Exploration Team to make the journey possible. Shirley, one-time manager of the Mars Exploration Project at the Jet Propulsion Laboratory (JPL), and current assistant dean of engineering at the University of Oklahoma and CEO of Managing Creativity (www.managingcreativity.com), knows that you have to dig deep and motivate to make a team work together flawlessly as one entity.

"This is an example of what occurs when creativity is sought, cultivated, and managed," says Shirley of her own management approach. "We formed and used a creative, diverse team to produce an innovative product within tight money constraints. When you manage creativity, you have to be ready to change the plan, be flexible," says Shirley, author of *Managing Martians* (Broadway Books), about creativity in the workplace. Shirley, the first woman to ever head a NASA program, was awarded the NASA Medal for Outstanding Leadership.

"You just have to keep revising. You must evaluate where you are throughout the process," suggests Shirley. "Command and control works just fine if you're running a sweatshop, but not if you're running a creative team. Anarchy doesn't work. Your team has to be motivated, but their energy must be directed toward a desired outcome. At the other end of the scale, slaves are not particularly productive and eventually will revolt. As a manager, achieving balance through teamwork—that area of productive, focused effort—is the secret to managing creativity."

SUMMARY

Internet startups are a different kind of beast. They attract the same types of talent that first sailed over from Europe to "discover" California: risk takers, dreamers, and daredevils. These people cannot be managed; they are cultivated, they are encouraged, and they are too smart to stay somewhere that doesn't treat them with respect. And they will walk, they will walk long, before they vest, if not before they even get a pink slip. And just like any other wild animal, they need to be tempted to come join you, and they will need to be treated with respect if you want them to stay.

If you trust your intuition and those working closely with you to make the right hiring decisions, you will, in turn, need to trust your brilliant employees to do their very best. If you follow a code of ethics and remember what it was like to be someone else's employee, you will hopefully be rewarded with an excellent company that will go on to become part of dot-com history.

CHAPTER 9

SAY BUH-BYE
Your Exit Strategy

T he exit strategy is the most controversial thing you'll consider once you have your revenue model in place. There
are many schools of thought on the subject. Some say you
absolutely need one; others are clear they won't believe it if
you do propose an exit strategy. I say that perhaps it's wise to
err on the side of being prepared. This is probably something a
dreamer like you doesn't have in the forefront of your mind, but
the exit strategy is something you should always have in a
PowerPoint slide ready to present if the pitch calls for it.

There are a lot of reasons for having an exit strategy—is the
first and foremost being that your investors want to know when
they can expect their money back. They're not a nonprofit after
all, and they will expect a return—a big return for the risk they
took to invest in you. So what's it going to be? Merger? Acquisition? IPO?

"You want to know their perception of what the exit strategy is," says Tom Bevilacqua, chief strategic investment officer for E*TRADE Group, Inc., and managing general partner of E*TRADE Venture Capital. "Sometimes they'll come in and say they want to do an IPO in six months; you look at the company, and you look at what they're doing, and you know it's not possible. I want to know what the company's strategy is. Is it an IPO? Is it an acquisition? And when will one of those liquidity events be likely? What kind of timeframe are we looking at? If you look at a company and they say that they want an IPO in an incredibly short time and they have crazy valuation expectations—well, that usually tells you that the CEO is pretty naïve."

Why is an exit strategy so important to some people? Obviously, venture funds would like to see returns on their money, but they want to know when you're planning on making a move that will allow them to get their money back. It's just business to these guys, nothing personal. Some angel groups and individual angels are well off, not bloody rich. This means for a well-off angel to invest in you, they'll want to know—in a good scenario—when they will see a return.

This information will also help them gauge your progress and let them knock off the milestones as you meet those challenges. And if you're not on target, you'll also feel the pressure to do something, especially if one of the angels is on your board. Other angel groups that are not into investing in technology for a quick buck and understand cycles, choose their members carefully know not to expect returns until the company is ready to do the right thing for it.

"No, I never have an exit strategy planned—you're not starting a company to exit. If you're starting a company to exit, you can save yourself a lot of trouble by not starting it in the first place."
—STEVE KIRSCH, founder of Infoseek, Mouse Systems, Frame Technology, and Propel

Different investors—angel and VC, individual and group—have different motivations for their investments. When they ask you what your exit strategy is, ask them about their expectation for your exit strategy.

Carol Sands, managing partner of The Angels' Forum, LLC, and The Halo Fund, has a philosophy about her investments that follows throughout her group.

"Investors are asking the wrong question if they ask the entrepreneur what their exit strategy will be," says Sands. "At The Angels' Forum, we want to invest in companies that are built to last. This means that the company has a plan for continuous growth and profitability. A truly successful company will have a choice of going public or being acquired. We all like having to make that choice. Give me that problem any day!"

THE FALLOUT AND CONSOLIDATION AHEAD

The IPO isn't what it used to be. As soon as you say that your plan is to go for an IPO during a pitch, you'll probably be greeted with rolling eyes. A good number of the CEOs I know who were planning on going public in 2000 and what kinds of companies pulled the paperwork because the market wasn't strong enough for them to go public. Now about 75 percent of those are looking for stronger partners to acquire them; the rest are looking to partner with younger companies with valuable technology, waiting for the market to beef up a bit before they try again.

Everyone has a different idea about what the future of dot-com will look like. Will there be another fallout in our future? Some are already bracing for it by accelerating their growth via mergers and acquisitions (M&A). Companies have been doing M&A for what seems like millennia. It's only in this new economy that these mergers and acquisitions have been done at such a frenzied pace. Startups are buying startups to beef up their technology, hoping it will be enough to carry them through the next patch of trouble in the market.

"One funny observation from my perspective is that, ever since we went public, people have been asking, 'When is the consolidation going to happen?' And my argument to that is, 'It's always been happening.' People have been buying other companies, consolidating, and trying to get scaled from the very get-go," says Joe Kraus, Cofounder of Excite@Home (which went public in '96 and merged with @Home in '99). "I think it's only recently that it's not so much that consolidation has been happening more rapidly but you're starting to see some reasonable pricing for that consolidation, and I do think it's happening at a little more rapid clip—that's for sure. I believe consolidation will continue. I think that the dynamics of scale continue to play here, meaning that the bay will continue to get bigger. Look at Excite@Home, Yahoo—those kinds of businesses work because they have tens of millions of customers. So I think the consolidation will continue—the age of promiscuous capital has come to a sunset. I don't know whether the sun is coming back up again, but I do think the whole notion of promiscuous capital will continue to fade."

GROWTH MAKES LIFE EXCITING

Making the decision to follow through with any exit plan can be sticky. Many people have personal reasons why they want to sell out after having worked so hard to build a company. There are so many millionaires floating around the Valley who have done just that.

You may get an offer for an exit and have to think about what you personally want to do, what your partners want to do, and what's best for your company. There's always a chance that your partners will offer you a buyout if you want to go your own way. Often enough, people are steeped so thick in the business that an offer broadsides them.

So now you're sitting around this boardroom after three years. You've come up on the radar of a company like Cisco or Microsoft—they want to buy you out. You know they already have a product like yours, with just slightly better technology. Your technology could be faster with more time, but by then they may have slaughtered you with their marketing dollars and left you twitching in the rearview mirror. A large corporation may see you as a threat to fragment the market. They see a simple solution, buy you out. The offer they have on the table will offer your people severance packages. It will allow you to return many-fold what your investors gave you (so there might be some pressure from the member of the venture arm or angel group sitting on your board). And you? You will have enough money in the bank to immediately start or invest in another company, and shed that little 27-foot sailboat you have down at the dock and buy that 80-foot and a membership at the harbor.

With such an obvious offer from the competition, you know they don't plan on doing anything with your wonderful product except keep it on a respirator long enough to salvage the customer list and pull the still beating heart of its technology out of it and transplant it.

Death? Yeah, somewhat. But that's your name all over that still-beating heart, the one being put inside of Bill Gates' or John Chambers' metaphorical chest, along with all of those other hearts they've consumed over the years. Can you look at this decision as an *it's only commerce* scenario? Or will they pull you away from the table, contracts signed, your knuckles white and still clinging, weeping hysterically. Will all that cash make the pain go away? You need to know your limitations before you talk about exit strategies. You'll have to do some soul searching for this one.

"We closed round A in January, 1995. We sat there with a buyout offer at the same time we were closing," says Joe Kraus, co-founder of Excite@Home. "A company named Verity wanted to buy us for $3 million, and we had $3 million in financing. We sat there in one of those many couch moments, where we had these two ratty couches and we put them together facing one another, three people on each side. We each gave this impassioned plea about what we wanted to do, started at about one in the morning, and we ended up split right down the middle. Three wanted to take the financing, and the three others wanted to sell. So the three others went for a walk and came back an hour later and said, 'We're in, let's do it.' We were so excited we wanted to go to Vegas, but there were no more flights, so we had our celebratory dinner at Denny's in Cupertino and we all had Moons Over My Hammy."

ECONOMIES OF SCALE

Many times in your entrepreneurial life you'll make decisions based on your wallet. Then again, maybe you'll make those decisions based on gut instincts, or intuition, as we women like to call it. Sometimes it will be your partners or your board who will make those decisions for you. One way or another, partnerships and acquisitions will one day become a part of your world, and you will have to make tough decisions.

"Probably our biggest set of mistakes [in the early days] was around this notion that we knew it was going to be big," says Joe Kraus, co-founder of Excite@Home. "The biggest mistakes relate to the word *scale* and our notion of not thinking about, or not preparing for, our business to be as big as it could be. A classic example, Lycos was originally a Carnegie Mellon University project they decided to spin out. We had an opportunity to bid for that technology. We had a million dollars in the bank and it was clear that the bid would be about $3 million. I couldn't see a way to bridge the gap. I thought, 'We don't have $3 million, how can we bid for them?' Plus, we're working on our own stuff. We didn't realize that the value of early consolidation would be tremendous. Instead of paying $3 million, we allowed a multi-billion dollar competitor to emerge.

"You're not thinking that way in the early days, you're just trying to survive," says Kraus. "So we didn't make an offer, but at least we didn't repeat the mistake. An example of that is when Netscape put their two buttons up for bid—the search and the directory buttons. There were three bidders for that spot: us, Infoseek, and an MCI offering. Nobody remembers that MCI actually tried to get into the portal business really early on. We had a million dollars then, and we bid three-million bucks and lost. But we didn't give up. We called them for twenty-one days straight. We sat in their lobby unannounced; we made pains in the ass of ourselves. And when MCI couldn't deliver, we got the deal back. We certainly wouldn't be here today in the position we are in had we not won that deal. You learn from your mistakes, hopefully. Particularly around scale.

"Opportunities don't come around very often, and you better jump on them, even if they mean spending more money than you have and figuring out a way to pay for them. One of the key lessons I always talk about is the value of pure persistence. Nothing has benefited us more—nothing—than just being persistent. I credit that lesson one-hundred percent to Vinod Khosla [the company's VC at Kleiner-Perkins]; he is the most persistent human I've ever met."

BIRDS OF A FEATHER FLOCK TOGETHER

As the CEO of Half.com, a startup located in Pennsylvania, Joshua Kopelman founded a company that immediately took off. Before he founded Half.com, he had just left Infonautics, a company he had founded that went public in 1996. He left

Infonautics with an investment from the company in 1999 and built Half.com. The company—based on the premise that a buyer and a seller can be put together to buy and sell mass market goods, with the website taking a 15 percent cut of the deal as a broker's fee—began receiving a lot of attention from auction bulletin boards. Things changed quickly for the company when it talked the town of Half Way, Oregon, into changing its name for a year to Half.com. The company placed a simple full-page map ad in the Industry Standard that said, *Welcome to Half.com, somewhere between eBay and Amazon. And not to mention Hell's Canyon and the Oregon Trail*, and history began to take motion.

"I was interviewed by Katie Couric live on the "Today" show, interviewed by *The Wall Street Journal, Time, Newsweek*," says Kopelman. "Half.com got known as the first dot-com company to own a ZIP code, the first dot-com town in the world. It was a small town, and we told them, 'We'd love to put our name on the map, we'd love to help you put your name on the map, it clearly could help tourism.' And we also helped them by building websites for all of the cottage industries in the town. We gave their school twenty Internet-ready computers and some small funds for economic development. It got us an incredible amount of visibility when we launched."

"We were more focused on a good business rather than building a good exit strategy. In all of my VC pitches, there was never a slide that said 'exit strategy.' We were not building this to do a quick IPO; we were not doing this quick acquisition. This was built to be a real, sustaining business."
—JOSHUA KOPELMAN, CEO of Half.com

Half.com immediately made itself a player by ramping up to a million users in no time at all, and they soon found eBay calling.

"The contact was, 'Hey you're in our space, what are you doing?' I was very apprehensive about it. I've been an eBay user since '97. I was a big fan and thought they were an incredible company. I didn't know what the call was about. So then we began some conversations, and there were a whole spectrum of things we could do together. We could do nothing, they could invest in us, we could buy ads on their site, we could partner together—these types of relationships take many forms. It was a process of discussing and brainstorming and holding a few meetings. We decided we would take it slowly.

"The site was just starting to get traction, and our tech team was working hours on end just to keep the site growing," says Kopelman. "We didn't know what they wanted, so we decided to not tell our employees because there was a good chance nothing would come of it. We didn't want anyone taking their eyes off the ball. We were very cautious; we didn't tell them anything confidential or sign any NDAs for at least a few months. Then, over time, they saw that we were growing, and we weren't going away."

"What ended up happening was that the management team, the culture of the company, the way the company evolved—it built a prepotency for rapid adjustment and rapid mutation."
—JOSHUA KOPELMAN, CEO of Half.com

Before and after the decision was made, Kopelman and his company had some other difficult decisions to make. "Ask anyone on my management team—I worry a lot. My fingernails are gnawed to nothing. As CEO, my job is to obsess, and I think of every little thing that could go wrong. The deal is still ready to close. Look at Columbia House and CD Now—they announced a great deal, and it fell through. We're still running the company and don't want anyone to take their eye off the ball. The real benefit that eBay provides us is that it's going to accelerate our growth. So I view it as an accelerating event to help us fulfill our mission rather than an exit. Our whole management team is staying on board and we're still hiring, so the basic strategy will stay the same.

"One of the things that the negotiations process reaffirmed for me was the similarities in culture [of company culture] and that was extremely important to me," says Kopelman of the deal. "I wanted to make sure it wasn't going to be an exit for me, I still wanted to make sure I wasn't giving up my baby and giving up my say in the baby as well. Part of the reason I liked the deal was that we were going to be running as a separate stand-alone company. And while [eBay was] going to be the sole shareholder of the company, I was going to be the president of the company, and the mission is still the same—let's grow this business.

"Everyone I met at eBay were just very smart people. The culture of the company was so similar to ours that, as we ultimately expanded the fact that we were talking to these guys, some of the members of our management team were all really hitting it off and saw the value that they had. The negotiations were not easy—these things are never easy. The deal was in the middle of the stock market readjustment. You look at their stock price today, fifty—it was over one-hundred while we were having some of these discussions. Both companies saw the value we could offer each other. They have fourteen-hundred employees right now, we have less than seventy, and I'd say we're a little more nimble. One of the benefits of a startup, one of the things about startups, is speed. Speed has been our whole culture here—speed of execution, speed of delivery—and I think that was something they wanted to maintain, as well. I was happy about that. I feel we are still in our infancy. I think we might have just finished the preface of the book; we haven't even gotten to chapter one yet."

"If you want speed, you don't lock yourself into anything—we signed no long term contracts [before the deal with eBay], not even for real estate."
—JOSHUA KOPELMAN, CEO of Half.com

"I really see myself and the company executing the plan," says Kopelman of what the acquisition means to the future growth of Half.com. "It freed me from dealing with fund-raising—and don't let any entrepreneur tell you it's less than sixty percent of their job. They're lying if they do. And it lets me focus on the long term and provides some incredible assets—the fact that they have over twelve-million members, and our original business plan didn't show us hitting twelve-million members until the year 2003. So it just gives us such a resource to tap into knowledge when we have ideas or problems.

"There is so much to be done here. We're only in four categories and we've identified over twenty-five categories we want to expand into. We're only in the U.S. now, and we want to go international. We're only in consumer goods; we haven't even talked about B2B goods. There are so many ways this concept can be expanded. You know you're really having fun at your job when you're not thinking of the next business but you're thinking about how to improve the current one. I wake up in the middle of the night not for ideas for a new business, but about what we really need to do at this one. I'm still in the honeymoon period. I like to think of myself as creating businesses and I don't think Half.com is ready at the point where I can say, 'It's a business, my job here is done.' "

MASTER OF HIS OWN DOMAIN

If there is one underdog startup team that all of the Bay Area is rooting for, it's craigslist.org. At the helm of this motley crew is Craig Newmark, CEO and founder. Newmark started the craigslist community in 1995, a site listing apartments, personals, announcements, etc., as a way to help his friends find apartments and jobs and built it one listing at a time. Craigslist was also the site people looked to for a listing of cool Net-related events. Then the site added jobs, personal items for sale and housing as the Bay Area's housing shortage began.

Now that the site has become a success and has local sites in Boston, New York City, DC, Portland, Seattle, Los Angeles, San Diego, Chicago, Sydney, and Melbourne, Newmark has more options than ever. The programmer-turned-entrepreneur never took a cent of venture funding and has boot-strapped the entire operation to profitability and is giving sites like Monster.com and other IT job sites a run for their money.

All of this has made the site a desirable acquisition or buyout possibility. The big issue for Newmark is sticking to his non-exploitative commitments. The site has no cookies or other embedded tracking code, and he wants to keep it that way.

Newmark is an ethical guy in this sometimes-sleazy dot-com business. He puts everything up to vote each time something on the site is changed, and the members of his community have a voice in what goes down. He requests feedback from the community regarding every significant issue, personally reads it all, and acts on the consensus, letting people know all about it. So chances are, if Newmark does take a buyout or partnership offer one step further, the readership will have a final say on the sale. Now these are not people who are stockowners, or people who even pay a membership fee...these are *his* people. The people he has committed to keep happy.

"We have no exit strategy whatsoever; we're in this for the long run, because we're about providing a modest platform for the human voice on the Net and restore some of the early values of Net culture."
—CRAIG NEWMARK, CEO, craigslist.org

"We want to preserve the spirit of the community," says a protective Newmark. "Basically we've had two solid offers. The first was a few years ago when [the site] was just me," says Newmark. "Microsoft's Sidewalk approached us about running banner ads. Just from that alone, I would have made enough to live comfortably. But, at that point, I was already an overpaid contract programmer. More recently, we were offered a buyout that would have included a few million plus equity. But the amount of control they wanted would have meant we turned corporate, which probably would have meant we would have killed the site, at least in spirit.

"As entrepreneurs, my team and I knew the company would be worth more if we just kept plugging away—so why risk the community for a quick gain? We're in it for the long haul and we intend to keep making it a better place for all of our users."

Newmark describes the buyout offer coming from a company whose model was building a collection of sites for IT professionals. "It was tempting, but the spirit of the site would have been damaged, and that would not have been cool. I don't see a buyout in the future. Right now, revenue-wise, we're making a comfortable living."

Craig has not let success go to his head. He drives an eight-year-old Saturn and seems to have both feet planted firmly on the ground. "My dream is to have craigslist everywhere, and to do so with a human voice and, thereby, change the Net a little and, thereby, change the world a little."

TAKING STOCK IN WHAT YOU HAVE

When Jim Drury, CFO and executive VP for StockMaster.com, decided to temporarily leave his position at BenefitStreet.com where he served as CEO, he was strapping himself in for a wild ride. He took StockMaster.com from six to 60 employees and proved you could successful run a company without raising much money.

"[Bringing stock updates to users] wasn't necessarily revolutionary, but that area was sticky," says Drury of the company when he took the CFO position and began pushing the company harder by finding more funds and developing strategies. "Even though StockMaster, at the time, was not one of the top ten financial sites, it still had a huge potential for market cap, and that's what we were able to achieve. Mark [Torrance, Stock-Master's chairman and CEO] had various buyout offers before and after I met him. It was this jewel that needed to execute on scalability, and then it would end up being fifty times the valuation of early offers."

StockMaster soon became a contender in the crowded market of stock sites. The company's assets soon included online stock charting, a premier source of in-depth online investment information, research tools, and customized investor-relations technologies.

"Then we hit that baby out of the ballpark," says Drury about the event that changed the company forever. "We ended up with a multi-party bidding war. We had hired an investment bank to supplement our own contacts. We did the typical analysis and made a list of all of the acquisitions candidates and strategic partners. We were going to look at either a large investment or an M&A. It was a long list a lot of people that would be interested in a finance site, and we had a lot of users—1.5 million registered users who spent a lot of time on our site compared to most sites. We actually got some good interest from Lycos, Alta Vista, and CNET; but the first written offer was from NBCi, and shortly after that, we had strong interest from AOL.

"And then Red Herring came in. We met with them while we had a written letter of intent signed by NBCi. We were chosen by Broadview Capital Partners, who were counseling Red Herring, and told [Red Herring] that they didn't have enough Internet users or owned technology, and they made a list of companies. Red Herring said, 'Sounds like a great company.' We listened to their pitch about why we should talk to them, and we said, 'We have a signed letter of intent, and we have to the end of the day to reach a deal.' We couldn't say who it was with. Mark was not at the meeting, and we called him and said, 'Do not sign that.' We met with them for a couple of hours. We postponed NBCi over the weekend—it was a Friday. It's not that there was a better synergy, or a better fit. We took a risk. It was a new party—it was like a new date. We had only known them for twenty-four hours. Now months have gone from a statement of intent to a binding agreement to a lot of integrating, and a closing is scheduled for July."

On May 16, 2000, Red Herring Communications acquired StockMaster.com and became part of the Redherring.com network.

M&A PRESS

A merger or acquisition is always a great excuse to write a press release and generate press for the files. This is a way for a company to throw as many partners' names in as possible and post some impressive statistics about what the new acquisition will do for the company's valuation.

The StockMaster.com acquisition tripled Redherring.com's user base, increased its team by 30 percent, added powerful tools and growing revenue streams, and brought exceptional engineering and technical capabilities to the network, propelling it to the forefront of financial content sites. The StockMaster.com acquisition follows the $31 million in equity funding Red Herring received from an investment led by Broadview Capital Partners, a late-stage private equity fund, with additional participation from ZDNet, which operates a leading Web destination. The money was raised to accelerate the development of Redherring.com as the site for the critical business and investing information needs of its users.

LATE TO THE DANCE

Scores of companies pulled their IPOs after April 2000. Why enter into a market that won't support you? Many CEOs are waiting to see what the market will do, anticipating the day they refile for the IPO. These are scary times filled with unpredictability.

"It is fascinating to see the change in which investors view the GirlGeeks business model, pre and post the April, 2000, market correction—as it is lovingly referred to. Before April, I stopped counting the number of times that people told the other co-founder and I that we weren't thinking big enough, we weren't moving fast enough. Every so often, we would stop and scratch our heads and wonder, 'Was there something to what they were saying?' But we knew that we were building GirlGeeks the right way, slow but sure. We want to be around for a long, long time and build the company with a foundation that works and can withstand the pressure of a volatile market and changing trends in the economy. So far, so good. We keep our burn rate low, consistently reanalyze our priorities, and we have been extremely fortunate to hire excellent individuals who know the value of a dollar."
—KRISTINE HANNA, CEO and president, GirlGeeks

"I had all of these fantasies that it would get better quicker, but pulling the IPO was good for us," says William Lohse, CEO of SmartAge. "Now, I'm concentrating on the next round. It's a challenge, but it's the same challenge as it's been my entire career. I've raised a lot of money during my career, and it was always the same thing except for the last two years [before April 15], those years were easy. We raised $50 million so far, and we're going to raise another $50 million and, if all goes well, this is the last cash we'll need to get to cash flow and profitability.

"It seems as though everything is timing," says Lohse. "You look back and learn from failure. So I ask myself 'What could I have done to get the company to go public sooner?' Now I can imagine a lot of things, but this feels so much like timing. Tigers are tigers, and cycles are cycles, and the market does what it does. The lucky thing is that we're performing, and the company is operating, and I have the best management team I've ever had in my entire career.

"The consensus is that pulling the IPO was a good thing, and we were just late to the IPO. Now we're bigger and in better shape and more mature. It's not like what companies had to do in the past to go public anymore. It seems like there's been uncertainty and confusion about what the matrix are, and how to deliver on those matrix and to bridge the gap of what they jokingly call growing into one's evaluations. If we fail, I will feel very bad—it would be $50 million of my friends' money so far. I've never lost money for anyone in my life, and I've made billions for my friends."

Lohse recently landed $35 million to continue building SmartAge to profitability.

SUMMARY

The thing about an exit strategy is that, one way or another, the odds are you'll probably one day be facing one. Whether you're trying to sell your technology because your company is drowning and you need a life preserver to exit gracefully, or because you're doing so well everyone is courting you for an M&A, you *will* come to a crossroads. Who knows? You may one day even be doing well enough (and the market may be strong enough) for you to file for an IPO. To ready for such an event, you need to get your team together and discuss the options. Make sure everyone is on the same page and thinking realistically, or you will have problems later.

EXECUTIVE SUMMARY AND SAMPLE DOCUMENTS

This book will be a great resource as you build your startup, but inevitably you'll want more information about a broad range of topics of concern when building a startup. Here's what you'll find in this appendix:

- An outline and excerpt from the business plan of iPrint, Inc.

- Sample contracts from *Internet Legal Forms for Business* by J. Dianne Brinson and Mark F. Radcliffe

- A copyright development and transfer agreement

- A website development and maintenance agreement

- A domain name assignment agreement

iPrint, Inc. First Executive Summary

iPrint.com was generous enough to allow me to share its executive summary, which it was in its early years. iPrint.com has a business that revolutionized the printing industry... The natural evolution of printing was a concept that flowed naturally into the Internet industry. I believe that companies will find protection from the fallout and consolidation ahead by using such transferable business models based in a real need.

iPrint, Inc.

Part I: Business Plan

Presented by:

Royal P. Farros, CEO

NASA Ames Research Center

Building N223 • Suite 108 • Mail Stop 223-5

Moffett Field, CA 94035

Telephone: 415.604.2410

Fax: 415.604.2470

E-mail: royal@iPrint.com

iPrint Discount Printing & CyberStationery Shop

www.iPrint.com

This document has been submitted on a confidential basis solely for the benefit of selected, highly qualified analysts and investors and is not for use by other people. It may not be reproduced, stored, copied, faxed, or distributed in any form without written permission from iPrint, Inc. By accepting delivery of this plan, the recipient agrees to return this copy to the corporation at the address listed above.

CONTENTS

EXECUTIVE SUMMARY

"The Internet will almost certainly have a stronger impact than the PC... a reasonable guess might put it ahead of the telephone and television but behind the printing press."

—The Economist, July 1, 1995

The bank ATM took the most popular *serviced* transactions and made them *self-service,* therefore changing the cost structure of the banking industry.

Enabled by the Internet, Amazon.com (NASD: AMZN) made the book buying process *self-service* and therefore more convenient, more efficient, and more cost-effective.

iPrint, Inc. will have these same effects on the commercial and quick printing industry, starting with the $20.6 billion stationery, business forms, and specialty advertising market.

Having created the only electronic commerce *environment* specifically designed to automate mass market custom printing over the Internet, iPrint allows print buyers to interactively create, proof, and buy professionally printed materials in a way that revolutionizes the printing industry.

In a near commodity-oriented industry, iPrint's self-service, "What-You-See-Is-What-You-Get," automated approach

- *dramatically improves* the customer experience.

- *drastically reduces* cost structure.

IPRINT'S MISSION

iPrint's mission is to be the online "connection" between print buyers and commercial printers, thus participating in virtually every target printing transaction in the new online world.

iPrint will accomplish this by partnering with commercial and quick printers, as well as with Internet organizations, that control specific production, customer segments, and traffic, essentially employing a "best neutral partner" strategy which will allow iPrint to scale quickly while raising an important barrier-to-entry for future competition.

TECHNICAL ACHIEVEMENT

iPrint has accomplished the very difficult technology component (Phase I) of its growth plan. iPrint has created—and is currently operating—one of the most sophisticated, interactive, revenue-producing e-commerce websites on the Internet, a formidable development achievement.

NOW OPEN FOR BUSINESS

The complete iPrint "e-tailing" environment for professional printing <u>has no direct competition</u> on the Internet. iPrint has received overwhelmingly positive customer approval, won numerous Web awards, including the prestigious WebMaster Top 50 Internet Site Award, and has garnered the following written accolades <u>that best sum up the iPrint opportunity</u>:

"iPrint will likely cause another **major shift** in how these [printed] products are bought and sold over the next several years."
—Hard Copy Supplies Journal, January 1997

"iPrint has shown that it has the technology to **achieve its aim**, and the company has attracted considerable press buzz as well as support from many printers and a couple of large technology companies."
—Jonathan Burke, Red Herring "Hits," Spring 1997

KEY BUSINESS PARTNERSHIPS

iPrint has made solid headway creating business partnerships. (Exhibit B has a complete list.) Here are four of note:

- **Sir Speedy**. The world's largest chain of quick printers. iPrint will create and host Sir Speedy's online custom print shop.

- The $4.3 billion **CUC International**. iPrint is the exclusive print shop in CUC's new "Business Advantage" membership club.

- **Netscape.** iPrint is Netscape's "Premier Example Site" for showcasing their new electronic commerce "Canvas" (kiosk) technology.

- **BCT**. The largest thermographer to the printing trade. BCT is iPrint's first commercial backend printer. BCT is partnering with iPrint in negotiations with chains such as Office-Max, the third largest office supply chain in the country.

LAUNCHING THE NEXT PHASE

With actual customer validation and the recent addition of our "clustering" (scaling) component, iPrint is now ready to ramp. iPrint, Inc. is raising $3 million in equity financing to launch the marketing and sales phase of the iPrint business opportunity.

YEARS	REVENUES	EXPENSES	PRETAX INCOME
1996	$0	$234,770	($234,770)
1997	$328,628	$1,325,066	($996,438)
1998	$8,012,293	$9,644,185	($1,631,892)
1999	$20,321,060	$20,613,881	$292,821

SAMPLE CONTRACTS

These sample contracts are taken from *Internet Legal Forms for Business*, by J. Dianne Brinson and Mark F. Radcliffe, a partner in the law firm Gray, Cary Ware & Freidenrich in Palo Alto. The domain name assignment agreement was authored by Katherine C. Spelman and Jason D. Firth, of Steinhart & Falconer, and revised by J. Dianne Brinson. *Internet Legal Forms for Business* and the latest Brinson/Radcliffe book, *Internet Law and Business Handbook*, are available for purchase at **www.laderapress.com**. (This book includes some of the forms set forth in this Appendix.) Sample chapters from the books are posted on that website.

COPYRIGHT DEVELOPMENT AND TRANSFER AGREEMENT

THIS AGREEMENT ("Agreement") is entered into by and between _____ (the "Client") and _____ (the "Contractor") on the _____ (the "Effective Date").

NOW, THEREFORE, in consideration of the promises and mutual covenants and agreements set forth herein, the parties agree as follows:

1. Engagement of Services. Contractor agrees to perform services for client as follows: _____ ("Project"). Contractor may not subcontract or otherwise delegate its obligations under this Agreement without Client's prior written consent. Contractor agrees to perform the services in a professional manner and to complete the Project by _____.

2.   Compensation.

2.1   Fees and Approved Expenses. Client will pay Contractor the fee of
_____ for services rendered by Contractor pursuant to this Agreement. Contractor will not be reimbursed for any expenses incurred in connection with the performance of services under this Agreement, unless those expenses are approved in advance and in writing by Client or listed in Exhibit A as Reimbursable Expenses.

2.2   Payment Due. Client will review the Work Product within
_____ (__) days after receiving it from Contractor to ensure that it meets the Project requirements stated in Section 1. If Client does not give written notice of rejection to Contractor within that time period (describing the reasons for the rejection in reasonable detail), the Work Product will be deemed to be accepted. Client will pay Contractor for services and will reimburse Contractor for previously approved expenses within _____ (__) days after acceptance.

3.   Independent Contractor Relationship. Contractor and Client understand, acknowledge, and agree that Contractor's relationship with Client will be that of an independent contractor and nothing in this Agreement is intended to or should be construed to create a partnership, joint venture, or employment relationship.

4.   Trade Secrets and Confidential Information

4.1   Third-Party Information. Contractor represents that his performance of all of the terms of this Agreement does not and will not breach any agreement to keep in confidence proprietary information, knowledge or data of a third party, and Contractor will not disclose to Client, or induce Client to use, any confidential or proprietary information belonging to third parties unless such use or disclosure is authorized in writing by such owners.

4.2   Confidential Information. Contractor agrees during the term of this Agreement and thereafter to take all steps reasonably necessary to hold in trust and confidence information which he knows or has reason to know is considered confidential by Client (Confidential Information).   Contractor agrees to use the Confidential Information solely to perform the Project hereunder. Confidential Information includes, but is not limited to, technical and business information relating to Client's inventions or products, research and development, manufacturing and engineering processes, and future business plans. Contractor's obligations with respect to the Confidential Information also extend to any third party's proprietary or confidential information disclosed to Contractor in the course of providing services to Client. This obligation shall not extend to any information which becomes generally known to the public without breach of this Agreement. This obligation shall survive the termination of this Agreement.

5.   Ownership of Work Product.

5.1   Definition. "Work Product" means the works of authorship conceived or developed by Contractor while performing the Project services.

5.2   Assignment. Contractor hereby irrevocably assigns, conveys and otherwise transfers to Client, and its respective successors and assigns, all rights, title and interests worldwide in and to the Work Product and all copyrights, contract and licensing rights, and claims and causes of action of any kind with respect to any of the foregoing, whether now known or hereafter to become known (except as stated otherwise in Section 5.3). In the event Contractor has any rights in and to the Work Product that cannot be assigned to Client, Contractor hereby unconditionally and irrevocably waives the enforcement of all such rights, and all claims and causes of action of any kind with respect to any of the foregoing against Client, its distributors and customers, whether now known or hereafter to become known and agrees, at the request and expense of Client and its respective successors and assigns, to consent to and join in any action to enforce such rights and to procure a waiver of such rights from the holders of such rights. In the event Contractor has any rights in and to the Work Product that cannot be assigned to Client and cannot be waived, Contractor hereby grants to Client, and its respective successors and assigns, an exclusive, worldwide, royalty-free license during the term of the rights to reproduce, distribute, modify, publicly perform and publicly display, with the right to sublicense through multiple tiers of sublicensees, and the right to assign such rights in and to the Work Product including, without limitation, the right to use in any way whatsoever the Work Product. Contractor retains no rights to use the Work Product except as stated in Exhibit B and agrees not to challenge the validity of the copyright ownership by Client in the Work Product.

5.3   Ownership of Components. Contractor will retain copyright ownership of the following components: _____ ("Retained Components"). However, Contractor grants to Client a royalty-free, worldwide, perpetual, irrevocable, nonexclusive license, with the right to sublicense through multiple tiers of sublicensees, to reproduce, distribute, modify, publicly perform and publicly display the Retained Components on any Web site operated by or for Client and in marketing material.

5.4   Power of Attorney. Contractor agrees to assist Client in any reasonable manner to obtain and enforce for Client's benefit copyrights covering the Work Product in any and all countries. Contractor agrees to execute, when requested, copyright, or similar applications and assignments to Client, and any other lawful documents deemed necessary by Client to carry out the purpose of this Agreement. Contractor further agrees that the obligations and undertaking stated in this Section 5.4 will continue beyond the termination of Contractor's service to Client. If called upon to render assistance under this Section 5.4, Contractor will be entitled to a fair and reasonable fee in addition to reimbursement of authorized expenses incurred at the prior written request of Client. In the event that Client is unable for any reason whatsoever to secure Contractor's signature to any lawful and necessary document required to apply for or execute any patent, copyright or other applications with respect to any Work Product, Contractor hereby irrevocably designates and appoints Client and its duly authorized officers and agents as his agents and attorneys-in-fact to act for and in his behalf and instead of Contractor, to execute and file any such application and to do all other lawfully permitted acts to further the prosecution and issuance of copyrights or other similar rights thereon with the same legal force and effect as if executed by Contractor.

6.   Return of Client's Property. Contractor acknowledges that Client's sole and exclusive property includes all documents, such as drawings, manuals, notebooks, reports, sketches, records, computer programs, employee lists, customer lists and the like in his custody or possession, whether delivered to Contractor by Client or made by Contractor in the performance of services under this Agreement, relating to the business activities of Client or its customers or suppliers and containing any information or data whatsoever, whether or not Confidential Information. Contractor agrees to deliver promptly all of Client's property and all copies of Client's property in Contractor's possession to Client at any time upon Client's request.

7.   Warranties. Contractor represents and warrants that:

(a) The Work Product was created solely by him, his full-time employees during the course of their employment, or independent contractors who assigned all right, title and interest worldwide in their work to Contractor.

(b) Contractor is the owner of all right, title and interest in the tangible forms of the Work Product and all intellectual property rights protecting them. The Work Product and the intellectual property rights protecting them are free and clear of all encumbrances, including, without limitation, security interests, licenses, liens, charges or other restrictions;

(c) Contractor has maintained the Work Product in confidence.

(d) The use, reproduction, distribution, or modification of the Work Product does not and will not violate the rights of any third parties in the Work Product including, but not limited to, copyrights, trade secrets, trademarks, publicity and privacy.

(e) The Work Product is not in the public domain.

(f) Contractor has full power and authority to make and enter into this Agreement.

8.   Indemnification. Contractor agrees to defend, indemnify, and hold harmless Client, their officers, directors, sublicensees, employees and agents, from and against any claims, actions or demands, including without limitation reasonable legal and accounting fees, alleging or resulting from the breach of the warranties in Section 7. Client shall provide notice to Contractor promptly of any such claim, suit, or proceeding and shall assist Contractor, at Contractor's expense, in defending any such claim, suit or proceeding.

9.   General Provisions. This Agreement will be governed by and construed in accordance with the laws of the United States and the State of _____ as applied to agreements entered into and to be performed entirely within that state between residents of that state. This Agreement, including any Exhibits to this Agreement, constitutes the entire agreement between the parties relating to this subject matter and supersedes all prior or simultaneous representations, discussions, negotiations, and agreements, whether written or oral. The Agreement may not be modified except by written instrument signed by both parties. No term or provision hereof will be considered waived by either party, and no breach excused by either party, unless such waiver or consent is in writing signed on behalf of the party against whom the waiver is asserted. No consent by either party to, or waiver of, a breach by either party, whether express or implied, will constitute a consent to, waiver of, or excuse of any other, different, or subsequent breach by either party. Contractor may not assign its rights or obligations arising under this Agreement without Client's prior written consent. Client may assign its rights and obligations under this Agreement. This Agreement will be for the benefit of Client's successors and assigns, and will be binding on Contractor's heirs, legal representatives and permitted assignees. If any dispute arises between the parties with respect to the matters covered by this Agreement which leads to a proceeding to resolve such dispute, the prevailing party in such proceeding shall be entitled to receive its reasonable attorneys' fees, expert witness fees and out-of-pocket costs incurred in connection with such proceeding, in addition to any other relief to which it may be entitled. All notices, requests and other communications required to be given under this Agreement must be in writing, and must be mailed by registered or certified mail, postage prepaid and return receipt requested, or delivered by hand to the party to whom such notice is required or permitted to be given. Any such notice will be considered to have been given when received, or if mailed, five (5) business days after it was mailed, as evidenced by the postmark. The mailing address for notice to either party will be the address shown on the signature page of this Agreement. Either party may change its mailing address by notice as provided by this Section. The following provisions shall survive termination of this Agreement: Sections 4, 5, 6, 7 and 8.

This Agreement is effective as of _____, 20____.

By_____   By_____

Typed name   Typed name

Title_____   Title_____

Address_____   Address_____

EXHIBIT A   Reimbursable Expenses

EXHIBIT B   Contractor's License to Use the Work Product

WEB SITE DEVELOPMENT AND MAINTENANCE AGREEMENT

This Agreement is entered into by and between _____ ("Client") and _____ ("Developer") on the _____ (the "Effective Date").

RECITALS

WHEREAS, Developer has experience in developing and maintaining Web sites for third parties;

WHEREAS, Client wishes to have Developer create a Web site for Client and maintain such Web site for Client, and Developer is interested in undertaking such work.

WHEREAS, Client shall employ a separate company to host its Web site.

NOW, THEREFORE, in consideration of the promises and mutual covenants and agreements set forth herein, Client and Developer agree as follows:

Section 1

DEFINITIONS

1.1   **Beta version** means a working version of the Web Site recorded in executable form on the specified medium with any necessary supporting software and data, which has been fully tested by Developer prior to delivery and which Developer believes in good faith to be bug free and to fully implement all functions called for in the Specifications.

1.2   **Client content** means the material provided by Client to be incorporated into the Web Site, as listed on Schedule "C."

1.3   **Development Schedule** shall be as set forth in Schedule "B" to this Agreement which lists the deliverable items contracted for ("Deliverables") and the deadlines for their delivery. Payment Schedule shall be as also set forth in Schedule "B."

1.4 **Developer Tools** means the software tools of general application, whether owned or licensed to Developer, which are used to develop the Web Site.

1.5 **Documentation** means the documentation for the software developed by Developer specifically for the Web Site and other material which implement the Web Site. Source materials are part of the Documentation.

1.6 **Enhancements** means any improvements to the Web Site to implement new features or add new material. Enhancements shall include modifications to the Web Site Content to make the Web Site operate on a Server System of a new ISP.

1.7 **Error** means any failure of the Web Site (i) to meet the Specifications and/or (ii) to operate with the Server System.

1.8 **Final version** means a non-copy protected and unencrypted disk master of the final version of the Web Site, recorded in executable form on the specified medium with any necessary supporting software and data, as to which all development work hereunder, and corrections to the Beta Version, have been completed and which meets the Specifications.

1.9 **ISP** means an Internet Service Provider which maintains the Web Site on the World Wide Web portion of the Internet. The ISP may change from time to time.

1.10 **Specifications** for the Web Site shall be as set forth in Schedule "A " to this Agreement.

1.11 **Source Materials** means (i) all documentation, notes, development aids, technical documentation and other materials provided to Developer by Client for use in developing the Web Site, and (ii) the source code, documentation, notes and other materials which are produced or created by Developer during the development of the Web Site, in such internally documented form as is actually used by Developer for development and maintenance of the Web Site.

1.12 **Server System** means the hardware and software system owned or licensed by the ISP.

1.13 **Web Site Content** shall mean (i) the graphic user interface, text, images, music and other material of the Web Site developed by Developer under this Agreement which is visible to World Wide Web browsers and (ii) software (including cgi scripts and perl scripts) developed by Developer under this Agreement to implement the Web Site. Web Site Content shall not include Developer Tools.

1.14 **Web Site** means the site to be developed for Client on the graphic portion of the Internet known as the World Wide Web which is described in the Specifications.

Section 2
DEVELOPMENT AND DELIVERY OF DELIVERABLES

2.1   Development; Progress Reports. Developer shall use its best efforts to develop each Deliverable in accordance with the Specifications. Developer shall first prepare a design for the Web Site. This design shall include drawings of the user interface, a schematic of how to navigate the Web Site, a list of hyperlinks and other components. All development work will be performed by Developer or its employees at Developer's offices or by approved independent contractors who have executed confidentiality and assignment agreements which are acceptable to Client. Developer agrees that no development work shall be performed by independent contractors without the express written approval of Client. Each week following execution of this Agreement during which any development and/or testing hereunder remains uncompleted, and whenever else Client shall reasonably request, Developer shall contact, or meet with Client's representative, and report all tasks completed and problems encountered relating to development and testing of the Web Site. During such discussion or meeting, Developer shall advise Client in detail of any recommended changes with respect to remaining phases of development in view of Developer's experience with the completed development. In addition, Developer shall contact Client's representative promptly by telephone upon discovery of any event or problem that will materially delay development work, and thereafter, if requested, promptly confirm such report in writing.

2.2   Delivery. Developer shall deliver all Deliverables for the Web Site within the times specified in the Development Schedule and in accordance with the Specifications.

2.3   Manner of Delivery. Developer agrees to comply with all reasonable requests of Client as to the manner of delivery of all Deliverables, which may include delivery by electronic means.

2.4   Delivery of Source Materials. Upon request by Client, but in no event later than the delivery of the Final Version, Developer shall deliver to Client all Source Materials.

Section 3
TESTING AND ACCEPTANCE; EFFECT OF REJECTION

3.1   Testing and Acceptance Procedure. All Deliverables shall be thoroughly tested by Developer and all necessary corrections as a result of such testing shall be made, prior to delivery to Client. Upon receipt of a Deliverable, Client shall have a period of _____ days within which to test the item (the "Acceptance Period") and to notify Developer in writing of its acceptance or rejection based on its test results with respect thereto. If Client has not given notice of rejection within the Acceptance Period, the Deliverable will be deemed to be accepted. No delivery of a Deliverable shall be considered complete unless and until Client has received all Documentation necessary to support the use and modification of the Deliverable. If Client accepts the Deliverable, the milestone payment for that Deliverable (set forth in Schedule "B") is then due.

3.2   Correction. If Client requests that Developer correct errors in the Deliverable, Developer shall within _____ days of such notice, or such longer period as Client may allow, submit at no additional charge a revised Deliverable in which such Errors have been corrected. Upon receipt of the corrected Deliverable, Client shall have an additional ___ days to test the Deliverable and either (1) accept it (making the milestone payment set out in Schedule "B"); or (2) request that Developer make further corrections to the Deliverable to meet the Specifications and repeat the correction and review procedure set forth in this Paragraph 3.2. In the event Client determines, in its sole discretion, that the Deliverable continues to include Errors after three attempts at correction by Developer, Client may terminate this Agreement.

Section 4
OTHER OBLIGATIONS OF DEVELOPER

4.1   Web Site Warranty. Developer represents and warrants that the Web Site (1) will be of high quality and free of defects in material and workmanship in all material respects; and (2) will conform in all respects to the functional and other descriptions contained in the Specifications. For a period of one year after the date of acceptance of the Final Version by Client (the "Warranty Period"), Developer agrees to fix at its own expense any Errors. EXCEPT AS STATED IN SECTION 8.1, DEVELOPER DISCLAIMS ALL IMPLIED WARRANTIES, INCLUDING WITHOUT LIMITATION, THE WARRANTIES OF MERCHANTABILITY, NON-INFRINGEMENT OF THIRD PARTY RIGHTS, AND FITNESS FOR A PARTICULAR PURPOSE.

4.2   Web Site Support. Developer also agrees to provide Client with the support services stated in Schedule "D" to maintain and update the Web Site on the World Wide Web during the Warranty Period at no cost to Client. Such assistance shall not exceed ___ hours per calendar month.

4.3   Maintenance Period. After the expiration of the Warranty Period, Developer agrees to provide Client with the services stated in Schedule "D," at Client's option, for _____ years after the last day of the Warranty Period (the "Maintenance Period") for an annual fee of _____ . Such maintenance shall include correcting any Errors or any failure of the Web Site to conform to the Specifications. Maintenance shall not include the development of Enhancements at the time of the notice.

4.4   Enhancements. During the Maintenance Period, if Client wishes to modify the Web Site, it may request that Developer provide a bid to provide such Enhancements. Developer shall provide Client a first priority on its resources to create the Enhancements over any other third party with the exception of obligations under contracts with third parties existing on the date of the notice. Such services shall be provided on a time and materials basis at the most favored price under which Developer provides such services to third parties.

Section 5
PROPRIETARY RIGHTS

5.1   Client's Ownership Rights. Developer acknowledges and agrees that except as stated in Section 5.3, the Web Site Content and Documentation, including but not limited to images, graphic user interface, source and object code, and any documentation and notes associated with the Web Site are and shall be the property of Client. Title to all intellectual property rights including but not limited to copyrights, trademarks, patents and trade secrets in the Web Site Content and Documentation is with, and shall remain with Client.

5.2   Assignment of Rights. Except as provided in Section 5.3, Developer hereby irrevocably assigns, conveys and otherwise transfers to Client, and its respective successors and assigns, all rights, title and interests worldwide in and to the Web Site Content and Documentation and all copyrights, trade secrets, patents, trademarks and other intellectual property rights and all contract and licensing rights, and all claims and causes of action of any kind with respect to any of the foregoing, whether now known or hereafter to become known. In the event Developer has any rights in and to the Web Site Content or Documentation that cannot be assigned to Client, Developer hereby unconditionally and irrevocably waives the enforcement of all such rights, and all claims and causes of action of any kind with respect to any of the foregoing against Client, its distributors and customers, whether now known or hereafter to become known and agrees, at the request and expense of Client and its respective successors and assigns, to consent to and join in any action to enforce such rights and to procure a waiver of such rights from the holders of such rights. In the event Developer has any rights in and to the Web Site Content or Documentation that cannot be assigned to Client and cannot be waived, Developer hereby grants to Client, and its respective successors and assigns, an exclusive, worldwide, royalty-free license during the term of the rights to reproduce, distribute, modify, publicly perform and publicly display, with the right to sublicense through multiple tiers of sublicensees and assign such rights in and to the Web Site Content and the Documentation including, without limitation, the right to use in any way whatsoever the Web Site Content and Documentation. Developer retains no rights to use the Web Site Content and Documentation except as stated in Section 5.3 and agrees not to challenge the validity of the copyright ownership by Client in the Web Site Content and Documentation.

5.3   Ownership of Components. Developer will retain copyright ownership of the following material: _____ ("Retained Components"). However, Developer grants to Client a royalty-free, worldwide, perpetual, irrevocable, nonexclusive license, with the right to sublicense through multiple tiers of sublicensees, to use, reproduce, distribute, modify, publicly perform, and publicly display the Retained Components on the Web Site or any Web site operated by or for Client and related marketing material.

5.4   Power of Attorney. Developer agrees to execute, when requested, patent, copyright, or similar applications and assignments to Client, and any other lawful documents deemed necessary by Client to carry out the purpose of this Agreement. Developer further agrees that the obligations and undertaking stated in this Section 5.4 will continue beyond the termination of this Agreement. In the event that Client is unable for any reason whatsoever to secure Developer's signature to any lawful and necessary document required to apply for or execute any patent, copyright or other applications with respect to the Web Site Content and Documentation (including improvements, renewals, extensions, continuations, divisions or continuations in part thereof), Developer hereby irrevocably designates and appoints Client and its duly authorized officers and agents as his agents and attorneys-in-fact to act for and in his behalf and instead of Developer, to execute and file any such application and to do all other lawfully permitted acts to further the prosecution and issuance of patents, copyrights or other rights thereon with the same legal force and effect as if executed by Developer.

5.5   License to Web Site Content and Client Content. Client grants to Developer a nonexclusive, worldwide license to reproduce and modify Client Content and the Web Site Content to develop and maintain the Web Site.

5.6   Internet Access. Client shall be responsible for obtaining access to the Internet through an ISP. Developer shall not be responsible for such access and shall not be considered a party to the agreement between ISP and Client. Although the Web Site will be hosted by the ISP, the ISP will not be a party to this Agreement nor will it be a third party beneficiary of this Agreement.

5.7 Licenses to Third-Party Content. _____ shall be responsible for obtaining and paying for any necessary licenses to use third-party content other than the third-party content listed on Schedule "C" as Client Content. Client shall be responsible for obtaining and paying for any necessary licenses to use third-party content listed on Schedule "C."

5.8 Licenses to Developer Tools. Developer shall be responsible for obtaining licenses for and paying license fees for any Developer Tools used in this project that are not owned by Developer.

5.9 Licenses to Use Other Software. _____ shall be responsible for obtaining a license to use _____ software and for paying license fees for such software.

5.10 Client's Domain Name. Client's domain name, _____, shall remain the sole property of Client. Developer acknowledges that Developer has no right to use Client's domain name other than in connection with the Web Site development and maintenance project covered in this Agreement.

Section 6
PAYMENT

6.1 Payment Schedule. The fees set forth in Schedule "B" shall be paid as provided in such Schedule.

6.2 Maintenance Fees. If Client chooses to have Developer perform maintenance and support service during the Maintenance Period, the annual fee stated in Section 4.3 shall be due thirty (30) days prior to the commencement date of each year of the Maintenance Period.

6.3 Taxes. Developer shall be responsible for the payment of all sales, use and similar taxes.

6.4 Expenses. Except as expressly stated in this Agreement or in a later writing signed by Client, Developer shall bear all expenses arising from the performance of its obligations under this Agreement.

Section 7
CONFIDENTIALITY

7.1 Confidential Information. The terms of this Agreement, the Source Materials and technical and marketing plans or other sensitive business information, including all materials containing said information, which are supplied by Client to Developer or developed by Developer in the course of developing the Web Site are the confidential information ("Confidential Information") of Client.

7.2   Restrictions on Use. Developer agrees that except as authorized in writing by Client: (i) Developer will preserve and protect the confidentiality of all Confidential Information; (ii) Developer will not disclose to any third party, the existence, source, content or substance of the Confidential Information or make copies of Confidential Information; (iii) Developer will not deliver Confidential Information to any third party, or permit the Confidential Information to be removed from Developer's premises; (iv) Developer will not use Confidential Information in any way other than to develop the Web Site as provided in this Agreement; (v) Developer will not disclose, use or copy any third party information or materials received in confidence by Developer for purposes of work performed under this Agreement; and (vi) Developer shall require that each of its employees who work on or have access to the Confidential Information sign a suitable confidentiality and assignment agreement and be advised of the confidentiality and other applicable provisions of this Agreement.

7.3   Limitations. Information shall not be considered to be Confidential Information if Developer can demonstrate that it (i) is already or otherwise becomes publicly known through no act of Developer; (ii) is lawfully received from third parties subject to no restriction of confidentiality; (iii) can be shown by Developer to have been independently developed by it without use of the Confidential Information; or (iv) is authorized in writing by Client to be disclosed, copied or used.

7.4   Return of Source Materials. Upon Client's acceptance of the Final Version, or upon Client's earlier request, Developer shall provide Client with all copies and originals of the Web Site Content, Client Content and Source Materials, as well as any other materials provided to Developer, or created by Developer under this Agreement. Not later than seven (7) days after the termination of this Agreement for any reason, or if sooner requested by Client, Developer will return to Client all originals and copies of the Confidential Information, Web Site Content, Client Content and Source Materials, as well as any other materials provided to Developer, or created by Developer under this Agreement, except that Developer may retain one copy of the Web Site Content and Source Materials, which will remain the Confidential Information of Client, for the sole purpose of assisting Developer in maintaining the Web Site. Developer shall return said copy to Client promptly upon request by Client.

Section 8
WARRANTIES COVENANTS AND INDEMNIFICATION

8.1   Warranties and Covenants of Developer. Developer represents, warrants and covenants to Client the following:

(a) Developer has the full power to enter into this Agreement and perform the services provided for herein, and that such ability is not limited or restricted by any agreements or understandings between Developer and other persons or companies.

(b) Any information or materials developed for, or any advice provided to Client, shall not rely or in any way be based upon confidential or proprietary information or trade secrets obtained or derived by Developer from sources other than Client unless Developer has received specific authorization in writing to use such proprietary information or trade secrets.

(c) Except to the extent based on Client Content used as licensed to Developer in Section 5.5 and on licenses obtained by Client pursuant to Sections 5.7 and 5.9, the use, public display, public performance, reproduction, distribution, or modification of the Web Site Content and Documentation does not and will not violate the rights of any third parties, including, but not limited to, copyrights, trade secrets, trademarks, publicity, privacy, and patents. The use of the Developer Tools in the Web Site Content and Documentation does not and will not violate the rights of any third parties, including but not limited to, copyrights, trade secrets, trademarks, publicity, privacy, and patents.

(d) Its performance of this Agreement will not conflict with any other contract to which Developer is bound, and while developing the Web Site, Developer will not engage in any such consulting services or enter into any agreement in conflict with this Agreement.

(e) The Web Site Content and the Documentation was created solely by Developer, Developer's full-time employees during the course of their employment, or independent contractors who assigned all right, title and interest worldwide in their work to Contractor.

(f) Developer is the owner of all right, title and interest in the tangible forms of the Web Site Content and Documentation and all intellectual property rights protecting them. The Web Site Content and Documentation and the intellectual property rights protecting them are free and clear of all encumbrances, including, without limitation, security interests, licenses, liens, charges or other restrictions.

(g) Developer has maintained the Source Material in confidence.

(h) The Web Site Content and the Documentation is not in the public domain.

8.2 Developer's Indemnity. Developer agrees to defend, indemnify and hold harmless Client and its directors, officers, its employees, sublicensees, and agents from and against all claims, defense costs (including reasonable attorneys' fees), judgments and other expenses arising out of or on account of such claims, including without limitation claims of:

(a) alleged infringement or violation of any trademark, copyright, trade secret, right of publicity or privacy (including but not limited to defamation), patent or other proprietary right with respect to the Web Site Content or Documentation unless based on the use of the Client Content or on licenses obtained by Client pursuant to Sections 5.7 and 5.9;

(b) any use of confidential or proprietary information or trade secrets Developer has obtained from sources other than Client;

(c) any negligent act, omission, or willful misconduct of Developer in the performance of this Agreement; and

(d) he breach of any covenant or warranty set forth in Section 8.1 above.

8.3 Obligations Relating to Indemnity. Developer's obligation to indemnify requires that Client notify Developer promptly of any claim as to which indemnification will be sought and provide Developer reasonable cooperation in the defense and settlement thereof.

8.4 Client's Indemnification. Client agrees to defend, indemnify, and hold harmless Developer and its directors, officers, its employees and agents from and against all claims, defense costs (including reasonable attorneys fees), judgments and other expenses arising out of the breach of the following covenants and warranties:

(a) Client possesses full power and authority to enter into this Agreement and to fulfill its obligations hereunder.

(b) The performance of the terms of this Agreement and of Client's obligations hereunder shall not breach any separate agreement by which Client is bound.

(c) The use, public display, public performance, reproduction, distribution, or modification of Client Content in accordance with the license granted to Developer in Section 5.5 does not and will not violate the rights of any third parties including, but not limited to, copyrights, trade secrets, trademarks, publicity, privacy, and patents. The use of third-party licensed material obtained by Client pursuant to Sections 5.7 and 5.9, if within the scope of the license, does not violate the rights of any third parties, including, but not limited to, copyrights, trade secrets, trademarks, publicity, privacy, defamation, and patents.

8.5 Obligations Relating to Indemnity. Client's obligation to indemnify requires that Developer notify Client promptly of any claim as to which indemnification will be sought and provide Client reasonable cooperation in the defense and settlement thereof.

Section 9
TERMINATION

9.1 Termination for Non-Performance or Delay. In the event of a termination of this Agreement by Client pursuant to Paragraph 3.2 hereof, Client will have no further obligations or liabilities under this Agreement. Client will have the right, in addition to all of its other rights, to require Developer to deliver to Client all of Developer's work in progress, including all originals and copies thereof, as well as any other materials provided to Developer by Client or third parties, or created by Developer under this Agreement. Developer may keep any milestone payments which have been paid or are due under Schedule "B," and such payments shall be deemed payment in full for all obligations of Client under this Agreement, including full payment for all source code, object code, documentation, notes, graphics and all other materials and work relating to the portion of the Web Site and the assignment or licenses of rights relating to the Web Site which has been completed as of the time of termination.

9.2 Termination for Convenience. Client shall have the right at any time to terminate this Agreement upon fifteen (15) days notice by giving written notice of termination to Developer. Developer shall immediately cease all work on the Web Site. In the event of such termination, Client's entire financial obligation to Developer shall be for then accrued payments due under the Development Schedule, plus the prorated portion of the next payment, if any, due with respect to items being worked on but not yet delivered at the time of termination. The pro-rata payment shall be calculated by determining what percentage of the total work required for the next milestone has been completed by the date of Developer's receipt of the termination notice.

9.3 Automatic Termination. This Agreement will be terminated automatically, without notice, (i) upon the institution by or against Developer of insolvency, receivership, or bankruptcy proceedings or any other proceedings for the settlement of Developer's debts; (ii) upon Developer making an assignment for the benefit of creditors; or (iii) upon Developer's dissolution.

Section 10
GOVERNING LAW AND DISPUTE RESOLUTION

10.1 Arbitration. The parties agree to submit any dispute arising out of or in connection with this Agreement to binding arbitration in _____ before the American Arbitration Association pursuant to the provisions of this Section 10.1, and, to the extent not inconsistent with this Section 10.1, the rules of the American Arbitration Association. The parties agree that such arbitration will be in lieu of either party's rights to assert any claim, demand or suit in any court action, (provided that either party may elect either binding arbitration or a court action with respect to obtain injunctive relief to terminate the violation by the other party of such party's proprietary rights, including without limitation any trade secrets, copyrights or trademarks). Any arbitration shall be final and binding and the arbitrator's order will be enforceable in any court of competent jurisdiction.

10.2 Governing Law; Venue. The validity, construction, and performance of this Agreement shall be governed by the laws of the state of _____ , and all claims and/or lawsuits in connection with agreement must be brought in _____ .

Section 11
MISCELLANEOUS PROVISIONS

11.1 Notices. For purposes of all notices and other communications required or permitted to be given hereunder, the addresses of the parties hereto shall be as indicated below. All notices shall be in writing and shall be deemed to have been duly given if sent by facsimile, the receipt of which is confirmed by return facsimile, or sent by first class registered or certified mail or equivalent, return receipt requested, addressed to the parties at their addresses set forth below:

If to Developer:

_____

_____

_____

Attn:_____

If to Client:

_____

_____

_____

Attn:_____

11.2 Designated Person. The parties agree that all materials exchanged between the parties for formal approval shall be communicated between single designated persons, or a single alternate designated person for each party. Neither party shall have any obligation to consider for approval or respond to materials submitted other than through the Designated Persons. Each party shall have the right to change its Designated Person from time to time and to so notify the other in writing of such change. The initial Designated Person for Client is _____ and for Developer is

_____.

11.3 Entire Agreement. This Agreement, including the attached Schedules which are incorporated herein by reference as though fully set out, contains the entire understanding and agreement of the parties with respect to the subject matter contained herein, supersedes all prior oral or written understandings and agreements relating thereto except as expressly otherwise provided, and may not be altered, modified or waived in whole or in part, except in writing, signed by duly authorized representatives of the parties.

11.4 Force Majeure. Neither party shall be held responsible for damages caused by any delay or default due to any contingency beyond its control preventing or interfering with performance hereunder.

11.5 Severability. If any provision of this Agreement shall be held by a court of competent jurisdiction to be contrary to any law, the remaining provisions shall remain in full force and effect as if said provision never existed.

11.6 Assignment. This Agreement is personal to Developer. Developer may not sell, transfer, sublicense, hypothecate or assign its rights and duties under this Agreement without the written consent of Client. No rights of Developer hereunder shall devolve by operation of law or otherwise upon any receiver, liquidator, trustee, or other party. This Agreement shall inure to the benefit of Client, its successors and assigns.

11.7 Waiver and Amendments. No waiver, amendment, or modification of any provision of this Agreement shall be effective unless consented to by both parties in writing. No failure or delay by either party in exercising any rights, power, or remedy under this Agreement shall operate as a waiver of any such right, power, or remedy.

11.8 Agency. The parties are separate and independent legal entities. Developer is performing services for Client as an independent contractor. Nothing contained in this Agreement shall be deemed to constitute either Developer or Client an agent, representative, partner, joint venturer or employee of the other party for any purpose. Neither party has the authority to bind the other or to incur any liability on behalf of the other, nor to direct the employees of the other. Developer is an independent contractor, not an employee of Client. No employment relationship is created by this Agreement. Developer shall retain independent professional status throughout this Agreement and shall use his/her own discretion in performing the tasks assigned.

11.9 Limitation on Liability; Remedies. Except as provided in Section 8 above with respect to third party indemnification, neither party shall be liable to the other party for any incidental, consequential, special, or punitive damages of any kind or nature, including, without limitation, the breach of this Agreement or any termination of this Agreement, whether such liability is asserted on the basis of contract, tort (including negligence or strict liability), or otherwise, even if either party has warned or been warned of the possibility of any such loss or damage.

IN WITNESS WHEREOF, this Agreement is executed as of the Effective Date set forth above.

[Client] [Developer]

By_____   By_____

Name_____   Name_____

Its:_____   Its:_____

Title_____   Title_____

SCHEDULE A   Specifications (attach)

SCHEDULE B   Development and Payment Schedule

Contract Signing: _____

Payment Due: _____

DELIVERABLES   Due Date:

Payment Due Upon Acceptance by Client

Delivery of Web Site Design

Delivery of Beta Version

Delivery of Final Version/Source Materials

TOTAL PAYMENT:

Bonus. Client agrees to pay Developer a bonus of $_____ which shall be payable to Developer in the event Developer delivers a Final Version of the Web Site which is acceptable to Client prior to _____.

SCHEDULE C   Client Content Item Owner

SCHEDULE D   Maintenance and Support Services

SCHEDULE E   Developer's Credit

DOMAIN NAME ASSIGNMENT AGREEMENT

WHEREAS [transferring party], [a _____ corporation having a principal place of business at _____][an individual residing at _____] ("Transferor"), has adopted, used and registered with Network Solutions, Inc. ("Registrar") [or other domain name registry] the domain name _____ (the "Domain Name"); and

WHEREAS [receiving party], [a _____ corporation having a principal place of business at _____][an individual residing at _____] ("Transferee"), is desirous of acquiring the Domain Name and the registration therefore;

NOW THEREFORE, for good and valuable consideration, receipt of which is hereby acknowledged, Transferor hereby transfers and assigns to Transferee all of Transferor's right, title and interest in and to the Domain Name and the registration therefore.

FURTHERMORE, the Parties agree as follows:

1   Transferee agrees to pay Transferor _____ dollars, payable [upon execution of this agreement] [upon completion of the transfer of the Domain Name].

2.   Transferor agrees to cooperate with Transferee and to follow Transferee's instructions in order to effectuate the transfer of the Domain Name registration in a timely manner. Specifically, Transferor agrees to prepare and transmit the necessary Registrar registration deletion template and/or to correspond with Registrar to authorize transfer of the Domain Name.

3.   Transferor warrants and represents that:

(a) Transferor has unencumbered rights in the Domain Name;

(b) Transferor properly registered the Domain Name with Registrar without committing fraud or misrepresentation;

(c) Transferor has the authority to transfer the Domain Name;

(d) Transferor has not received any claim from a third party that the use of Domain Name violates the rights of such third party;

(e) Transferor has not used the Domain Name for any illegal purpose; and

(f) to the best of Transferor's knowledge, the use of the Domain Name does not infringe the rights of any third party in any jurisdiction.

4.   This agreement is governed by the internal substantive laws of the State of _____. If any provision of this agreement is found to be invalid by any court having competent jurisdiction, the invalidity of such provision shall not affect the validity of the remaining provisions of this agreement, which shall remain in full force and effect. No waiver of any term of this agreement shall be deemed a further or continuing waiver of such term or any other term. This agreement constitutes the entire agreement between the Transferor and Transferee with respect to this transaction. Any changes to this agreement must be made in writing, signed by an authorized representative of both parties.

IN WITNESS WHEREOF, the Parties have caused this document to be executed by their authorized officers on the date(s) indicated below.

Transferor

By _____

Name _____

Title _____

Date _____

Transferee

By _____

Name _____

Title _____

Date _____

ONLINE AND OFFLINE RESOURCES FOR ENTREPRENEURS

I n this appendix, you will find information about the following entrepreneurial resources:

- Online Resources
- Books
- Organizations
- Software

ONLINE RESOURCES

Check out these great online resources for entrepreneurs:

http://www.artemisventures.com This is venture capitalist Christine Comaford's website, where you'll find some fabulous articles written by Christine that talk about the funding process.

http://www.Garage.com Guy Kawasaki's website has a few great resource lists. You can be added to a list that includes a ton of your peers, all of whom are going through the same thing that you are. You can also find information about the Garage.com boot camps and other conferences for professionals in the business.

http://www.Business2.com Track what's going on in the industry.

http://www.DotComDivas.net This site, founded by Elizabeth Carlassare, author of DotCom Divas, is a really fabulous place to start your entrepreneurial journey.

http://www.forbes.com/magazines/ Check out all of Forbes' mags ASAP to find out what's going on in the industry, and who is making it happen.

http://www.FuckedCompany.com Get all the dirt on tech startups. This info may save you from making the wrong partnerships or alert you to some great acquisitions possibilities.

http://www.LaderaPress.com Check out J. Dianne Brinson and Mark F. Radcliffe's website, which has great information about cases effecting multimedia and Internet law. Here you can download an entire book of contracts (including the ones in this chapter) to help you firm up the legal side of your dot-com.

http://www.StartupFailures.com A fabulous site founded by entrepreneur Nick Hall. It connects entrepreneurs with each other to share lessons learned.

http://www.startups.com This is a company that helps startups move from concept to funding and beyond. It has some great resource lists. Check it out.

http://www.redherring.com Red Herring offers online articles about the industry that can be helpful when you're keeping tabs on the competition.

http://www.vFinance.com This online resource is all about entrepreneur funding, and it was ranked one of the top 100 sites by entrepreneur.com, the online division of *Entrepreneur Magazine.*

http://www.craigslist.org This is a great site to post listings for your team and employees. You can also subscribe for free and see what new dot-coms are posting, and whether your competition is getting a foothold. It's also a great place to look for a place to live if you're going to one of the many major cities craigslist.org covers, or just want to find a date in a new city.

http://www.venturewire.com Subscribe to Venturewire to get an e-mail listing every day of who is getting funding and from whom.

http://www.Fool.com The Motley Fool is a great place to sign up on a list where you can find information every day about technology companies and what they're doing in the market.

http://www.sba.gov/starting/indexbusplans.html The SBA's business plan outline can guide you when you're developing the plan for your dot-com.

http://otl.stanford.edu Stanford's Office of Technology Licensing has great links for entrepreneurs.

http://www.goldenparachute.com This is a professional networking site with community and resources.

`http://www.nasdaq.com` Check IPO and stock news.

`http://www.FWE.org` Hey, if you're a woman in technology, join this group. I think you'll be really pleased about the quality of people you meet through the Forum for Women Entrepreneurs. There are chapters located throughout the country.

`http://www.WITI.org` The Women in Technology Foundation is another women's-based organization that holds conferences across the country at which you can hear fabulous people in technology talk about how they did it. You can also join local chapters to meet technologists who are looking for jobs or who might make good partners.

`http://www.GirlGeeks.com` GirlGeeks is really cool women's organization that will lead you to finding others like yourself. They have some great chats with leaders in technology, a free mentors program and an online technology courses.

`http://www.SVEC.org` The Silicon Valley Engineering Council is a great website to link to any of its member organizations. You can meet other technologists and entrepreneurs at your local chapter event.

`http://www.TiE.org` An organization chartered by entrepreneurs, corporate executives, and senior professionals. With roots or interest in the Indus region, the explicit goal of this organization is to benefit all entrepreneurs, would-be entrepreneurs, and professionals with an interest in entrepreneurship.

`http://www.WomensTechCluster.org` This outstanding San Francisco incubator gives women-owned companies an exciting opportunity to grow.

`http://www.workit.org` At this site, you can find resources for incubators and accelerators, tech events, etc.

http://www.NVST.com   This is a great place to list your investment opportunity, and it also has a great resources page.

http://www.webmergers.com   Webmergers is the research-backed marketplace for Internet opportunities.

BOOKS

These are the books entrepreneurs should read:

Accidental Empires: How the Boys of Silicon Valley Make Their Millions, Battle Foreign Competition, and Still Can't Get a Date
Robert X. Cringely (Addison Wesley, 1992)
A former Stanford professor and foreign correspondent provides a detailed overview of the personal-computer industry, ranging from the technological breakthroughs of Intel and IBM to visionary entrepreneurs such as Steve Jobs (cofounder of Apple) and Bill Gates (Microsoft). Cringely's thorough analysis concludes that most of the major companies will need to redefine their mission due to the new engineering developments already in the works.

Confessions of a Venture Capitalist: Inside the High-Stakes World of Start-up Financing
Ruthann Quindlen (Warner Books, 2000)
A venture capitalist offers insights and lessons about how the venture capital economy and Silicon Valley are radically changing the world we all live in.

DotCom Divas: E-Business Insights from the Visionary Women Founders of 20 Net Ventures
Elizabeth Carlassare (McGraw-Hill, 2001)
Provides an inspirational look at women who founded dotcom companies. Carlassare gives people an honest looks at the ups and downs of being an entrepreneur.

eBoys: The First Inside Account of Venture Capitalists at Work
Randall E. Stross (Crown Publishing/Random House, 2000)
Randall E. Stross, author of books on Microsoft and Steve Jobs, gives an inside account of life within a Silicon Valley venture capital firm that made investments into such companies as eBay and returned a Silicon valley record of 100,000 percent.

How to Drive Your Competition Crazy: Creating Disruption for Fun and Profit
Guy Kawasaki, Rick Kot (editor), Michele Moreno, Scott Adams (Hyperion, 1996)
The author of *Selling the Dream* and *The Macintosh Way* provides advice on how to help companies get and maintain the lead.

The Nudist on the Late Shift and Other True Tales of Silicon Valley
Po Bronson (Random House, 1999).
A series of essays intending to capture the spirit of Silicon Valley, from life with a group of Java programmers to the rise of Sabear Bhatia from a starving immigrant and engineering student to cofounder of Hotmail.

Rules for Revolutionaries: The Capitalist Manifesto for Creating and Marketing New Products and Services
Guy Kawasaki, Michele Moreno (Harperbusiness, 1999)
A former chief evangelist at Apple Computer and a business strategist who now works with high-tech startups in Silicon Valley lays out instructions and advice to aspiring entrepreneurs on how to succeed in business. The author presents insights drawn from his own personal experiences and the experiences of leading innovators such as Amazon.com, Dell, Hallmark, and Gillette.

Selling the Dream: How to Promote Your Product, Company, or Ideas—and Make a Difference—Using Everyday Evangelism
Guy Kawasaki (Harperbusiness, 1992)
The bestselling author of *The Macintosh Way* explains his successful business approach to selling, marketing, and managing.

The Monk and the Riddle: The Education of a Silicon Valley Entrepreneur
Randy Komisar, Kent L. Lineback (contributor)
(Harvard Business School Press, 2000)
The author intertwines the story of his own career with that of two fictional entrepreneurs to show how deals are made and businesses get started in Silicon Valley. Komisar stresses how venture capitalists and headhunters think and operate, the importance of passion and vision, and his own philosophy of success and fulfillment.

The New New Thing: A Silicon Valley Story
Michael Lewis (W.W. Norton & Company, 1999)
Profiles the technology entrepreneur Jim Clark, founder of Silicon Graphics, Netscape, and Healtheon. The narrative discusses Clark's entrepreneurial ideas and sheds light on the history of the Internet.

The Silicon Boys and Their Valley of Dreams
David A. Kaplan (William Morrow & Company, 1999)
A senior writer at Newsweek gives a historical survey of Silicon Valley that covers the ways and means of the individuals and their companies that made it big, ranging from the origins of HewlettPackard to Netscape and Yahoo!.

Engineering Your Start-up: A Guide for the High-Tech Entrepreneur
Michael Baird (Professional Publications, Inc.)
Entrepreneurs will find this book extremely helpful when looking for straight-up, practical information.

Internet Law and Business Handbook
J. Dianne Brinson and Mark F. Radcliffe
(LaderaPress.com)
A comprehensive, practical guide to the legal and business issues that arise in various aspects of using the Internet for setting up business websites and personal Home Pages, putting existing material on the Internet, creating material for the Internet, using material found on the Internet, and e-commerce laws. Includes disk with

ORGANIZATIONS

Here is a list of great organizations for entrepreneurs:

http://www.fwe.org

http://www.TiE.org

http://www.WITI.org

http://www.GirlGeeks.com

http://www.SVEC.org

One of the largest and most well respected organization with huge ties into the industry is the Silicon Valley Engineering Council. Check out its website at www.SVEC.org to find links to local chapter of the groups listed below.

Members of the Silicon Valley Engineering Council follow:

AIChE, American Institute of Chemical Engineers

ASCE, American Society of Civil Engineers

ASM Intl, American Society of Materials International

ASME, American Society of Mechanical Engineers

AVS, American Vacuum Society

CSPE, California Society of Professional Engineers

IEEE, Institute of Electrical and Electronic Engineers

NSBE, National Society of Black Engineers

SAE, Society of Automotive Engineers

AMPE, Society for Advancement of Materials & Process Engineers

SWE, Society of Women Engineers

WSV, Workforce Silicon Valley Engineering Consortium.

Silicon Valley Engineering Council's affiliate members include:

AES, Audio Engineering Society

AIAA, American Institute of Aeronautics and Astronautics

APWA, American Public Works Association

ASSE, American Society of Safety Engineers

ASHRAE, American Society of Heating, Refrigerating, and Air Conditioning Engineers

ASQ, American Society of Quality

ASQ, Statistics Task Group; CASE, Case Alumni Association

CHAC, Computer History Association of California

ECSCV, Engineers Club of Santa Clara Valley

EOS/ESD Electrical Overstress & Electrostatic Discharge Society

IEEE CPMT, Components, Packaging, & Manufacturing Tech

IEEE LEOS, Laser Electro Optics Society

IIE, Institute of Industrial Engineer

ISA, International Society of Measurement and Control

INCOSE, International Council on Systems Engineering

LM, Lockheed Martin

NATEA, North America Taiwanese Engineers' Association

OSNC, Optical Society of Northern California

PATCA, Professional and Technical Consultants Association

The Electronics Museum of the Perham Foundation

SAME, Society of American Military Engineers

SBE, Society of Broadcast Engineers

SCS, Society for Computer Simulation

SHPE, Society of Hispanic Professional Engineer

SME, Society of Manufacturing Engineers

SMPTE, Society of Motion Picture and Television Engineers

SPIE, International Society for Optical Engineering

SOCE, Society of Concurrent Engineering

SOFTWARE

The Multimedia Contracts Disk, by J. Dianne Brinson and Mark F. Radcliffe (www.LaderaPress.com), is a disk that contains all 56 contracts found in *Multimedia Contracts*, a 600-page book packed with contracts that have actually been used in the multimedia industry.

INDEX

Note to the Reader: Page numbers in **bold** indicate the principle discussion of a topic or the definition of a term.

S

St. John, Jeff, 118
SallyRichards.com, 13
Sand Hill Challenger Race Car
    Derby, **114**
Sands, Carol
    on angel involvement, 47–48
    on business plans, 38–39
    on entrepreneur attractiveness,
        39–45
    on entrepreneur courage, 9, 40–41
    on entrepreneur rudeness, 30, 47–48
    on exit strategies, 227
    on investor reputation, 44–45
    on profitability, 40–41
sba.gov/starting/indexbusplans.html, 269
scale, economies of, **230–231**
Schneier, Bruce, **167–170**
school, hiring people just out of, 198
Schwab, 177
Scott, Ridley, 172
SEC (Securities Exchange
    Commission), 43–44
*Secrets and Lies: Digital Security in a
    Networked World* (Schneier), 167,
    169
securing IT against hackers, **160–170**.
    See also IT.
    cost of, 165
    using Counterpane, 168–169
    and customer fraud, 164
    Dept. of Justice example, 166
    hacker characteristics, 162–164
    hacking tools, 165
    Half.com example, 160–162
    information value and, 165
    national security and, 166–167
    versus real world security, 164, 168,
        170
    reporting to police/FBI, 166
    and viruses, 166
seed rounds, **61**
Selling the Dream (Kawasaki), 273
selling out, **229–230**

SendMail, 15
SFWOW.org, 211
Shanks, Tom, **205**
shared visions, **205**, 214, **218–219**
Shatner, William, 126, 129, 190
Shirley, Donna, **223**
Shockley, William, **219–220**, 222
silent film industry, 5
*The Silicon Boys and Their Valley of
    Dreams* (Kaplan), 273
Silicon Snake Oil (Stoll), 161, 162
Simpson, O. J., 18
Sir Speedy, 133, **245**
Skolman, Stuart, 119
smart money, **38**, 47
SmartAge.com, 23, 129, **134–135**,
    239–240
Sobieski, Ph.D., Ian Patrick, 15, 49–50
Social Security records, 209
software resources, **276**
Speilberg, Steven, 1
Spencer, Graham, 10
Spencer, Teri, 149–151
Spottiswood, John
    on branding Match.com, 179–182
    on partnerships, 130, 139
    on technology issues, 147–148
Springboard2000.org, **91**, 92
Stanford Office of Technology
    Licensing website, 269
star power, basing dot-coms on, **18–22**
StartupFailures.com, 268
startups.com, 269
stealing ideas example, 70–71
Stewart, Martha, 18
stickiness, 8, **21**
stock
    common versus preferred stock,
        65–66
    in hiring executive teams, 73
    as incentive, 201, 203, 214
    stock options for employees, 66–68
StockMaster.com, 237–239
Stoll, Clifford, 161, **162–165**